THE THEATRE OF SIMON STEPHENS

Jacqueline Bolton is Senior Lecturer in Drama and Theatre at the University of Lincoln. In addition to publishing widely on Simon Stephens, she has published in *Studies in Theatre and Performance* and *Contemporary Theatre Review* (*CTR*), edited a special issue of *CTR*, 'David Greig: Dramaturgies of Engagement and Encounter' (2016) and contributed book chapters to *Modern British Playwriting: Voices, Documents, New Interpretations: The 2000s* (2013) and *British Theatre Companies: From Fringe to Mainstream Vol. II* (2015). In 2020, she published a co-edited volume *debbie tucker green: Critical Perspectives*. She is currently co-editing a volume on the stage and television works of Dennis Kelly (2022).

Also available in the Critical Companions series from Methuen Drama:

CRITICAL COMPANION TO NATIVE AMERICAN AND FIRST NATIONS THEATRE AND PERFORMANCE: INDIGENOUS SPACES
Jaye T. Darby, Courtney Elkin Mohler and Christy Stanlake

THE DRAMA AND THEATRE OF SARAH RUHL
Amy Muse

THE THEATRE OF AUGUST WILSON
Alan Nadel

THE THEATRE OF EUGENE O'NEILL: AMERICAN MODERNISM ON THE WORLD STAGE
Kurt Eisen

THE THEATRE AND FILMS OF CONNOR MCPHERSON: CONSPICUOUS COMMUNITIES
Eamonn Jordan

IRISH DRAMA AND THEATRE SINCE 1950
Patrick Lonergan

For a full listing, please visit www.bloomsbury.com/series/critical companions/

THE THEATRE OF
SIMON STEPHENS

Jacqueline Bolton

Series Editors: Patrick Lonergan and Kevin J. Wetmore, Jr.

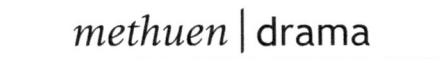

LONDON • NEW YORK • OXFORD • NEW DELHI • SYDNEY

METHUEN DRAMA
Bloomsbury Publishing Plc
50 Bedford Square, London, WC1B 3DP, UK
1385 Broadway, New York, NY 10018, USA
29 Earlsfort Terrace, Dublin 2, Ireland

BLOOMSBURY, METHUEN DRAMA and the Methuen Drama logo are trademarks of Bloomsbury Publishing Plc

First published in Great Britain 2021
This paperback edition published 2023

Copyright © Jacqueline Bolton and contributors, 2021

Jacqueline Bolton has asserted her right under the Copyright, Designs and Patents Act, 1988, to be identified as the author of this work.

For legal purposes the Acknowledgements on p. vii–viii constitute an extension of this copyright page.

Cover design: Ben Anslow
Cover images © Tristram Kenton

All rights reserved. No part of this publication may be reproduced or transmitted in any form or by any means, electronic or mechanical, including photocopying, recording, or any information storage or retrieval system, without prior permission in writing from the publishers.

Bloomsbury Publishing Plc does not have any control over, or responsibility for, any third-party websites referred to or in this book. All internet addresses given in this book were correct at the time of going to press. The author and publisher regret any inconvenience caused if addresses have changed or sites have ceased to exist, but can accept no responsibility for any such changes.

A catalogue record for this book is available from the British Library.

Library of Congress Control Number: 2021938168.

ISBN: HB: 978-1-4742-3864-9
PB: 978-1-3502-4960-8
ePDF: 978-1-4742-3866-3
eBook: 978-1-4742-3865-6

Series: Critical Companions

Typeset by Deanta Global Publishing Services, Chennai, India

To find out more about our authors and books visit www.bloomsbury.com and sign up for our newsletters.

CONTENTS

Acknowledgements	vii
Introduction: Contextualization	1
1 Tension	**13**
The Royal Court, London, and Royal Exchange, Manchester	15
Bluebird	20
Christmas	23
Herons	27
Port	33
Country Music	37
On the Shore of the Wide World	42
Conclusion	46
2 Transgression	**49**
Motortown	52
Pornography	57
One Minute	65
Harper Regan	68
Sea Wall	75
Punk Rock	78
Conclusion	83
3 Juxtaposition	**87**
Wastwater	92
The Trial of Ubu	102
Three Kingdoms	107
Conclusion	120
4 Contradiction	**123**
Morning	125
Secret Theatre	132
The Curious Incident of the Dog in the Night-Time	135
Conclusion	153

Contents

5	**Critical Perspectives**	**157**
	Can't Help Falling in Love: Simon Stephens's 'Late' Plays (2014–19) *Caridad Svich*	157
	Pornography's European Directions: Germany and France *Mireia Aragay*	175
	Precursive Texts in the Work of Simon Stephens: *Motortown, Birdland, Punk Rock* *James Hudson*	189
	The Directors *Andrew Haydon*	206

Notes	219
Bibliography	230
Notes on Contributors	243
Index	245

ACKNOWLEDGEMENTS

This book took a long (*long*) time to write. There are a number of treasured colleagues and friends who I need to recognize for the intellectual and emotional support they selflessly gave throughout the research, discussion and writing of this volume. Sincere and enduring thanks to: Siân Adiseshiah, Cassandre Balosso-Bardin, David Barnett, Peter Boenisch, Gilli Bush-Bailey, Ruth Charnock, Basil Chiasson, Christina Delgado-Garcia, Kate Dorney, Catriona Fallow, Clare Finburgh-Delijani, Sue Healy, Nicholas Holden, James Hudson, Louise Lepage, Lianna Mark, Kyla Pennington, Trish Reid, Graham Saunders, Anna Scheer and Hanna Wroe. A special thank you to Siobhan O'Gorman and the mighty Women who Tick. You lads carried me over the finishing line.

I would like to reserve a special mention for Dan Rebellato, a guiding inspiration to me whose incisive and illuminating scholarship undergirds many of the arguments advanced in this book. It was he who set me on this course by – quite whimsically, I think – once asking me at a conference whether I had read Stephens's plays and would I like to write about them. I hadn't (well, I'd seen a production of *Motortown* in German which I hadn't understood) but I said yes anyway. Thank you for asking me, Dan.

Many thanks for the grace, patience and excellence of the contributors to this volume: Caridad Svich, Mireia Aragay, James Hudson and Andrew Haydon. Thank you to all the actors and directors who over the years have given me their time to talk all things Simon Stephens and British theatre: Gordon Anderson, Niamh Cusack, Marianne Elliott, Sarah Frankcom, Ramin Gray, Sean Holmes, Katy Rudd, Nick Sidi, Adrian Sutton, Nicolas Tennant, Luke Treadaway and Nicola Walker, your contributions offer invaluable insights into the book's core concerns.

A huge thank you to Mark Dudgeon and Lara Bateman, together with the series editors, at Methuen Drama. Words cannot express my gratitude for your unstinting patience and generosity.

The final debt of thanks is owed to Simon Stephens, whose encouragement, endorsement of and enthusiasm for this work has made me a better thinker and a better writer. You get a special mention at the end, you know, Simon.

Acknowledgements

Copyright acknowledgements

Parts of Chapter 2 appeared first in Bolton (2013) 'Simon Stephens', in Dan Rebellato (ed.), *Modern British Playwriting 2000-2009: Voices, Documents, New Interpretations*, London: Methuen Drama; Bolton (2014) 'Introduction and Commentary' in Simon Stephens, *Pornography*, vii–lxxiv, London: Methuen Drama; and Bolton (2015) 'Introduction' in *Harper Regan*, 3–24, London: Methuen Drama. Parts of Chapter 4 appeared first in Bolton (2016) *The Curious Incident of the Dog in the Night-Time: GCSE Student Guide*, London: Methuen Drama; and Bolton (2016) '"Changing the Conversation": Simon Stephens, Sean Holmes and Secret Theatre', *Contemporary Theatre Review*, 26 (3): 337–44. These are reprinted with kind permission from Methuen Drama and Taylor & Francis.

INTRODUCTION
CONTEXTUALIZATION

Being a playwright is like pissing in a wet suit. It gives you a lovely warm feeling and nobody ever notices.[1]

Simon Stephens is one of the UK's most prolific, most celebrated and most travelled playwrights. In the first two decades of his career, world premieres of over thirty original works have been staged across the United Kingdom, Germany, the United States and Japan, and his plays have been translated into over twenty languages. Accolades for his award-winning plays range from the 2001 Pearson Award for Best New Play (for *Port*), via the *Theater Heute* award for Best Foreign Playwright of the Year (in 2006, 2007, 2008, 2011 and 2012), to the trove of Olivier and TONY Awards garnered for his stage adaptation of Mark Haddon's 2003 novel *The Curious Incident of the Dog in the Night-Time* (2012). In 2015, *Curious Incident* achieved canonical status as a set text on the GCSE English Literature syllabus in England and Wales (one of only two plays written since 1987 to enter the curriculum),[2] and his plays *Mctortown* (2006), *Pornography* (2007), *Punk Rock* (2009) and *Morning* (2012) routinely feature on college and university Theatre Studies syllabi throughout the UK and beyond. Simon Stephens has definitely been noticed.

This volume itself testifies to the demand from students, scholars, theatre-makers and spectators of contemporary theatre alike for an extended scrutiny of his oeuvre. *The Theatre of Simon Stephens* is not only the first full-length treatment of the playwright's original stage works (previously attended to only in the short formats of book chapters and journal articles);[3] this study further distinguishes itself by being the first to be granted full access to Stephens's personal archives: a (paper and digital) collection of diaries, letters, working notes and play drafts dating from 1999. The insights yielded by these unpublished materials supplement and augment the play analyses advanced in the following chapters, as well as illuminate and contribute to broader contemporary debates on theatre and theatre-making in the UK. These personal archival materials also, however, reveal the extent to which an appraisal of Stephens's career through the conventional markers of personal success – numbers of plays produced, awards won, entry into a canon already replete with white males – fails to recognize and do justice to the value of a working life fired primarily by the pleasures, trials, novelties and innovations of artistic collaboration.

In twenty years of writing for theatre, Stephens has worked with actors, directors, designers, dramaturgs, musicians, lyricists and choreographers based in the UK and Europe to create a dramaturgically diverse body of plays, musicals, adaptations, performance texts and monologues. His works contain characters written for specific actors (Danny Mays as Danny in *Motortown*, Lesley Sharp in *Harper Regan* [2008], Andrew Scott in *Sea Wall* [2008], Rinat Shaham in *Carmen Disruption* [2014]); are crafted, in the words of director Sarah Frankcom, with 'a complete understanding of what the director's modus operandi is going to be' (qtd in Costa 2016: 389); and, furthermore, are typically 'wrought' (a favoured word in Stephens's vocabulary) in response to not only the architecture of a specific theatre, but also its 'heritage, and the history of [its] culture [. . .] [its] trajectory and tradition' (Stephens qtd in Jester and Svich 2018: 206). While this aspect of his playwriting becomes more pronounced when he begins to write for specific theatres in Germany, Chapter 1 demonstrates how Stephens's proclivity to write *into the auditorium* of the commissioning theatre can be discerned in even his earliest plays.

Stephens's contribution to theatre, moreover, is not limited to his published plays but extends also to 'the modes of working he has sought to promote' in the UK subsidized theatre sector (Barnett 2016: 305). An appreciation of 'theatre' as not only an artistic medium but also a working industry is, Stephens attests, 'really central to my work [. . .] I like the machine of the theatre [. . .] I love the idea of being a theatre worker, infinitely more than I like the idea of being a writer' (2013a). Since being appointed as Writer in Residence at the Royal Court Theatre, London, in January 2000, Stephens has also held residencies at the Royal Exchange, Manchester (2000), and the National Theatre, London (2006), and between 2001 and 2005 was Writers' Tutor for the Royal Court's Young Writers' Programme, mentoring a generation of then emerging playwrights including Lucy Prebble, Laura Wade, Mike Bartlett and Duncan Macmillan. In 2009 he joined the board of the new writing company Paines Plough, and in 2014 became an Associate Playwright of the Royal Court. Between 2009 and 2014 Stephens also served as Artistic Associate to Sean Holmes at the Lyric Hammersmith, London, during which time he was instrumental to the design and launch of 'Secret Theatre' in 2013. This project – discussed further in Chapter 4 – established at the Lyric a resident acting ensemble that, over a series of months that

Introduction

became years, staged a repertoire of classic plays and new works, adopting a model of theatrical production that departed from, and explicitly sought to change, established ways of working within mainstream, subsidized, building-based theatre in Britain.

Secret Theatre was directly informed by Stephens's experiences of working in Europe, and his subsequent embrace of continental aesthetics, production processes and collaborators. To give some indication of the popularity of Stephens's plays within the European repertoire, between 2003 and 2015 twenty of his plays were produced ninety-six times in German-speaking nations alone; productions were also staged in a host of other European countries, including Spain, France, Hungary and Scandinavia (Barnett 2016: 305). In addition to close working relationships with UK directors including Marianne Elliott, Sean Holmes and Katie Mitchell (discussed in Chapter 3), to date Stephens has also worked on world premieres with such leading figures in European theatre as Patrice Chéreau (*I Am the Wind* [2011]) and Ivo van Hove (*Song From Far Away* [2015])

Stephens's engagement with European theatre cultures and traditions provides a key context for this volume's discussion and analysis of his work both as a 'writer' *and* a 'theatre-worker'. Stephens is, however, careful to parse two aspects of his dialogue with European theatre practice. The first of these is that his is not 'a very considered, or very cerebral, or intellectual position' but one of simple 'enthusiasm':

> So, for example, I came back from seeing *How to Explain Pictures to a Dead Hare* [2009] by [the Estonian theatre company] Teater No99, and went up to Sean [Holmes]'s office and just said 'it's fucking brilliant! We have to get an ensemble! We have to – it's fucking brilliant!' So, it's not very thoughtful or considered, it's just: 'it's fucking amazing, what they're doing is amazing'. (2013a)

The second aspect Stephens emphasizes is that: 'it's worth being specific about [this enthusiasm]: it's [for Sebastian] Nübling: it's not necessarily other directors':

> I [have seen] productions of my plays in Germany and actually sometimes they're not doing anything that different to what English directors do. Sometimes they're doing the same thing but just not as well. The one director who again and again smashes it out of the field

3

is Nübling. And he's the one I've learned from. He's the one who've I've gone 'fuck, you can do *that* to *Herons* or you can do *that* to *Punk Rock*'. (Ibid.)

Of the European directors that Stephens has worked with, it is Nübling with whom he has collaborated most often, on productions including *Pornography* for the Schauspiel Hannover and Deutsches Schauspielhaus, Hamburg; *The Trial of Ubu* (2010) for Schauspiel Essen and Toneelgroep Amsterdam; *Three Kingdoms* (2011), a co-production between Teater No99, Tallinn, Munich Kammerspiele and the Lyric Hammersmith, London; and *Carmen Disruption* also for the Deutsches Schauspielhaus, Hamburg. Indeed, it was Nübling's production of Stephens's 2001 play *Herons – Reiher* (2003) – which launched Stephens's career as a major modern dramatist in German-language theatre: no less than eight further productions of *Herons* were staged across Germany before the decade was out, together with seven productions of *Port*, twelve productions of *Motortown*, six productions of *Pornography* and eight productions of *Harper Regan*; by 2016, *Punk Rock* had had fifteen productions staged across German-language countries since its UK premiere at the Lyric Hammersmith, in a co-production with the Royal Exchange, Manchester, in 2009.[4] While Stephens readily attributes his success in Germany to having 'a great German agent' (2010a) – Rowohlt Theater Verlag – it is clear that a synergy exists between Stephens's work and the directorial approaches to staging texts in Germany that in years past have been decried or derided by British directors, playwrights and critics as 'auteur-led' (Billington 2009a: online), a feature of the British theatre establishment that is discussed further in Chapters 2 and 3.

Explanatory accounts of this synergy are multiple, and future scholarship will build upon the observations offered in this book. The following chapters explore those features of Stephens's dramaturgy and working practice which present themselves as being particularly responsive to a German-language theatre culture which, in the words of Erika Fischer-Lichte, places 'particular emphasis on the performance as an autonomous work of art' (2008: 360). '*Regietheater*' is the term ascribed to the directing styles and practices of a host of leading German (Swiss, and Austrian) directors of the twentieth- and twenty-first centuries – Peter Zadek, Peter Stein, Frank Castorf, Claus Peymann, Michael Thalheimer, Christoph Schlingensief, to name only a few – whose directorial approaches apprehend not only the text of a play 'but also the actors' bodies and space as a material that has to be worked upon and transformed in the process of mise en scène

Introduction

(Fischer-Lichte 2008: 370–1).[5] *Regietheater* often displaces the text from its conventional position as the generative matrix for performance: in line with a director's vision for a production, a play-text may be rewritten, edited, spliced, fused and/or collided with other texts, and ideas that have been conceptualized in words may be transposed onto other layers of theatrical presentation such as space, design, music, costume, rhythm and actors' bodies. In *Regietheater*, performance is not 'regarded as derivative but as an art form by itself'; that is to say, in Fischer-Lichte's pithy phrase: 'Theatre is not the representation of a reality, but a reality of its own' (2008: 371, 365).

Despite surface affinities with what might loosely be called 'social realism', Stephens's idiosyncratic dramaturgy often departs from the appearance of a hermetically sealed fiction, exposing its artifice through an acute acknowledgement of live performance as an agent of meaning-making. Stephens's fascination with acting – 'I love', he writes in his preface to *Plays 2*, 'watching actors become characters. I love then watching them become actors again'; his affection for 'spare stages', in which 'the infrastructure and the mess and the business of theatres [is] revealed to me'; and the value he places on inviting audiences to 'engag[e] with the fact that what [they're] watching is fundamentally metaphorical. It's made up' (2009: xvi), describe a writer alert to, and inspired by, the energy and autonomy of live performance. It may be argued that, by choosing to write for a medium dependent upon the co-presence of actors and spectators, *all* playwrights are necessarily attuned to the potentialities of 'liveness' in the theatre; what distinguishes Stephens's career from that of his contemporaries, however, is his willingness to relinquish – and to urge others to challenge – a model of theatre-making, engrained within mainstream subsidized English-language theatre, in which 'the writer is the *artist* and the director is the *interpreter*' (Whybrow 2007, emphasis added).[6] A key claim of this book is that Stephens's development as a playwright may be tracked against his increasingly sceptical attitude towards the writer's authorial function in theatre, and that this attitude has played a fundamental role in enabling – perhaps even authorizing, in the sense of imparting legitimacy to – a renewed questioning of theatrical structures and aesthetics which has impacted the work of emerging and established writers, directors and actors in the UK. In order to fully appreciate the distinctiveness of Stephens's contribution to theatre practices and discourses, it is necessary to consider the broader theatrical contexts which framed and informed Stephens's early career.

New writing is 'literary, not performance based' and 'an individual playwright is at the centre of the theatre-making process', Aleks Sierz confidently pronounces in his book *Rewriting the Nation: British Theatre Today* (2011: 44, 50). The centrality of the playwright within theatre-making processes is a feature of British theatre that has variously been celebrated, lamented and, at times, contested.[7] Indeed, 'British theatre' is, in terms of forms and practices, a diverse ecology of independent, commercial and subsidized, touring and building-based, small-, medium-, and large-scale companies; it is not a monolithic entity but a living, teeming landscape, inhabited differently according to where and how an artist intersects with the industry.[8] Nevertheless, the shadow of Shakespeare stretches long and, since the inception of the Arts Council of Great Britain in 1946, prestige and influence have consistently been conferred upon the single-authored play-text (a work of 'dramatic literature') through mechanisms of subsidy, the inauguration of competitions and awards, and grassroots organization of writers' groups. In 1975, the status of playwrights – and their role in the theatre-making process – was cemented through the founding of the Theatre Writers Union (TWU). The TWU played an instrumental role in protecting playwrights from financial exploitation, establishing principles of commissioning fees and standardizing terms relating to royalties, options and future productions. In addition to its oversight of fiscal matters, however, the TWU also established a 'bill of rights'. This bill 'guaranteed the playwright the right to approve or prevent any changes in their play, to be consulted over the choice of directors and actors, as well as over casting and marketing, and to attend rehearsals' (Edgar 2013: 1) – moreover, to be paid to attend rehearsals. These stipulations codified working relations between playwrights and directors in the UK and prepared the ground for future debates over 'New Writing' and practices of new play development. When in the mid-1990s the profile of new writing for the theatre was significantly raised – thanks in part to the Royal Court's headline-grabbing programme of 'new' plays by 'new' playwrights, which featured works from Sarah Kane (*Blasted*, 1995), Jez Butterworth (*Mojo*, 1995), Martin McDonagh (*Beauty Queen of Leenane*, 1996) and Mark Ravenhill (*Shopping and Fucking*, 1996) – the cultural capital accrued by the 'discovery' of a 'new voice' directed the creative energy of an adrenalized industry towards not new wri*ting*, per se, but new wri*ters*. This focus, shored up by the primacy of playwrights within production processes (as laid down by the TWU), in turn produced a specific discourse around 'New Writing' (capital 'N', capital 'W') which was formalized by the institution of a tier of 'Literary Management' in theatres, the function of which was to support and stimulate an emergent 'New Writing industry'.[9]

Introduction

This discourse (or rhetoric) – evident in industry reports, job descriptions, interviews with playwrights and directors, newspaper articles and features, and at dedicated conference symposia – lionized the 'authenticity' and 'vitality' of a playwright's 'unique voice', an energetic affirmation of an 'individual's vision' that encouraged models of theatre-making in which 'the collective process of theatrical production is harnessed in the service of an individual voice' (Derbyshire 2008: 131). The vogue for 'first' plays by 'new' playwrights at the turn of the millennium, moreover, created a climate in which was 'much more lucrative to discover writers than to keep working with them' (Waters 2007). Not only could support for the maturation of dramatic craft not be assumed, but the pursuit of the 'undiscovered' foreclosed on second productions of even successful contemporary plays, denying playwrights the opportunity of seeing how a second creative team might interpret and stage their work. In what remains a saturated industry, a playwright in the UK will usually only witness a single – by default definitive – production of their play, the aim of which will likely be 'to serve the text' (another key phrase of the 'New Writing industry'). Liz Tomlin, however, has queried prevailing attitudes that 'the pre-performance text [is] a reliable guide to the intended meaning of the final production', to be realized 'with the minimum of "treatment"' from the director and her creative team (2007: n.p.), and W. B. Worthen has observed that this approach to the writing and staging of dramatic texts casts the stage as no more than a 'printing press', a means through which to 'reproduce an already existing play' (2010: 2). David Lane, reflecting on new play development in the 2000s, has similarly noted how such conditions militated against the writing of a play that 'fully exploits, within its composition, the risks and tensions of live performance' (2010: 128).

Since the mid-1990s, the development of new plays and playwrights has become a key activity of not only specialized new writing houses but also regional theatres in receipt of regular Arts Council funding;[10] indeed, Stephens's generation benefited from a significant uplift in theatre subsidy specifically earmarked, as declared by the then Arts Council England Chairman Gerry Robinson, for the production of 'much more new work and [the] encouragement of living writers' (2000: 14). Over the course of his career, however, Stephens's enthusiasm for artistic collaboration, his curiosity towards people and places and, not least, the significant privilege of seeing his plays staged in multiple productions across wildly variant theatrical cultures have enabled him to look at British theatre from the perspective of an outsider, emboldening him to question and challenge some of the foundational assumptions and conventions which structure, in particular, the relations between playwrights and directors. 'The instinct of most directors', Stephens has said,

> is to go 'what does the writer think?' And actually, I don't fucking know, it's not interesting, it's not interesting what I think. What's interesting is your response to that text: embrace that and go with that and fly with that and I'll completely get behind you. (2013a)

Where establishment British theatre has historically looked to its playwrights to take the political temperature of a community, society or, indeed, nation,[11] this is a model that by the mid-2010s Stephens rejects absolutely. For Stephens, '[t]he role of the writer in theatre is to offer provocations to a company of actors as they try to make a night out in the theatre, not to describe how the world is or ought to be. Who fucking knows THAT anymore?' (2016: 5). Stephens's tone here is flippant but consistent with a dramatic oeuvre preoccupied by questions of how to live in the perceived absence of abiding teleological structures which explain and make sense of a globalized world. As I have argued elsewhere, characters in Stephens's plays do not pronounce upon, or argue the relative validity of, a coherent political stance, but rather seem to engage in an ongoing improvisation of moral, societal and familial values, an improvisation engendered by the erosion of such ideological certainties as organized religion, elected government and the nuclear family (Bolton 2013: 103–4). While often this erasure is the source of anxiety, grief and despair in his plays, the increasing instability of 'axes of identity' – previously 'established by what jobs we did. Or where we came from [. . .] Or what religion we had. Or what our gender was'[12] – at times also features in Stephens's oeuvre as a source of liberation and inspiration:

> As we become more aware of our position within a global context, we become aware that the behaviour and the assumptions that sit under this behaviour that have always defined us are not innate. Other people do things differently to us. Maybe we got it all wrong.[13]

'Playwrights', Stephens reflected in 2008, 'ask the question "what are these people doing? And why are they doing it?"'.[14] His inquisitiveness regarding 'the assumptions that sit under behaviour' has not spared the industry within which he works (why should it?)[15] and, consonant with a worldview

Introduction

suspicious of 'any play that champions a political idea with unquestioned coherence, or with any lack of doubt' (Stephens 2005a: xii), his ongoing practical enquiries into the role and function of a playwright within theatre-making processes lead him to conclude that 'theatrical experiences are never pure articulations of any kind of authorial voice':

> The author's intentions, as revealed in their plays, are only ever starting gestures towards an evening in the theatre. This gesture will be refracted through the prisms of theatre architecture, social geography, audience make up, audience size, design, casting and rehearsal. [. . .] [T]he best we can do is acknowledge this refraction and celebrate our right as theatre artists to attack our work with confidence. (2016: 229)

By inviting collaborators to regard his play-texts less as a destination to arrive at *in* performance than a point of departure *for* performance, Stephens has, more than most British playwrights, worked to dislodge literary-critical approaches to the staging of dramatic texts which privilege the individual artist as creative genesis and source. In apprehending the liveness of theatre as an active element of a play's dramaturgy, Stephens advocates for more inclusive notions of both 'text' and 'authorship' within contemporary practice and discourse. His recasting of the playwright-artist/director-interpreter model retains the potential to unsettle unhelpfully settled 'priorities regarding creation, definition, ownership, value, and meaning' in critical and creative discourse (Lane 2010: 130) – that is, to offer and promote alternatives to the status quo.

The Theatre of Simon Stephens is divided into four chapters and four essays, the latter gathered together under 'Critical Perspectives'. The first four chapters draw upon and synthesize Stephens's unpublished archival materials, original interviews with Stephens and his collaborators, theatre reviews and existing scholarship in order to advance extended analyses of the plays from Stephens's professional debut, *Bluebird*, which received a short run in the Royal Court Young Writers' Festival 1999, to the critically acclaimed, globally successful, theatrical juggernaut which is *The Curious Incident of the Dog in the Night-Time*. Textual and thematic analyses of the plays are complemented by considerations of the theatre cultures within which the play and its production emerge, and the 'assumptions and behaviours' which underpin aesthetic choices are examined in order to advance a dramaturgical analysis of Stephens's theatre inclusive of the mechanisms by which it is realized.[16] The titles of these four chapters –

'Tension', 'Transgression', 'Juxtaposition' and 'Contradiction' – admit to a degree of whimsy but, nevertheless, seek to identify and foreground key dynamics in Stephens's dramaturgical development as a writer. Following the structure of Stephens's archive, and in order to reflect the playwright's discovery of new horizons and new collaborators, these chapters are, for the most part, organized by the chronological order in which the plays were produced; as personal journeys are neither strictly linear nor unidirectional, however, where certain plays share structural and thematic similarities, these have been paired together.

'Critical Perspectives' is given over to other voices in academia and theatre. The first of the four essays is Caridad Svich's 'Can't Help Falling in Love: Simon Stephens's "Late" Plays (2014–19)'. As Svich notes, it seems a 'tad absurd' to mount a retrospective when the playwright is in the middle of his career; for the purposes of this book's periodization, however, Svich attends to the plays that come after *Curious Incident*. Her essay addresses the playwright's theatrical output between 2014 and 2019, a staggeringly productive period for the playwright in which nine plays were staged in five years across Manchester, Hamburg, London, New York and Cardiff. Svich identifies in these 'hotel plays', as she terms them, an emergent 'unease' with, even 'distrust' of, the theatrical form, 'as Stephens is at once catapulted to global fame' through the phenomenon of *Curious Incident*. Through detailed readings of these most recent plays in relation to Stephens's 'capacity to reinvent himself as a writer', Svich celebrates Stephens's restlessness, lauding his unwillingness to ever settle – 'even when you think he has'. In the second essay, '*Pornography*'s European Directions: Germany and France', Mireia Aragay proceeds from Stephens's refusal to '"stay at home" in his role as a playwright' to discuss two European productions of Stephens's *Pornography*: Sebastian Nübling's at the Schauspiel Hannover (2007) and Laurent Gutmann's at La Colline Théâtre National Paris (2010). Through close reading of scenographic and acting choices, Aragay offers a comparative analysis of these productions, focusing on the former's 'visual dramaturgy' in the form of 'surging images' (van den Berg 2008: 7), and the latter's dramatization of what Gérard Wajcman has described as the 'age of hypervisibility' (La Colline 2010: 15). Noting Stephens's relinquishment of authorial control, Aragay argues that these productions demonstrate 'in practice' what it means to state that 'in theatre "there's no purity of text which is received by a reader"' (Stephens qtd in Radosavljević 2014: 267). Following Aragay, James Hudson's 'Precursive Texts in the Work of Simon Stephens: *Motortown*, *Birdland*, *Punk Rock*' similarly troubles notions of

Introduction

purity, in the senses of singularity and originality, through his identification of Stephens's 'repeated strategy' of redeploying 'recently historical and contemporary popular culture' in his reinterpretations of classic, continental, avant-garde texts: specifically, *Woyzeck* (1913) by Georg Büchner, *Baal* (1923) by Bertolt Brecht and *Spring Awakening* (1906) by Frank Wedekind. Casting a penetrating gaze into Stephens's oeuvre, Hudson observes and dissects the playwright's 'promiscuous appropriation' of influences to argue that 'his imaginative process as a playwright is always, in essence, adaptive'. Concluding the volume are edited extracts from interviews with six key directors of Stephens's work, conducted and introduced by Andrew Haydon. Here, Marianne Elliott, Sarah Frankcom, Ramin Gray, Sean Holmes, Katie Mitchell and Carrie Cracknell discuss their experiences of working with Stephens's plays, providing valuable insights into their interpretation and staging of plays including *Port, Harper Regan, On the Shore of the Wide World* (2005), *Motortown, Pornography, Morning, Wastwater* (2011) and *Birdland* (2014).

This volume argues Stephens's place as a major contemporary playwright whose works will undoubtedly feature in future histories of British and European twenty-first-century theatre. The analyses of his oeuvre contained within these pages are offered with same curiosity as to their reception as Stephens gifts to his plays, and in the hope that they provide useful 'starting gestures' to future scholarship on his as yet unwritten works (Stephens 2016: 229). Stephens's is a powerful and distinctive theatrical voice that will continue to excite and enthral for years to come.

CHAPTER 1
TENSION
BLUEBIRD (1998) · *CHRISTMAS* (2003) · *HERONS* (2001) · *PORT* (2002) · *COUNTRY MUSIC* (2004) · *ON THE SHORE OF THE WIDE WORLD* (2005)

The launch of Stephens's career coincided with the relaunch of the Royal Court Theatre, London, at the turn of the millennium. This relaunch comprised, firstly, the appointment of Ian Rickson to the post of Artistic Director in 1998 and, secondly, the company's return to its Sloane Square premises after a multi-million-pound refurbishment in 2000. As incoming Artistic Director, Rickson shifted the theatre's agenda for new writing away from approaches that had prized (and arguably fetishized) 'new' plays by 'new' playwrights towards a model of new play development which would commit to supporting playwrights beyond their first production. As Stephens attests, it was a shift in the theatre's priorities that, while perhaps not as '"radical" or "sexy"' as the hype generated around 'new writing' in the 1990s, 'did allow playwrights to develop and flourish over time' (qtd in Haydon 2013: 68). In January 2000 Stephens was appointed Playwright in Residence at the Royal Court – a diary entry dated 4 January 2000 boldly states: 'Today, I started life as a writer'[1] – marking the inception of a close working relationship with the theatre which, at the time of writing, spans two decades.

The Royal Court's role in promoting, sustaining and shaping Stephens's work during the early years of his career is central to his subsequent success as a playwright; a more rounded account of these formative years, however, ought also to acknowledge Stephens's early association with the Royal Exchange, Manchester. The years 1998 and 2000 are again significant: in 1998 Marianne Elliott, who joined the theatre in 1995 as Associate Director, was appointed co-Artistic Director and, in 2000, Sarah Frankcom – who would go on to become Artistic Director in 2008 – was appointed Literary Manager. One of their first actions was to invite Stephens on attachment to the Royal Exchange; on his first visit in February 2000, Stephens's diaries record his apparent surprise at finding himself referred to by the company as 'Writer-in-Residence': 'I'm not entirely sure how I can reside in two theatres at once'.[2] Over the course of 2000–2002, Stephens – who was born and grew up in Stockport, a large town on the outskirts of Manchester – spent several extended periods at the Royal Exchange, working alongside Frankcom, observing the rehearsal rooms of Elliott, and meeting actors, such as Nick Sidi, who would become life-long friends and collaborators. His first commission for the theatre, *Port* (2002), was – unusually, given Stephens's then relative obscurity – produced on the theatre's main stage and won the Pearson Award for New Playwriting. Between them, Elliott and Frankcom have commissioned and/or directed nearly a dozen of Stephens's plays over the past two decades, responding to and drawing out both the jagged psychological detail of his characters and the irreverent disregard for playwriterly authority for which his work is renowned. Stephens continues to work with both directors, providing Elliott with the first new play to be produced by her theatre company, Elliott & Harper Productions (*Heisenberg: The Uncertainty Principle* [2017]), and Frankcom with her final production as Artistic Director of the Royal Exchange (*Light Falls* [2019]).

This chapter charts Stephens's development as a playwright from 1998 to 2005, during which time seven stage plays were produced in as many years. My intention is to offer a reading of these plays, and the formal and thematic characteristics they exhibit, that attends to the theatrical institutions within which they were conceived, written and produced. Drawing upon private notes made by Stephens during his residencies at the Royal Court and the Royal Exchange, I wish, on the one hand, to posit the influence of theatre cultures and discourses upon the written play-text, and, on the other, to attempt an account of the qualities that make Stephens's theatrical voice so distinct. Uniquely among his peers, 'residing in two theatres at once' meant that the mentorship offered to Stephens at the Royal Court was complemented by the concomitant opportunity to practice, contrast and question these principles in the rehearsal rooms of the Royal Exchange: a large-scale, in-the-round, theatre located in the heart of a city two hundred miles north of London. This observation is not intended to pit the Royal Court and Royal Exchange in opposition to, or competition with, one another but rather to recognize the distinctive environmental conditions in which Stephens learned and developed his craft, and to acknowledge the domestic theatrical culture(s) in which his writing was recognized, supported and championed before international acclaim followed. Stephens's personal notes and diary entries from this

Tension

period offer a historical record of the prevailing discourses circulating in practices of new play development within UK subsidized theatre at this time; a subjective record that is patchy and partial, of course, but one which nevertheless reveals something of the lessons and impressions available to an apprentice playwright at these theatres in the early 2000s.

The Royal Court, London, and Royal Exchange, Manchester

As Writer-in-Residence at the Royal Court in 2000, Stephens assisted the then Literary Manager, Graham Whybrow, providing feedback on solicited and unsolicited scripts; watching shows free of charge; and sitting in on rehearsals of in-house productions. He was introduced to networks of directors, producers, playwrights and actors and, most importantly, attended an intensive week-long writing course during which established playwrights and directors including Stephen Jeffreys, Hanif Kureishi, Max Stafford-Clark, David Lan, Ian Rickson and Dominic Cooke held workshops with selected writers. In 2015, when delivering a workshop to emerging playwrights at the Royal Exchange, Stephens refers to this course as 'the week that defined my next fifteen years [. . .] The things I learnt and the things I thought about in that week sustained me and galvanized me for the following years' (Stephens 2015c: 2). His notebooks from this period capture some of the approaches to, and techniques of, playwriting taught in these sessions, including Stephen Jeffreys's workshop on the manipulation of time and space; a seminar by David Lan on dramatic narrative; Ian Rickson on the significance of location; and Dominic Cooke on character objectives, behavioural tactics and 'transitive verbs' (a workshop derived in part from the directorial practice of 'actioning' established by Max Stafford-Clark, the Royal Court's former Artistic Director).

A culture of mentorship and training for its emerging playwrights has endured at the Royal Court, albeit to varying degrees and in different guises, since the first Writers' Group was established by George Devine in 1958.[3] Stephens's account of his first meeting with Stephen Jeffreys in June 2000 is suggestive of this legacy, and intimates an established master/apprentice approach to pedagogy at the Court:

> I went for lunch with Stephen Jeffries [sic]. I felt a little like Luke Skywalker, hanging on his words of advice [. . .] Stephen Jeffries [sic] is seen as a patron, a father, to an entire generation of Royal Court

Writers. There are good reasons for this. He has a towering intellect. He is a good man.

As we stood on the corner of Sloane Square he asked to see my hand. Confused, I thought he wanted to see the time so I showed him my watch. But he held my hand and turned it palm upwards. 'Ah, you've got it', he exclaimed quietly.

– What?
– My acupuncturist told me that this (he pointed to a break in the lines of his own left palm) is writer's hook. You've got it too. There. Only yours goes downward.

It was a magical, generous gesture. Like a beautiful card trick. He turned to go but before he left he looked over his left shoulder, smiled and told me 'keep at it'. I walked off, grinning from ear to ear.[4]

Stephens's anecdote is illustrative of a culture of 'a sort of [. . .] "respect for [your] elders"' that the director Gordon Anderson remembers prevailing at the Royal Court in the early 2000s (2010). Indeed, the language used to describe the development of writers at the theatre during this time – playwrights were 'schooled [. . .] taught and encouraged' (Gompertz n.d.: online) by a Writers' 'Tutor' – is suggestive of a teacher/pupil dynamic in which an older generation passes down knowledge to a younger one.

A central axiom within these principles, one to which Stephens returns most in his notes, is 'characters' desires are the engine of theatre'.[5] A diary entry from 16 May 2000 records the following from a conversation with Graham Whybrow:

A scene consists of a dramatic action – the playing out of the behavioural tactics a character uses to get what he or she wants.

A drama consists of a story which propels a character into progressive states of crisis.[6]

Later that month, Stephens records the following:

Narrative is born out of desire and learning what characters want. Identifying the specific nature of desire is a keen way to structure insight – political, emotional, philosophical. [. . .]
Stories dramatize desire.

Tension

Plays play out the conflict of this desire.
Desire is the human response to political/emotional situations.
We are what we want.[7]

The claim that 'narrative is born out of desire' is accompanied by the proposition that 'desire is a politically specific phenomenon',[8] a perspective that suggests that what and how we desire is a social phenomenon that can be collectively constructed, directed, frustrated and exploited. If the substance of dramatic action is the repertoire of behavioural tactics characters adopt to get what they want, then it follows that the playwright's task is, firstly, to create complex and beguiling characters and, secondly, know these characters intimately, so as to understand not only *what* they 'want' but also *how* they would go about 'getting it'.

There is, in the notes Stephens makes during these workshops, a further dimension to consider: while the action of a scene may be driven by the desire of a character, the most compelling drama is that which 'inserts a tension between the desire and the action'.[9] Fear may be dramatized by depicting efforts to remain calm, for example; failure may be communicated by dramatizing the attempt to succeed. According to this dramaturgical model, if there is no tension between what the character wants and the behavioural tactics they employ to get it, then the space to engender an engaged act of interpretation is foreclosed and, effectively, the role of the audience nullified. While this dramatic model takes as axiomatic the idea that theatre audiences are not passive voyeurs but interpretative agents within the live event, it also, arguably, implies a fairly prescriptive range of spectatorial activity: to look for, and correctly diagnose, subtext; to identify and appreciate psychological complexity; to assume a discrepancy and fixed relation between 'inward' and 'outward' appearances; and, through a 'uniform transmission' of meaning, to 'get out' that which the playwright has 'put in' to the play: 'What the spectator *must see* is what the [playwright and] director *makes her see*' (Rancière 2009: 14, original emphasis).[10] Interestingly, this is a model of dramatic writing that would later be challenged by the German director Sebastian Nübling when working on Stephens's *Three Kingdoms* (2011) – 'Sebastian [. . .] enjoy[s] it when text *articulates* idea, rather than text *releasing* idea through sub-text, so I [wrote] text that made ideas explicit' (Stephens qtd in Bolton 2012b: vii, original emphasis) – and, indeed, later of Stephens's works (*Carmen Disruption* [2014], *Nuclear War* [2017]) explore the fusion of, rather than tension between, intention and utterance.

During the same period at the Royal Exchange, Stephens was mentored by Sarah Frankcom; attended shows free of charge; was introduced to producers, directors and actors and invited into rehearsals. In June 2000, Stephens sat in on rehearsals for Marianne Elliott's production of *As You Like It*; ten years later, Stephens recalled still being 'haunted' by the experience of that production (2010). The scattered and sketchy notes that he makes during this time suggest a novice nonplussed by the rehearsal practices and rituals encountered in these professional contexts – specifically, the time devoted to reading and discussing the play. Noting admiringly how Elliott establishes, through 'application to the text', 'a democratic collective authorship – a spirit of the company', Stephens is nevertheless taken aback by 'this process of textual interrogation – how long will it last?!'.[11] Similarly, in rehearsals for Richard Brinsley Sheridan's 1779 play *The Critic*, directed at the Royal Exchange by Matthew Lloyd in October 2000, Stephens notes the 'rigorous analysis of language' in the rehearsal room, describing it as a 'remarkably intellectual procedure': 'I am always struck', he writes, 'by the tension between [an] urban, contemporary environment and the aseptic intellectual rigour of this kind of textual analysis'.[12] 'The level of work that actors bring to their texts is remarkable', he writes, 'there is a might, a bewildering might, to watching these people debate the meaning of this text in phenomenal detail in a rehearsal room in the centre of Manchester'.[13] Some doubt as to the purpose of this debate and analysis, however, is also expressed: 'Why do you think it is important?' he writes rhetorically; 'How much of an objectified notion of how this scene ought to play can you bring?'[14] Stephens may have articulated this question verbally, as his notes also record an answer: 'By establishing this level of textual analysis so early, this acts as a firm foundation [for the actors' work]'.[15] This only raises further questions, however, as he describes the actors' 'vulnerable obsession' with establishing character and contemplates the labour of acting:

> How vulnerable is an actor onstage – naked? Frightening? Is this [textual work] a process of solidification – of comforting? A strange idea that these people will play different characters in this play later in their careers [. . .] An odd, odd, thing for an actor to do – seeking desperate solace in the solidity of a character.[16]

Observing these directors and actors read, interpret and work with playtexts, axioms of dramatic craft that in one context are presented as ahistorical

– as simply 'true' – are, in another, called into question. While the declarative statement 'the juice which the actors revel in here is the juice of the clash of objectives. This is as true of contemporary drama as it is of classics, Shakespearean or indeed Restoration comedy'[17] suggests a playwright who has assimilated a self-certifying authority, elsewhere his notes express caution. Discussions in Lloyd's rehearsal room, for example, invite Stephens to consider the 'well-made play' as a particular understanding of form that is 'socially specific' and so, necessarily, a 'politically loaded notion'.[18] He writes that such a consideration 'casts an interesting light' on the 'unquestioning assumption' of the structures of a well-made play articulated in a 'lecture' by 'S[tephen] Jeffries' [sic] at the Royal Court.[19] These dual residences gave Stephens privileged access to the practices of a variety of directors and actors, a vantage point from which he is able to question the apparent self-evidence of established convention and ask '[but] is that pursuit historically [culturally, socially] specific?'[20] This access extended, moreover, not only to differing models and methodologies of writing and directing but also to contrasting stage auditoria and architecture. Where *Herons* and *Country Music* were conceived for the small black box studio space of the Theatre Upstairs, for example, *Port* and *On the Shore of the Wide World* were written for the Royal Exchange's 700-seat, in-the-round, main stage. The physical scale of the latter theatre can be glimpsed in not only the larger casts but also the longer timescales employed by these plays – months and years rather than hours and days.

The six plays considered in this chapter[21] – *Bluebird, Christmas, Herons, Port, Country Music* and *On the Shore of the Wide World* – evidence the development of Stephens from what Frankcom has described as a playwright working 'on instinct' to one who understands 'that there [is] a real craft to be learnt about playwriting' (2010). Written while on attachment to the Royal Court and Royal Exchange, these plays are marked by a considered attention to the ways in which identity is shaped by the class, gender, family and the geographical location into which individuals are born. These plays sit comfortably within established traditions of social realism in their portrayal of working-class urban environments, reliance upon demotic speech and design of narrative structure: the protagonists of these plays are not only 'the embodiment of the play's moral or political values', as Stephen Lacey puts it, but also 'the structural centre of the narrative, whose dilemmas are the chief sources of the dramatic conflict and who precipitate the significant action' (1995: 68). As I have argued elsewhere, however, Stephens's early plays also evince a sensibility which tests and perhaps revises established ideas of realism and naturalism, even as they subscribe to a naturalistic rationality (Bolton 2013: 102–3). This chapter expands on this argument by focusing on those moments in Stephens's plays where a broadly realist narrative is somehow troubled – suspended, interrupted, contradicted – by its live performance. In these moments, theatrical articulation appears to *exceed* fictional narrative; the corporality of objects and bodies appears to *vie* with their referential function. My contention is that, irrespective of the fictional context in which they occur, these momentary disturbances in the mimetic economy of realism are generative of a sense of *delight* for spectators. I use the term 'delight' as Bert O. States translates it, as a sense of '*wrappedness* in the [stage] image [. . .] for its autonomous life, or liveliness' (1985: 9–10). The complex density of meaning generated by these moments of tension feeds into a dramaturgical gesture that Dan Rebellato, writing about Stephens's early works, identifies as an emphasis upon 'affirmation, optimism and care' (2005: 174). This chapter builds on Rebellato's reading of the empathetic gesture in Stephens's writing to consider the treatment of hope in these plays. Hope is here not equated with optimism, though this word features often in Stephens's own lexicon. I adopt rather the formulation offered by Ernst Bloch in *Principle of Hope* (1954), glossed by Peter Thompson as 'the way in which our desire to fill in the gaps and find something that is missing [takes] shape' (Thompson 2013: 3). Thompson observes that the subtitle to Bloch's work 'could well have been "something's missing"': the phrase 'contains within its apparent simplicity a philosophical depth to do with presence through absence [. . .] which allows an investigation of the question of what is possible and what might become possible' in the world (Thompson 2013: 11). The tension between 'what *is* (possible)' and 'what *might become* (possible)' provides a thoughtful definition of the collective gesture made by the plays explored in this chapter.

Bluebird

Bluebird premiered at the Theatre Upstairs as part of the Royal Court's Young Writers' Festival in December 1998, directed by Gordon Anderson. The play presents a series of glimpses into the experiences of Jimmy Macneill, a Manchester-born taxi driver ferrying 'fares' across London at night (Stephens 2005a: 11).[22] These fleeting interactions with an unrelated sequence of strangers appear as dramaturgically discrete episodes; they also, however, emerge from and belong to the city of London at night and, in this way, are curated by specific times and locations. Jimmy and his car – a Nissan Bluebird – provide continuity across all the scenes; despite this, however, we learn little about our protagonist other than he lives in 'Bluebird Towers' (14), is separated from his wife and, it gradually emerges, witnessed his daughter killed in a car accident. Interspersing these episodes – which range from a few lines to several pages of dialogue – are brief scenes in which we see Jimmy attempt to contact his estranged wife, Clare. In the play's final extended scene, a conversation between Jimmy and Clare, we discover that it was Jimmy who was driving the car that killed his daughter. In the five years that have since elapsed, Jimmy has lived in his car, saving his earnings so that when he and Clare finally meet – on the anniversary of their daughter's death – Jimmy is able to present her with £100,000 in cash.

> **Clare:** I can't take this. [. . .]
> **Jimmy**: I have no need for it. It is about as useful to me as a suitcase full of drawing pins. Or envelopes. Or shoelaces [. . .] This isn't an apology. It's not a bribe. It's not any kind of attempt to compensate or make up for what I did [. . .] It is simply that I have something in my possession that I don't want and I thought that I would get in touch with you so that I could let you have it. I wanted to see you, Clare. I'm so glad that you came. (70)

Bluebird contains a number of themes and motifs that will recur across Stephens's oeuvre: noir as generic convention ('the man with a past', the city as character, a world seen from the perspective of an outsider); desire and the inability to act upon it; and a keen alertness to physical sensation, particularly when it seems weirdly disconnected from the self. The play also inaugurates a recurring trope in Stephens's work: a protagonist who is isolated, adrift, removed from or otherwise at odds with his or her environment, whose character emerges only through an eclectic series of encounters with others (see *Port*, *Motortown* [2006], *Harper Regan* [2008], *Carmen Disruption* [2015], *Nuclear War* [2017] and *Maria* [2019]). Indeed, the dramaturgical template laid down by *Bluebird* – a single narrative spun from a singular protagonist – captures the dialectical tension of despair and hope that is definitive of Stephens's writing during this period. The emotional heart of the play does not (cannot) rest simply with the battered loneliness of Jimmy: the 'engine' of the drama lies in the dynamic relation between his anonymous isolation and the supporting cast of (equally anonymous) 'fares' that he encounters (the most compelling drama is that which 'inserts a tension between the desire and the action': Jimmy longs for connection but chooses anonymity). In the face of his apparently abject situation, Jimmy discovers that he nevertheless derives 'an endless source of inspiration' from the 'arbitrary nature of that social interaction' (53) to which he, as a cabbie, is privy. It is not that any of these social interactions – including his temporary reunion with Clare – lead to any profound transformations within Jimmy's situation but they do, occasionally, serve to forge a fleeting connection with another human being. The dramatization of such connection is handled by the playwright with an odd balance of naivete and self-conscious irony in the conversation between Jimmy and train engineer Richard:

> **Richard**: Do you believe in the intransience [*sic*] of love?
> **Jimmy:** You what?
> **Richard:** What about the communicability of the human spirit?
> **Jimmy:** Those are very odd questions.
> **Richard**: They're about the most important questions in the whole fucking world, Jimmy. Give me an answer.
> **Jimmy**: Yes. I do. [. . .] Unquestionably. (26–7)

A few moments later, the possibility of a meaningful connection between strangers is both delicately affirmed and gently ironized; it is in this conversation with Richard that the audience first learns Jimmy's name – but only because Richard speaks in a Scots dialect, using 'pal', 'man' and 'Jimmy' to punctuate his speech. When Jimmy arrives at Richard's destination, he turns to him:

> **Jimmy:** You want to know something quite funny?
> **Richard:** What's that, pal?
> **Jimmy**: That's actually my name. Jimmy. It's actually my fucking name an all. That's seven pound, mate. (27)

The need for a connection – or, to put it another way, *intimacy* – with another person defines the gesture of many of Stephens's plays. A commitment to psychological realism in theatre can afford the opportunity of intimacy between strangers (one of whom, bizarrely, is fictional). The empathy required for a sense of intimacy to manifest between spectator and character is, arguably, a humanizing – and hopeful – energy: to recognize one's 'self' in an 'other' is to encounter, joyfully or reluctantly, an unanticipated commonality.

Christmas

Stephens's first commissioned play began life in 1998 as *You Keep Going and Then What?*. Despite being rejected by the Royal Court in 1999, Stephens kept working on this play, which went through several iterations – including *Phil Piratin Is Dead*[23] and *The Past Boys* – before assuming its final form as *Christmas*. Directed by the actress Jo McInnes, who had played Clare Mcneill in *Bluebird*, *Christmas* premiered in December 2003 at the Pavilion Theatre, Brighton, before transferring to the Bush Theatre, London, in January 2004.

Like both *Bluebird* and Stephens's later play *Herons*, the drama takes place on the night of a significant anniversary. It is the week before Christmas Eve in a pub just off the Roman Road in East London. The landlord, Michael Macgraw, is on the brink of bankruptcy and repossession, on account of a dwindling custom caused by Macgraw's refusal to refurbish, serve food or prohibit smoking – a refusal, that is, to acquiesce to the encroaching gentrification of the East End. He is joined by two of the pub's regulars, an 'ugly, exasperated' man in his late twenties called Billy Lee Russell (this character makes his first appearance in *Bluebird*) and Giuseppe Rossi, an Italian barber in his late sixties who made his home in London several decades ago (Stephens 2005a: 78).[24] Russell is reeling from the recent discovery that the dad he never knew died before he was born in a fire on Christmas Eve that was most probably 'an insurance grift that got fucked up' (86). The three men pass the time smoking roll-ups and drinking beer until an outsider disturbs their sanctuary: Charlie Anderson, a Manchester-born postman in uniform, who brings with him an expensive cased cello and, initially at least, a taciturn silence. Over the course of the evening, chatter, banter and jokes are interspersed by moments of menace and physical confrontation instigated by a brooding, sometimes shaking, Anderson. In the aftermath of an angry confrontation between Russell and Anderson, it emerges that eight months previously Anderson's wife was killed in an attempted burglary. They had met in Macgraw's pub fifteen years ago, a week before Christmas Eve.

The published play-text is prefaced by a dedication to Stephens's dad, G. N. Stephens, who died from cancer exacerbated by alcoholism in Stepping Hill Hospital, Stockport, in January 2001. Diary entries and earlier drafts show that Stephens substantially reworked the play over Christmas 2000. In August 2001 Stephens wrote to his agent Mel Kenyon telling her that, following a week's workshop with actors (including Jim Norton who appeared in Conor McPherson's 1997 pub drama, *The Weir*), he 'would love to see it staged': 'I think it has a darkness and a beauty that is worthy of my continued faith. It is a play that feels soaked in booze and grief and for obvious reasons feels very personal and important to me'.[25]

A play about absent fathers and sons, *Christmas* is steeped in nostalgia for the past and, ostensibly at least, deeply suspicious of the future. 'All these fucking City boys' (88) are moving in, barber shops are being replaced by 'hair design specialists' (95) and people these days 'want everything fast and covered in plastic' (95). Anticipating in rudimentary form the politics of later plays, the play is both a mourning for, and warning against being blind to, the erosion of a particular way of life. The emotional conflict at the heart of the play inheres in the stasis of characters who want, but are not able, to change.

In his preface to *Plays 1*, Stephens emphasizes that while he had wanted to be a writer from a young age, he 'never formally studied playwriting' and, before the age of eighteen, 'went to the theatre seven times, at most' (2005a: viii, vii). During the course of 2000–2001, diary entries record Stephens voraciously reading the Western dramatic canon, encountering, sometimes for the first time, plays by Sophocles, Aeschylus and Euripides; Shakespeare; Feydeau; as well as American classics by Arthur Miller, Eugene O'Neill and David Mamet (whose work Stephens admires while regarding the man as 'a misogynist').[26] His most effusive appreciation, however, is reserved for the plays of Anton Chekov. *Three Sisters* (1900) is 'a work of tremendous cumulative sadness', and *Uncle Vanya* (1897) is extraordinary for its 'overpowering compassion. For missed sorry lives. For the need to seek permanence in work. For the inability to find love anywhere'.[27] When *Christmas* transferred to the Bush Theatre in 2004, most reviewers compared it (unfavourably) to what they identified as a recent spate of 'pub plays' at new writing venues (Conor McPherson's *The Weir* [Royal Court], Owen McCafferty's *Closing Time* [2002, National Theatre] and Doug Lucie's *The Green Man* [2003, Bush Theatre]). Eugene O'Neill's 1939 *The Iceman Cometh* was identified as this genre's 'bibulous grandfather' (Taylor 2004). In his introduction to the play, however, it is not to O'Neill that Stephens

Tension

pays tribute but to Chekov and, specifically, *The Cherry Orchard* (1903). Seeing in what was then his own local a 'pub that had fallen out of time', it struck him that this 'worked accidentally as some kind of metaphor for the disappearance of the traditional working-class man. As a sector of society that, like Chekov's aristocracy, had become redundant without even realising it' (2005a: ix). Indeed, there is fun to be had spotting emotional resonances with – and intertextual references to – Chekov's play in *Christmas*.[28] Stasis provides the prevailing mood and the characters' sense of home is permanently held in tension: Rossi originally hails from Rome, Macgraw from County Wicklow, Ireland, Anderson from Manchester and Russell still lives with this mum. The notion of returning home may be idly toyed with in conversation but its execution is as impossible as the return to a Moscow that exists only in the remembrances and imagination of the three sisters Serghyeevna. 'People live in times', as Rossi declares. 'They live in places. And as soon as the place goes then the person goes too. If you move on then you change' (97).

These sideways glances towards a canon of work steeped in a longing for *what might have been* accrue another layer of significance when read alongside what might be described as an uncanny form of 'ghosting': an *implied* narrative, independent of the dramatic fiction proper. In the last third of the play, and over the course of about fifteen pages of dialogue, Charlie Anderson takes a specific, intense and unexplained interest in Billy Lee Russell: stage directions tell us that Anderson '*stays looking at Russell*' (117) after the latter has finished speaking; his glance '*lingers*' on him (118) after the conversation has moved on; and he '*stares*' at Russell as the younger man drinks (120). Anderson begins to question Russell about his work, his living arrangements and about whether his mother knows that Russell has taken to talking to strangers on Roman Road: 'I just think she'd be a bit surprised is all' (123). He plays a game of charades at Russell's suggestion, then begins to talk over him as though he isn't there. Finally, Anderson asks Billy about his dad and, strangely, doesn't seem to believe Russell's response:

Russell: He's dead.
Anderson: Oh yeah?
Russell: Yeah. Can I see your cello?
Anderson: When did your dad die, Billy? Billy?
Russell: Before I was born. Can I?
Anderson: Really?

> **Russell**: Yes.
> **Anderson**: That's a diabolical fucking tragedy. (131)

Even more oddly, given that Russell has been nothing but amicable towards the unexpected guest, Anderson then turns on Russell, taunting him:

> **Anderson**: [...] Did you have a very hard time at school, Billy? Did you, though? I bet you fucking did! I bet you had a cunt of a time, eh, Billy? What did they used to say to you? What did they used to do? (*Singing.*) 'Where's your daddy gone?' That was before it was fucking fashionable and all, wasn't it? No fucking daddy. Poor bastard, eh? (132)

When this, unsurprisingly, blows up into a stand-up argument, the strained intensity of emotion between the men is more suggestive of an estranged father-and-son relationship than two strangers meeting for the first time in a pub:

> **Russell**: What kind of a fucking cunt are you
> **Anderson**: (*squeezes his eyes closed tight, then looks straight at him*) I'm not a cunt, Billy. [...] I'm your fucking guardian angel, mate. [...] You're so fucking young. [...] You've got to start taking control over your life, Billy, because it is just going to piss away –
> **Russell**: You what?
> **Anderson**: (*talking over him*) – in this place. And that would be too horrible to even think about. (132–3)

As the dramatis personae reliably informs us that Billy Lee Russell is twenty-nine and Charlie Anderson is thirty-five, the biographies of these characters make a father–son relationship impossible. Yet the impression persists: Anderson's advice is accompanied by an unguarded attempt '*to touch Billy's face*' (133) – one of a handful of moments in the play when any kind of physical contact is made – and his final act, a gesture of atonement for his previous behaviour, is to offer Russell the cello in which the latter takes such interest: 'You want it? I'll leave it for you, Billy, if you fucking want it, son, you can fucking have it' (134).

What the text produces here is a momentary but potent disjunction between a realist narrative and its theatrical articulation, a disjunction which itself produces an alternative – perhaps utopian – narrative in which Russell encounters the father he never met. The affective work of this moment relies precisely on its logical impossibility, as the hopeless beauty of what *cannot be* simultaneously invokes and affirms *what might have been*. The image of the two men appears as a double exposure, pointing to the space between dramatic fiction and live situation. Rebellato has noted several moments in Stephens's plays 'where the utilitarian flows of ordinary life are interrupted by something terribly delicate or hopelessly beautiful' (2005: 176). In this confrontational exchange between two characters, what we might describe as the 'utilitarian flow' of realism's mimetic economy – the one-to-one exchange of signifier for signified, individual actor for individuated character – is interrupted and a 'terribly delicate' dramatic aporia conjured. What *is* momentarily co-exists with what *might be* – or might have been – and the sniff of a possibility of something better works to affirm the importance of imagination, optimism and care.

Herons

Set by the lock and housing estates of the Limehouse Cut and River Lee in east London, *Herons* deals with the social, emotional and psychic disturbances caused by the assault and drowning of a schoolgirl, Racheal King, one year before the action of the play. The play's protagonist, once again Billy Lee Russell, is here a fourteen-year-old, bullied by Scott and his mates Aaron and Darren. Billy is a target because his dad witnessed Rachael's assault and informed on Scott's older brother and cousin, who were convicted and are now serving ten years in prison. While Scott's stalking of Billy escalates from verbal abuse to threats of physical violence, Adele – who denies being Scott's girlfriend – befriends Billy. When Billy finally stands up to Scott, the fifteen-year old goes berserk and attacks Billy by anally raping him with a beer bottle. In retaliation, Billy takes the gun his father uses to 'shoot the herons' (Stephens 2005a: 165) and confronts Scott.[29] Terrified and pleading for his life, Scott begs forgiveness:

> Scott: I'm sorry. I'm sorry. I'm sorry. I'm sorry. It wasn't me. [. . .] I try. I try. I try. I try. [. . .] I try so fucking hard Billy, but it's so fucked. [. . .] Please don't hurt me, Billy. [. . .] I'm so very scared. I don't want to die, Billy. (222–3)

Billy doesn't shoot Scott. The play ends quietly with Billy announcing to his dad and Adele, with absolute conviction, that he has decided to leave the Limehouse Cut and go 'somewhere where there's sea' (232).

Stephens delivered *Herons* to the Royal Court at the end of his residency at the theatre and it was directed by Simon Usher at the Royal Court Jerwood Upstairs in May 2001. A letter from Stephens to his agent in August 2000 testifies to the craft of playwriting absorbed over the previous year and, for the insight it offers into Stephens's process, is worth quoting at length. The letter accompanied Stephens's second draft of *Herons*, which he had revised in light of Kenyon's feedback:

> I have tried as far as possible to cut those chunks of heightened, poetic language that didn't serve the play in any way. In doing this I have removed nearly every reference to the canal, to the water, etc. [. . .]
>
> I have tried as far as possible to clarify each character's individual objective. And then to clarify their journeys to achieve these objectives [. . .] The biggest process of clarification concerned Billy and his dramatic action. I needed to clarify exactly what Billy wanted, what his objective was, what it was born out of, how he realised that objective and how that realisation could be dramatized.
>
> I used a model that Dominic Cooke talked about. He said that when he directs he works on the analytic faith that characters are fuelled by three types of objectives. The super objective, the main line objective and the scenic objective. The super or spiritual objective describes what they want out of life. The main line objective describes what they want out of the moment in their life dramatized in the play and contributes to the realisation of this super objective. The scenic objective describes, unsurprisingly, what they want out of each scene and goes to contribute towards the main line objective and therefore the spiritual objective. Looking at it this way every line, every gesture, every pause, should in some way serve towards realising what the character wants out of life. Although this model may be considered to be rather reductive (and may explain why directors always seem to be very cautious around people – they must think everyone is trying to realise their individual spiritual objective all the fucking time!!!) it is nevertheless useful. I have tried to apply this to Billy's journey.[30]

Stephens further specifies Billy's spiritual objective as 'to make himself secure' – a dilemma the protagonist resolves by deciding that 'he needs to escape' from the 'environment that he lives in, from the viciousness of his contemporaries, from the cruelty of his mother and the stasis of his father'.[31] At the end of the five-page letter, he apologizes for 'being so wordy' but explains the 'urgency' he feels 'to get the fucker right': 'I feel a huge commitment to this dramatic world', he writes, 'and more towards the world that I see and the people that I have met that have informed this world and these characters'.[32]

The play is prefaced by two epigraphs, the first of which is taken from Blake Morrison's *As If* (1997), a first-hand account of the trial and conviction of Robert Thompson and Jon Venables. Thompson and Venables were ten years old when, in February 1993, they abducted two-year-old James Bulger from a Merseyway shopping centre. His body was discovered two days later on a railway line; he had been tortured and killed with bricks and an iron bar. The excerpt from Morrison's book reads as follows:

> Can children, whose sense of right and wrong is newer but dimmer, fresher but fuzzier, act with the same clear moral sense? Do they grasp that badly hurting someone is much more wrong than stealing and truanting [. . .]? Do they have a sense of the awful irreversibility of battering a child to death with bricks? Can death have the same meaning for them as it has for an adult? I submit, your Honour, that the answer to these questions is no, no, no and no. (Morrison 1997: 99)

In notes for the play, the question to which Stephens repeatedly returns is: 'What kind of culture can lead a child to be so emotionally battered that he or she could kill a person?'[33] In his preface to *Plays: 1*, Stephens writes of *Herons* that he wanted to 'dramatize working-class teenagers with all of the honesty, cruelty and insight they could display. I wanted to capture their vibrant, violent language. I wanted to write a play about the British poor that was as hopeful and poetic as it was tough' (2005a: x). To this end, Stephens returned to Eastbrook School, Dagenham, where he had taught for two years, and conducted interviews with a dozen or so former pupils, the transcripts of which remain in his archives. Although not directly replicated in *Herons*, the experiences articulated by these teenagers – their hopes, grievances, beliefs and fears – suffuse the play's environment, language and imagery.

The play's portrait of childhoods damaged by domestic violence, mental health issues, crime and economic instability prompted both Aleks Sierz

(2001) and Michael Billington (2001) to invoke the epithet 'in-yer-face', and more than one reviewer identified what Alastair McCauley described as a 'strong current of Royal Court realism about adolescent violence' (2001). To appraise the play, as Charles Spencer opined, as merely a 'front line report from the sink estates', however, is to overlook the significance of the play's second epigraph (2001). This comes from the television dramatist and journalist Dennis Potter in a Channel Four interview broadcast in 1994:

> But the nowness of everything is absolutely wondrous, and if people could see that, you know. There's no way of telling you, you have to experience it, but the glory of it, if you like, the comfort, the reassurance. . . . The fact is, if you see the present tense, boy do you see it! And boy can you celebrate it. (Potter qtd in Bragg 1994)

Potter's words are suggestive of an aesthetic, or phenomenological, attitude to the world-involving nature of experience, in which reality is accessed through 'the sensation of things as they are perceived and not as they are known' (Sklovsky qtd in States 1985: 21). This is a reality assessed in terms of its *enworldedness*: not just the material fact of an object (or action), nor what it symbolizes, but the object (or action) in its own totality and the totality of existence to which it belongs. The affective dynamic at work in *Herons*, as Stephens suggests in notes for the play, is that of 'the tension between the awesome and the ordinary';[34] a 'tension' between the social injustices, compromises and disappointments of an economically deprived, 'ordinary' urban environment and the solace and strength to be found in the 'awesome' beauty of the natural world. Stephens's play draws on and reworks this tension into a metaphor for 'the resilience of children in the face of crippled circumstances'.[35] His notes for the play include the following:

> The sky this weekend has been huge and blue. The clouds crisp. I will write about the astonishing way in which this happens in my play for the Royal Court. [. . .] A world in which battered children try to make sense of their lives and in the face of impossible fucking odds discover hope, innocence, beauty, humour. Blue sky. White clouds.[36]

'In this sense', Stephens writes in a letter to Mel Kenyon, 'this play is an almost irresponsibly optimistic play about the beauty of the detail of things and the way in which that beauty can serve to sanctify'.[37]

Tension

The phrase 'irresponsibly optimistic' is an echo of Edward Bond's 'Author's Note' for *Saved* (Royal Court, 1965). There are indeed strong visual and thematic correspondences between the two plays, not least the acting out of (self)destructive drives against the vulnerable of society. Where *Saved* frames a critique of the cultural and spiritual impoverishment that issues from a capitalist organization of society, however, *Herons* grounds its proto-political stance within a phenomenological, affective engagement with the natural environment. In his compelling discussion of Stephens's early plays, Dan Rebellato notes that 'despite or because of their urban settings, the natural world seems a gateway to an alternative world of values' (2005: 176). In *Herons*, these values manifest and clash in the interpersonal conflict between Billy, who spends much of the play by the canal fishing, and his tormentor Scott who, with his gang of Aaron and Darren, spends his time at the canal drinking, smoking and littering. Billy's fishing particularly irritates Scott, who cannot understand such an apparently redundant activity: 'What's the point of throwing them back in, Billy? Waste of time, eh?' (159). Billy's explanation – 'when they come out of the water. They flash. They're all silvery. They look just magnificent' (162) – 'opens up a glimpse of something beyond means-end thinking' (Rebellato 2005: 176). This feeling is 'aesthetic' but it 'is ethically grounded, too' (ibid.). Early in the play, Billy rages at the way his peers treat their environment: 'there is litter, pissy fucked litter everywhere. And it's kids that have left it [. . .] People don't care. Do they? Even about trees and that? People just, why do they, just fucking, the way people treat trees around here is despicable!' (178). Billy's passionate appreciation of the useless beauty of the natural world finds its converse in his persecutors' contempt for the pointlessness of nature:

Aaron: [. . .] See that tree?
Darren: Yeah.
Aaron: I hate that tree.
Darren: Right.
Aaron: I piss on that tree.
Darren: Right.
Aaron: Tree! I piss on you! From great, great, unthinkable heights.
Darren: Right!
Aaron: And what does the tree do?
Darren: The tree?
Aaron: What does it do?
Darren: The tree does . . .
Aaron: What does it fucking do, Darren?

Darren: Nothing.
Aaron: Fuck all.
Darren: Diddley squat.
Aaron: Stupid green motherfucker. (201–2)

This disdain for nature's unproductiveness invokes and is juxtaposed by Billy's 'affirmation of values beyond utility' (Rebellato 2005: 177). When Billy aims his father's gun at Scott, Scott's 'desperate pleading to be spared is a revelation to Billy, who sees in it a glimpse of some fundamental value' (Rebellato 2005: 176):

> Billy: It was funny [. . .] He wanted so badly to live, Adele [. . .] I thought there must be a reason for him wanting to stay alive so badly [. . .] I realised [. . .] the way that things are wonderful. The way that colours work. The sound of things and the way they smell, Adele. [. . .] And I started to figure out how everything joins up, Adele [. . .] The blue sky. And the flowers in the towpath. [. . .] Everything is just joined up. (228–9)

What Billy experiences is the value of the 'present-tense', the wondrous 'nowness of everything', which here translates into 'a kind of ethical ecology, in which our recognition of the useless beauty of the natural world is continuous with (perhaps a ground of) our respect for the value of one another' (Rebellato 2005: 176). While critics responded to the 'Royal Court realism' in the play, *Herons* is not intended to serve as an investigation into the social causes of violence; indeed, it may be truer to say that the play is interested less in the 'objective reality' posited by social realism than it is in the phenomenological processes of perception which continually synthesise and construct this 'reality'. 'I want', Stephens writes in his notes, 'to dramatize the awe of these children at the horrors they experience – a horror which in itself is an example of some vestige of life, hope, possibility. IF YOU ARE SENSITISED TO THIS THERE IS HOPE FOR YOU' (original emphasis).[38] Asserting hope as fundamental to the condition of being human renders Billy's wish that Scott will 'never, not for one second, ever know what it is to hope' (208) particularly excoriating.

The totality of 'present-tense' experience finds an artistic equivalence in the 'nowness' of live performance. Indeed, this sense of our interconnectedness ('everything is just joined up') is 'not merely stated but is embodied in the staging' of *Herons* (Rebellato 2005: 177). The play contains no scene divisions: once the action starts it runs continuously. At several points in the narrative, 'two separate events overlap visually and the actors' exits and entrances exceed and overflow the movements of their characters' (ibid.). As the first scene between Billy and his father is drawing to a close, for example, Michelle Russell (Billy's mother) enters, though '*neither Charlie nor Billy acknowledges her*' (171). A few lines later, however, Charlie turns to leave and '*exchanges a long glance with Michelle as he exits*' (172). This momentarily conjured pocket of irreality nudges the play out of a realist dramaturgy and, consequently, the where and when of Billy and Michelle's following conversation is obscured. When this geographical and temporal obfuscation is repeated in their second and final encounter there is a vague possibility that Billy is simply imagining, or hallucinating, their conversation – just as Adele imagines that she has seen Racheal's ghost.

The distinction between real and imagined experiences is also blurred later in the play when Scott, Aaron and Darren '*surround* Billy *and* Adele, *but remain around the peripheries of the stage for now, allowing them to continue [talking] uninterrupted*' (181). The dialogue continues for several more lines before Scott speaks: 'We was just thinking about you [Billy]' (182). This line is heard by Billy but not by Adele, who instead reaches out to '*touch Billy's face*' then leaves the stage (ibid.). In narrative terms, this gesture does not take place in front of Scott, who would otherwise go berserk; as a concrete theatrical gesture, however, it takes place between two actors in a way that leaves spectators to wonder at this implied narrative. Did this moment 'really' happen (elsewhere?) in the play's world, or is it something Billy, or indeed Adele, imagined? We might regard these overflows, or excesses, of narrative realities as breaching even the boundaries of the play: the implied father-son narrative in *Christmas*, for example, is here realized in the relationship between Billy Lee and Charlie Russell; indeed, *Herons* marks Billy Lee Russell's third appearance in Stephens's first three plays, a figure to be understood not so much as the solid incarnation of a singular character than as an instantiation of feelings of vulnerability, neglect and resilience. 'Billy' also appears in Stephens's next play, *Port*; this time he is Billy Keates, brother to Rachael – the name of the girl whose drowning precipitates the action of *Herons*.

Port

Stephens's attachment to the Royal Exchange, Manchester, meant that throughout 2000–2002 he returned several times to Stockport, a place he had not lived in for any length of time since leaving for university in 1989. An impressionistic sketch of his hometown, recorded in a diary entry from July 2001, provides a vivid portrait of the themes and characters that inhabit his 'Stockport plays' from this period:

> I arrived early [at Stockport station] and had time to stare out over the town in this light with this big blue light and everything looked clear and kind of hazy and all at once. The flats on Lancy Hill and behind the Town Hall [. . .] the stacks from all the chimneys of the mills and factories. And I was trying to figure out whether the sadness that I felt seemed to touch the place was a projection of my own sadness or if it was actually that the feel, the atmosphere, the truthful tangible face of Stockport is of a culmination of terrible fear and disappointment and loss.
> This is a town built around a brewery. It is a town soaked in alcohol. [. . .]
> Also this is a town built around transport routes. The River Mersey; the huge noble incredible viaduct; the A6 (all my childhood the sense that London and Scotland were both down the road from me would intoxicate my imagination); [. . .] and the flight path into and out of Manchester. I was always aware of the presence of places but never really appreciated how present they were. [. . .]
> This is also a town that nestles in a valley. I never noticed, as a child, just how *present* the Pennines are. It must evoke freedom and also isolation.
> So I think of flight and I think of repression and I think of the nature of the men, their tattoos, their aggressive sexuality, their self-mythologizing [. . .] And the way in which the architecture dates here so that it always looks shit and grotty and odd.
> And I get the strangest sense of disappointment because of the strength of the desire and its inarticulacy.[39]

Port opens in 1988 with an eleven-year-old Racheal Keates sat in a Vauxhall Cavalier parked at Lancashire Hill, a housing estate in Stockport, with her mum, Christine, and six-year-old brother, Billy. It is midnight on a weekday and they have been thrown out of their flat by Racheal's dad. The following scene takes place in 1990; Rachel's mum has left, she and Billy live with their dad, and her granddad is in hospital dying. Over the next six scenes, in two-year intervals, we watch Racheal cope with the successive disappointments and betrayals meted out to her by family members, friends and lovers. With a regularity that becomes normalized, she is threatened, accused, humiliated, exposed, exploited, objectified, judged, denied and physically assaulted. These aggressions are both gendered and classed: Racheal spends some time talking to Chris about her enthusiasms and fears, only for the latter to respond with 'You've got really lovely tits' (Stephens 2005a: 271),[40] and Rachael's grandmother refuses to lend her the deposit on her flat because she has no faith that Racheal can manage her finances (288). In 2002, aged twenty-four, she leaves her physically abusive husband, Kevin, spending some time in York before returning to Stockport. Seeking out Danny, she allows her heart to be broken as she asks, knowing he'll say no, if he would leave his wife and child for her. In the play's final scene, Rachael and her brother Billy, recently released from yet another stint in prison for petty crime, are back in a parked car outside their old housing estate. Racheal asks her brother what he thinks of her leaving Stockport again, 'but for a long time this time' (336). Billy tells her that she should: 'You can't do, all your life, you can't do things just for me. Or for Dad. Or any of that [. . .] This place is just, it's odd. You should go and look at stuff' (336–7). That the play ends with Rachael making modest plans to reorient herself in life returns us to the fundamental importance of being able to imagine better futures.

The epigraph which precedes the play, taken from Raymond Carver's short story 'Chef's House' (1981), sounds the drama's notes of regret and desperate hope:

> 'Suppose, just suppose, nothing had ever happened. Suppose this was for the first time. It doesn't hurt to suppose. Say none of the other had happened. You know what I mean? Then what?' I said. (Stephens 2005a: 234)

In a programme note to the play, Stephens describes *Port* as exploring the 'psychological catastrophe of the catastrophic distribution of wealth in this country and [. . .] the absolute miracle of hope in the face of such catastrophe'.[41] The play's repeated references to characters 'being mental, or mad, or weird' suggests that this reconciliation of hope with catastrophe is both traumatic – how do we live like this? – and necessary – how else do we live?[42]

Directed by Marianne Elliott in November 2002, *Port* won the Pearson Award for New Playwriting, Stephens's first professional accolade. While thematically the play explores and expands upon the then emerging preoccupations of Stephens's work – family, death, grief, stasis, resilience – in other respects *Port* contrasts interestingly with his three previous plays. Working for the first time with a female creative team – Elliott, Frankcom and designer Rae Smith – *Port* is the first of Stephens's plays to feature a female protagonist and also the first to be set in Stockport. Written at a time when, by his own admission, Stephens was just starting 'to figure out how stages work' (2005a: xi), *Port* was also Stephens's first play to be imagined outside the architectural parameters of a generic black-box studio space. The physical height of the theatre's steeply tiered auditorium – no seat is more than thirty feet from the stage – is exploited in the play's opening scene, where Christine Keats ignores her kids to '*stare fixedly up at the fifth-floor flat*' (237) from which she has been locked out by her husband. The play-text's stage directions state that the drama's multiple locations are to be '*evoked by space, detail and lighting rather than replicated*' (236), suggesting the open flexibility of the theatre's in-the-round stage, and Racheal's observation of the 'many transport routes [that] cut through this place' (269) is visually echoed by the 'crossroads' created by the four double doors placed diametrically opposite one another around the Royal Exchange's stage.

Port's engagement with the 'fundamentally metaphorical' quality of theatre is bolder than that of Stephens's previous three plays. Its demands upon actors are greater – the actors playing Racheal and Billy must age over the course of thirteen years (from eleven to twenty-four and six to nineteen respectively) and it is the first of his plays to use doubling to create, through strategic visual resemblance, greater emotional resonance. In rehearsal notes for *Herons*, Stephens sets down that 'The actors are not the character, the actor is a sign of this character. [This] creates the magical tension between the audience and performance that is intrinsically theatrical.'[43] By the time *Port* is written, however, this idea of 'actor as "sign"' has been animated by an enthusiasm for the 'infrastructure and the mess and the business of theatre' as itself sparking affects, intuitions and meanings. The labour, or technology, of acting itself is exploited in order to animate the play's themes, as the stage directions which preface the play state specifically that the actor playing Racheal must remain on stage throughout: '*Inbetween scenes we should be able to observe the adoption of nuances of physicality, aspect and dress that the actor employs in order to dramatize her increasing maturity*' (236). The character list tells us that one actress is to play both Racheal's mum (aged twenty-nine) and grandmother (aged seventy-four) –

a dramaturgical decision which crystallizes in the body of an actor the play's preoccupation with the passing of years – and one actor is to play both Racheal's dad (thirty-four) and boyfriend (twenty-eight), underscoring ideas to do with repetition, circularity and – given the boyfriend's abusive behaviour towards Rachel – the necessity of breaking fixed patterns.

To watch one actor 'live' two distinct 'lives' within the bounded 'life' of the performance, moreover, seems also to resonate poetically with the play's preoccupation with death. The oxymoronic state of 'being dead' is something that Racheal is 'fixated [with], appalled by [. . .] and drawn to at once':[44] her earliest memory is of a dead bird, she touches her grandad's corpse, and dreams of the ghosts of two children who died when she was young. Her fascination, however, is not simply with the gruesome or irreversible fact of death itself: it is this absolute finality in combination with the inexorable forward movement of time that captures and captivates her imagination. Reflecting upon a girl, Sarah Briard, who was knocked down by a car, Racheal relates: 'She was ten. Imagine that. Imagine being ten and you're dead. All the stuff she wanted to do, all that stuff. She's never, ever going to do that now' (248). Paul Castle's older brother was a 'thick cunt' for throwing himself 'off a bridge over M62' but what's really 'nuts' is that Racheal and her mates are 'older than he was now. Paul Castle's older than his older brother' (271). Death stalks *Port* but so too do ghosts in the form of lives and histories that are either cut short or missed out on entirely by accidents of birth. Watching actors play multiple roles within a performance, spectators are perhaps reminded of, or invited to reflect upon, the multiple potentialities latent within any one individual.

Country Music

As part of his residencies at both the Royal Court and the Royal Exchange, between 2001 and 2003 Stephens led playwriting courses at HMP Wandsworth and HMP Grendon, a Pupil Referral Unit in Salford, and Youth Offending Teams in Kensington and Chelsea. A diary entry from December 2000 describes Stephens's work with excluded pupils in Salford, about whom, he writes, 'there is a huge amount that needs to be said':

> Many of these kids were quite battered. They were damaged, cut up. They'd been abused or served time in secure units. They'd robbed, used drugs badly, hurt other people. Been let down by parents, been

fucked about by teachers, their families, their peers [. . .] They found it difficult to concentrate [. . .] They were scared to speak. Or they were violent and abrasive.

And what we did over the course of those three weeks was we earned their trust. And we produced a monologue and a scene from each student. And had their work directed and performed by professional actors. It made me hugely proud. Of them and their work. I came to like them more than I could have possibly predicted. I was in awe of their honesty, their ability to trust and their commitment. I never wanted to find out about what had happened to them or what they had done. They wrote with conviction, honesty [. . .] When they watched their scenes they watched with real joy, glee, wonder, pride.

It made me realise how blessed Oscar is.[45]

It made me realise how fragile his security is.

And also how unfair. People don't choose the families into which they were born.[46]

Dedicated to the 'teachers and writers' Stephens worked with at Wandsworth, Grendon, Salford and Kensington and Chelsea (2009: 74), *Country Music* tells the story of Jamie Carris (played in the premiere by Lee Ross, who played Billy Lee Russell in *Christmas*), compressing twenty-one years into four two-hander scenes. We meet Jamie in 1983 at the age of eighteen, in a stolen car parked at a service garage on the A13 in Essex (this is, perhaps, the 'arse end of the A13' to which Russell refers in *Christmas* [Stephens 2005a: 105]). He is with Lynsey Sergeant, aged fifteen, who he has just sprung from the care home in which they first met. They are planning their escape to Southend, a discussion which – even before it emerges that Jamie has earlier that evening glassed a man, Gary Noolan, before stabbing a teenage boy – already carries strains of a deliberate, almost ruthless, naivete born of a sense of futility. Scene Two takes place eleven years later, in 1994. Jamie is being visited in prison by his younger brother, Matty. Jamie is serving fourteen years for killing a man called Ross Mack who, the text implies, sexually abused Jamie at his former care home. We learn from the brothers' conversation that Matty fell in with Mack's gang while Jamie was serving time in a Young Offenders Institution and we are invited to believe that Jamie killed Ross in order to protect his younger brother. Matty has come to tell his brother that Lynsey, with whom Jamie had a child some years before, has met another man and moved to Sunderland. Scene Three takes place ten years

Tension

later. Jamie, recently released from prison, is now thirty-nine and meeting his seventeen-year-old daughter for the first time since she was four. He struggles with the meeting, and is desperate for her to have some memory of him other than the time she found a wasps' nest behind their flat. He is even more desperate for her to forgive him, but Emma – resolutely, though without cruelty – will not be coerced into this intimacy:

> **Jamie**: I never wanted to be separated from you. Not ever.
> **Emma**: I know.
> **Jamie**: I've wanted to see you every day. All the time.
> **Emma**: That isn't my fault.
> **Jamie**: I wanted so many things for you.
> **Emma**: That doesn't mean anything.
> **Jamie**: It does to me.
> **Emma**: But it doesn't. Not really. (Stephens 2009: 128)[47]

In an echo of *Bluebird*, the scene ends with Emma neither agreeing nor refusing to see her dad again; she takes the scrap of paper bearing the phone number of his place of work but makes no promises.

A disruption of chronological time ends the play as the final scene takes us back twenty-one years to the hours before Jamie's decision to glass Noolan. Jamie is eighteen again and he is lying stretched out on a hill under a '*hot bright sky*' (131) on a beautiful summer evening with Lynsey. They talk; Jamie declares his intention to break her out of the care home so that she can come and live with him; Lynsey is sceptical and anyway happy to return to the care home. She starts laughing and reminds him of the time she found him 'fucking hanging there' (135) – a reference to a suicide attempt that Lynsey interrupted. She asks to see the bruises that remain on his neck and, in return, shows him a scar on her thigh that she got falling out of a tree when she was young; they kiss, '*slightly clumsily*' (136). Jamie threatens to go after Noolan; when Lynsey warns Jamie not to, he challenges her: 'stay with us, then' (137). The moment succeeds in dramatizing a moment previously stated in Stephens's *Christmas*: '"You poor fucker. You have no idea. Do you? Eh?" Right at that time in his life he has no idea what is about to happen him' (2005a: 105). A short, taut play, *Country Music* aspires to the 'emotional range that country music singers can achieve in three chords and one and a half minutes' and is structured accordingly, with 'the repetition at the end mirroring the way country music ends with a refrain of the opening verse' (Innes 2011: 450).

Stephens records the following thoughts in his notes for the play:

> To what extent are we defined by others by our actions? To what extent are we defined by ourselves by our actions? To what extent can people be paralysed by what they have done, by that definition? Because a postman murders someone he becomes a killer. That is his noun. Nouns are often frozen verbs . . . what action is most defining? Is it always fair?[48]

Through the figure of Carris, *Country Music* dramatizes the way people can be 'defined by singular moments', subsequently 'unable ever to redefine themselves as anything else' (Stephens 2009: xiv). Stephens is once again writing for the intimate claustrophobia of the Royal Court's black-box studio and the simple, static, sequence of four tightly-written scenes allows for a forensic study of human relationships. As with *Bluebird*, the play's protagonist is revealed only through his interactions with others; such exposition nevertheless pulses with action and emotion as the dialogue stutters, halts, surges, falls silent, explodes, broods and surprises. The drama of these scenes emerges less from the substance of the stories, reports and anecdotes told by the characters than by the way this information is delivered, demanding interpretation: as readers and spectators, it seems as though we discover a character at the same time *as the character discovers himself*, as when Matty finds himself embarrassed by his brother or Lynsey discovers just what Jamie is capable of doing.

The emotional heart of the play lies in the third scene, where Jamie's pride in Emma is made all the more poignant by her everydayness: having left school at sixteen, she works as a receptionist in a dentist's office, a job which she 'love[s]' and wants to 'stick at' so that she can train to become the office manager (115). Jamie finds this 'incredible' and reckons that Emma 'must've been a right boffin' at school (116). 'No. Not really' she replies. 'Must've been, though', he insists. 'I wasn't', Emma states simply. Jamie appears similarly overwhelmed by Emma's 'hair' (110, 121) and her 'clothes' (115) but, other than the hair being wet from her showering before she visited, the play-text does not specify that there is anything particularly unusual about her attire. Emma's defining characteristic is her self-possession before a father she elects to call Jamie. Small gestures such as eating the sweet he gives her are conscious acts of kindness but Emma also knows the limits of what she is and isn't prepared to do: she is prepared to visit Jamie at the B&B but will not go for a walk with him; she will have a cup of tea but will not take off her coat; and while she will not be drawn into a false intimacy she does reveal something about herself that, perhaps, she has never told anyone:

> **Jamie**: Tell me one thing that you want.
> **Emma**: I can't think.
> **Jamie**: Please tell me.
> **Emma**: I'd like to fly a plane.
> **Jamie**: I think that's brilliant, that. That stops me breathing. (128–9)

The play received mixed reviews on its premiere. While Charles Spencer celebrated it as 'a marvellous and moving new play' (2004), Nicholas de Jongh dismissed it as 'a contrived sob story' (2004b) and Michael Billington puzzled over its 'elliptical quality' (2004). The most impassioned review, however, came from Alistair McCauley, for whom *Country Music* was 'an accomplished piece of work', indeed 'faultless', except that (warming to a theme introduced in his review for *Herons*) it seemed 'an excessively polished version of The Royal Court Play' (2004). While complimenting the compassion of the writing, the 'strong [. . .] never stale' rhythm of the dialogue, and the performances of the actors, McCauley also cautions against the influence of a too-rigid 'house style' upon the writing. His review opens:

> *How to write your own play for today's Royal Court Theatre Upstairs.* [. . .] Go for (a) sociology, (b) rhythm. Some or most of the characters should be under 18. Most or all should come from at best a working-class background and it helps if at least one is involved in serious crime. Catch the detailed sonorities of their social milieu. Apply to this intensely demotic speech such classical devices as stichomythia. We hope you enjoy your visit to Sloane Square. (2004)

McCauley's review reveals more about London-centric theatre-going habits than it does about Stephens's then emerging style. By mid-2004 Stephens had had six professional productions – *Country Music* marks a hat-trick of plays in 2004 alone – staged across London, Manchester, Sheffield and Brighton. Fourteen publications reviewed *Country Music* (according to reviews collected in *Theatre Record*), yet only four London critics travelled to Manchester to see *Port* and of these only one, Charles Spencer, saw both *Port* and *Country Music*. McCauley's concern that Stephens seemed 'to be following [Royal Court conventions] rather than extending himself' (2004) would be roundly answered the following year, as the expansiveness of Stephens's theatrical vision – released in Manchester by the 'epic grandeur' of the Royal Exchange's main stage but until this point concentrated within the 'dirty claustrophobia' of black-box studios in London[49] – was channelled into a domestic drama conceived on an epic scale. Directed by Sarah Frankcom, by then Associate Director at the Royal Exchange, *On the Shore of the Wide World* premiered at the Royal Exchange in April 2005 before transferring to the National Theatre, the first production to symbolically unite Stephens's two theatre 'families' located at either end of the M6.

On the Shore of the Wide World

In a programme note for *On the Shore of the Wide World* (henceforth *On the Shore*) Stephens admits that it was only when working at the Royal Exchange that he 'found the courage to turn to Stockport for stories and characters for my plays':

> It is the place where I was born and raised but for reasons I may never understand I was never able to write about it properly for years [. . .] I think that [*On the Shore*. . .] is the play that I have been plucking up the courage to write for the last ten years.[50]

Divided into four parts and forty-one scenes, *On the Shore* dramatizes three generations of the Holmes family living in Stockport over a period of nine months in 2004. Part One of the play leisurely introduces us to Peter and Alice Holmes, their sons Alex and Christopher, and Peter's parents, Charlie and Ellen. The generations are distinguished from one another by the various stages of their relationships: Alex and his girlfriend, Sarah, are on the brink of losing their virginity together – a source of some heartache for Christopher, who decides he is in love with Sarah (and buys her a photo of footballer Roy Keane to prove it); Peter and Alice's marriage is tiring a little; and Ellen is grimly locked into a marriage with Charlie who continues to weather his alcoholism. In a bold manipulation of conventional dramaturgy, the central dramatic action which propels the subsequent three acts takes place not in front of the audience, as a logical consequence of a cause-and-effect narrative, but offstage, *between* Part One (February 2004) and Part Two (May 2004). Indeed, audiences are denied full knowledge of what has taken place until Scene Four of Part Two; glancing comments from characters induce an unspecified sense of unease until Peter, caught off-guard, reveals to a near-stranger that Christopher, his youngest son, was recently killed in a road accident. The apparent carelessness of this revelation, together with Peter's halting yet simple delivery of the facts – 'my youngest. He was out on his bike [. . .] There was. He was hit by a car' (Stephens 2011a: 67)[51] – carefully orchestrates an audience's emotional response, and is indicative of a playwright assured in his command of dramatic – and theatrical – material. In a play replete with hauntings of various kinds – the ruins of the Bluebell Hotel where Christopher makes his den; the alternative, or future, lives not lived; the love affairs denied; and the memories of Stephens's own father in hospital – *On the Shore* also conjures, in the extraordinary scene which opens Part Four, as 'real' a ghost as it may be possible to in theatre.

It is two weeks after Sarah and Alex, following Christopher's accident, left Stockport for London. Things have gone badly, Alex has behaved like a 'complete wanker' (115), and Sarah has returned by herself. She is picked up at the station by a taxi driver who, the stage directions to the 2005 published edition of the play insist, '*must be played by the same actor who plays Christopher Holmes*' (Stephens 2005b: 2). The driver asks what Sarah was doing in London and she tells him that she has left her boyfriend without telling him. 'I know it's not any of my business', the driver tells Sarah gently, looking back at her through his '*rear-view mirror*', 'but I think you should tell him' (2005b: 108). In a fleeting moment of stage action which resonates with the uncanny, utopian exchange in *Christmas* between Billy Lee Russell and his 'fucking guardian angel' Charlie Anderson (Stephens 2005a: 132), the male actor's body becomes host to a fictional character *other* than the one he appears to be playing. This twofold layering of fiction upon the singular reality of an actor's body creates a weird sense of double exposure, as 'Christopher' is superimposed into the scene in order to reach out to and guard over Sarah:

> **Sarah**: What?
> **Taxi Driver**: I think you should.
> **Sarah**: Do you?
> **Taxi Driver**: It's really difficult, isn't it?
> **Sarah:** What is?
> **Taxi Driver**: Just, the whole business of, you know, being very complicated.
> *Pause.*

> **Sarah**: Are you a bit mental?
> **Taxi Driver**: I think you should call him.
> **Sarah**: You don't know what you're talking about.
> **Taxi Driver**: I bet you do and all. I bet you. (2005b: 109)

From this point onwards in the play, each subsequent scene pivots on a small act of reparation for past errors, of restoration to damaged relations, up until and including the play's closing scene in which the three generations gather together for a Sunday roast dinner. In this way, the structure of the play dramatizes the efforts and resolve of its characters to reconcile, repair and recover from the drama's several bruising narratives of desire, fear, loss and regret.

In a further metatextual twist, it is interesting to note that this scene between 'Christopher' and Sarah has itself become something of a ghost, printed in the 2005 edition of the play but omitted from the version included in *Plays: 3* (2011). The scene was in fact cut by Frankcom during previews of the play's premiere at the Royal Exchange in April 2005. Reflecting on this decision in her interview with Andrew Haydon for this volume, Frankcom explains:

> In terms of the architecture of the play it's a scene that doesn't bear any relationship to any other, either tonally, or in terms of narrative. It's completely out of the blue. I couldn't make the scene work, and the actor couldn't make the scene work, so on the first or second preview I cut it [. . .] Of course, now it's the scene that interests me most about the whole play. (See pp. 209–10)

Placed within an otherwise 'well-made play that for all intents and purposes feels like it fits into the Royal Court realism tradition', Frankcom identifies this scene as a defining moment in Stephens's development as a writer: '[he's] really starting to say: "I completely and fundamentally reject that [realist tradition]; I'm much more interested in expressionism, I'm much more interested in non-naturalism, I'm much more interested in how this is realized physically"' (qtd in Costa 2016: 388).

The scene typifies a theatrical quirk of Stephens, described by the American director Christian Parker as a 'dramaturgy [that] reaches toward the audience' (2016: 395). These moments simultaneously capture and release an *excess of life*, a vitality which is not straightforwardly correlated to a defined emotion or affect but which instead invites a complex absorption and *wrappedness* in the stage image. The stage picture restores that which is absent, missing, past – the character of Christopher – through the presence of an actor who offers advice on the future of another character. The tangle of time and subjectivity expressed in the scene possesses a kind of 'quasitranscendental vitalism', an 'innate and irrepressible hope' that the density of meaning contained in this moment is received by a spectator alive and alert to its potential significations (Thompson 2013: 4). In a first draft of programme notes for the National Theatre's 2013 revival of *Port*, Stephens describes that play as 'about making sense of the inevitability of death and through that the urgency of living a life with eyes as wide open as you can get them to be'.[52] All of the plays collected in this chapter articulate that urgency, and scenes such as this between Sarah and 'not-Christopher' exact that demand quite literally.

On the Shore belongs to the 'transitional times' that Christopher muses upon (39). The internet makes its first incursions into Stephens's dramatic imagination in *On the Shore*, an observation which might seem trivial were it not for the influence it would consequently exert over not only the thematic content but also the sourcing, treating and mediating of dramatic material for future works. *On the Shore* was the first play Stephens wrote with access to the internet on his home computer; that the internet features in the consciousness of his characters – as when Christopher tells Sarah that his 'hobby' is 'Googling' (20), or Paul, a minor character, declares his amazement with Ebay ('Ebay's extraordinary. Get anything' [53]) – announces its steadily defining role within popular culture. In preparatory notes for the play, Stephens muses on 'the size of the world and the size of the universe and the overwhelming force of time. [*On the Shore*] is a play about the contradiction [that is] our awareness of this size and the way in which we live in small moments that change entire lives'.[53] The experience of this contradiction became more acute during the 2000s as consciousness of a new global reality was facilitated in the West by the mainstreaming of individual access to the World Wide Web. Unlike Stephens's earlier works, the dramatic cosmos conjured by *On the Shore* is no longer bounded by the comforting presences of local geographies and histories; such cosy familiarity as these may engender is now shot through with references to global political and cultural events, the contemporaneity and 'virtual proximity' (Baumann 2003: 62–5) of which disturb the hermetically settled dramatic narrative. References to phenomena such as Al Qaeda, the War on Terror and online pornography, for example, foreshadow the murkier moral universes that

Stephens would explore further in his following two plays, *Motortown* (2006) and *Pornography* (2007). As such, *On the Shore* may be regarded as both Stephens's most accomplished expression of theatrical craft in the first five years of his career, and as containing in embryonic form(s) the more expansive, geo-political preoccupations that animate his later works.

Conclusion

Dan Rebellato elegantly describes the early works of Stephens as plays that 'expose themselves, flirt willingly with naivety, and bruise easily' (2005: 177). The collective gesture of Stephens's first plays for the Royal Court and Royal Exchange might be defined in terms of journeys: from hunger to hope; from adversity to discovery; from fear to resilience; from social realism to something more theatrically expansive. Stephens has, rightly, been described as a Romantic (Bradley 2006; Anderson 2010) and, as Gordon Anderson relates, his plays have drawn criticism from some for being 'naïve or old-fashioned sometimes' (2010). For his part, Anderson's view is that 'Simon just has hope for better outcomes':

> And I think that is romantic in a way, maybe, but god, that's really important. And I think that he lives by that [. . .] his sense of 'we can do more than we are' [. . .]. It's that sort of belief in people, and in the potential of people, that makes him a particularly special voice, I suppose. (2010)

The plays from *Bluebird* to *On the Shore* reveal also a playwright testing the theatrical potential latent within a printed play-text, the reading of which Stephens describes as combining 'the oddness and difficulty of reading an instruction manual with the work of the imagination involved in reading a poem' (2011a: viii). It is not only that there is an increasingly economic use of stage directions; their purpose also shifts across these plays: in *Bluebird*, they imagine scenography ('*Headlights of a taxicab fill the stage* [. . .] *lighting becomes full but moody, neon, night-time*' [2005a: 3]); in *Christmas* they sketch in environmental and biographical detail; and in *Herons* full character descriptions accompany the prefatory list of dramatis personae. Character descriptions are also provided in *Port*, though these are now supplemented by the provision of dates, (real) locations and times:

Tension

'*1998. A parked Vauxhall Cavalier in the car park of the flats on Lancashire Hill in Stockport* [. . .] *It is midnight*' (2005a: 237). These geographical and temporal markers become even more specific in *Country Music* – '*Friday 15 July 1983, 2am. A parked Ford Cortina in the car park of a service garage on the A13 east of Thurrock*' (2009: 77) – though here only character ages, and not descriptions, are supplied. This is the format that Stephens reprises for *On the Shore* and, in both these plays, the stage directions' attention to character *action*, not character description, is more pronounced. Characters are no longer proscribed in advance to actors; actors are instead invited to improvise around and in response to the environmental conditions and behaviours disclosed in the text. 'Actors love working on [Stephens's] plays', attests the director Ramin Gray, 'he feeds them with all of the things they want' (2010). Anderson echoes these sentiments: 'actors love [. . .] working on Simon's scripts, it's food and drink to them. Quite often actors will tell you that they're having to cover for a script, they're having to cheat to make it sound real. But actors have always really, really responded to Simon's writing' (2010). Though it becomes more pronounced in later works, it is possible to detect even in these early plays Stephens's subtle recalibration of the play-text's function from that of instruction or illustration, to evocation or suggestion; from texts as blueprints from which to build productions (the play as 'instruction manual') to texts as prompts to imaginatively engage with (the play as 'poem').

These shifts in Stephens's deployment of language and text suggest a playwright increasingly attuned and responsive to the importance of (bodily) co-presence and liveness in theatre. The increasing command over his medium can be witnessed too in the deliberate and unexpected gaps in dramaturgy and characterization – when Christopher dies between Parts One and Two in *On the Shore*, for example, or the opacity of decisions made by Racheal in *Port* – which expect, or engender, audiences alert to the events unfolding *for them*. In the words of Frankcom, Stephens's plays from this period produce performances in which 'every minute of stage time is entirely about what happens to the people [characters] that audiences are experiencing and what they do to each other' (2010). A fierce investment in potentiality (of people, places, things) over mere actuality is poignantly rendered in these dramatic narratives; but it is captured too in those mimetically disrupted moments of *wrappedness* which 'challenge cynicism [. . .] and demand a corresponding openness from their audiences' (Rebellato 2005: 178). 'There is a sense of openness, air, and generosity in his manipulation of time and space, and in his characterizations', writes

Christian Parker, which 'invites the audience to see themselves in the moral dilemmas and existential struggles of his characters' (2016: 395). With these plays, Stephens discovers both the performer's and the spectator's active role in creating the theatrical event and, with growing confidence, exploits the liveness of this performer-spectator encounter.

CHAPTER 2
TRANSGRESSION
MOTORTOWN (2006) · *PORNOGRAPHY* (2007) ·
ONE MINUTE (2003) · *HARPER REGAN* (2008) ·
SEA WALL (2008) · *PUNK ROCK* (2009)

Chapter 1 identified *On the Shore of the Wide World* (2005) as a transitional play in Stephens's career, tracking the emergence of both murkier moral compasses and bolder theatrical visions in his writing. Sarah Frankcom, who directed the original production, pinpoints Part Four, Scene One – in which the actor playing a character who dies early in the play returns as a different, minor, but dramaturgically significant character – as the moment she realized the influence of Stephens's next significant mentor and collaborator: Sebastian Nübling. In her interview with Andrew Haydon for this volume, Frankcom relates Nübling's reaction to her production of *On the Shore* at the Royal Exchange:

> I just remember him saying to me afterwards how *horrified* he was that that scene wasn't there! And I remember thinking [of Simon], 'Oh, this is really interesting, you're having parallel relationships. There are two things happening here. There's how you are working within a very traditional, very UK theatre-writing system, and there's also how you are starting to develop some of your sensibilities somewhere else'. (See p. 210)

This chapter attends to the 'parallel relationships' with European theatre – and specifically Sebastian Nübling – that Stephens cultivated in the mid- to late-2000s, a period that he credits with interrogating his 'perception of what plays could be' (2015a: xi). In 'Skydiving Blindfolded', a keynote delivered at the 2011 Berliner Theatertreffen, Stephens paid fulsome tribute to the director, identifying five key lessons learned from him: that 'theatre is physical', 'multi-authored' and 'art'; that 'language is noise'; and that 'the English are polite and arrogant' (2011b: online). This final maxim

Stephens derives from the attitudes towards 'European' theatre voiced by his colleagues in England:

> There is an assumption that I continue to confront when I talk about my work in Germany to other English theatre makers. It is the same assumption they have always had. They talk about it in the way people used to talk about food in England in the seventies and football in the eighties. It wasn't proper food. It wasn't proper football. It's not proper theatre. (ibid.)

In his introduction to *Plays: 2*, Stephens writes of hearing British practitioners describe British theatre as being 'the best in the world' (2009: xix). 'The same people making those claims', he continues, 'often mock the experimental nature of German theatre. I can't share their confidence in their own industries or their contempt for others' (ibid.). 'Travel', he continues in 'Skydiving Blindfolded',

> has allowed me to see the assumptions sitting under our methods of working in the UK, our deference to the author, our hunger for success, our need to interpret meaning through language and our distrust of the non-naturalistic, as being culturally specific, not innate, and also, at worst, as being limited or small-minded [. . .] I couldn't have known that if I hadn't have travelled. [. . .] My assumptions were interrogated, my techniques exposed. This allowed me to take control of them. It empowered me. It exhilarated me. And it frightened me too. (2011b: online)

This chapter places Stephens as a UK playwright whose work (in the fractious years leading up to the 2016 EU Referendum, in which the UK voted to leave the European Union) 'illustrat[es] the permeability of a new generation of European sensibilities, open to the generative potential of travel and collaboration' (Fowler 2016: 328). Where Stephens's earlier plays are imaginatively preoccupied with claustrophobic familial relationships, intensely imagined locations and images of personal escape from these restrictive environments, these later works are alert and responsive to concerns – political, economic and ecological – more accurately defined as global. In a lecture delivered in Hannover in 2008, Stephens quotes Raymond Carver's suggestion that all you need to do to be a writer is to 'stare open mouthed in wonder at the world'.[1] Stephens continues to stare in wonder but the world he stares at is 'in chaos':

> Our paradigms have collapsed. Our horizons have been altered [. . .] The global population increases exponentially [and] as it does so, the demand on resources becomes intolerable [. . .] The consequences will be ecological as well as criminal. There will be massive population movement away from the increasingly uninhabitable equatorial regions towards the South and, more probably, the North of the globe. Economically and psychologically this seems to be very difficult to sustain. It seems to be difficult to police. [. . .] Extrapolating from UN and UK Governmental figures, solace seems to be being found in increasing narcotic dependency, increasing alcohol use, increasing use of pornography or the prostitution of trafficked teenage girls, increasing acts of dissociated violence, increasing religious fundamentalism. [. . .] At the same time meteorological systems seem to become increasingly chaotic [and] of course, too, the ice caps seem to be melting.[2]

This portrait of twenty-first-century disaster is all the more enervating for its hypodermic-like presence in Western consciousness: these images, headlines, facts, statistics, warnings and threats hum behind our eyes and in our fingertips through a proliferating number of screens, keeping the consequences of these particular phenomena 'a constant on the peripheries of our imagination, almost too unthinkable to think about, but undeniable'.[3] For Stephens, these 'curious' shared, recycled images widely circulated via the internet and social media – 'we've all watched the towers burn. We've all seen Bin Laden's videos' – have indeed 'provided a global shared vocabulary that feels as dissociated as any I could imagine'.[4]

The conception and execution of these plays (and, indeed, their circulation throughout Europe and beyond) is informed and enabled by the mass communication technologies that proliferated alongside Stephens's writing during the decade. Five of the six plays discussed in this chapter take as their point of departure an event that was recalibrated as spectacle(s) and extensively broadcast across 24-hour rolling news and multiple media platforms: the 2003 invasion of Iraq led by US and UK armed forces (*Motortown*); the suicide bombings on the London tube and bus network by four British men on 7 July 2005 (*Pornography*); the abduction and murder of schoolgirl Milly Dowler in March 2002 (*One Minute*); the moral hysteria surrounding crimes of paedophilia, which arguably reached its height in June 2000 when the redtop *News of the World* launched its controversial 'Name and Shame' campaign (*Harper Regan*); and the Columbine high school shooting of April 1999, in which two American teenagers killed thirteen students before killing themselves (*Punk Rock*). In these plays, a world in which 'access to corners of the world previously uncharted is immediately accessible' becomes one in which knowledge is severed from narratives of progress, or from being an intrinsically desirable end in itself, and instead lurks guiltily in the psyche.[5] What we see in these plays is an ongoing exploration of the relationship between political idea and its articulation through aesthetic form, a series of creative experiments infused and enlivened by Stephens's exposure to aesthetics and approaches encountered on the stages and in the rehearsal rooms of European theatre.

Motortown

In his introduction to *Plays: 2*, Stephens describes the plays produced between 2003 and 2008 as profoundly informed by 'two ruptures' (2009: xi). The first of these ruptures occurred on 11 September 2001 (9/11), when nineteen members of the militant Islamic group al-Qaeda hijacked four American planes, crashing two into the Twin Towers of the World Trade Centre, New York. Nearly 3,000 people died in the attacks, including the 246 civilians and 19 hijackers aboard the four planes. In response to the 9/11 attacks, the United States, supported by the United Kingdom, declared a 'Global War on Terror' and, in October 2001, US and allied forces invaded Afghanistan in order to depose the Taliban, a political regime suspected of harbouring al-Qaeda terrorists. In March 2003, the 'War on Terror' was also invoked to justify the invasion of Iraq. The governments of the US and the UK claimed that Iraq's alleged possession of biological and nuclear weapons – 'Weapons of Mass Destruction' (WMD) – represented a threat to their national security. A US-led coalition conducted a surprise attack, leading to the capture and subsequent execution of the Iraqi dictator Saddam Hussein. While both the US and UK governments submitted evidence that a pre-emptive military strike was both necessary and justifiable, Iraq's alleged possession of WMDs has never been substantiated.

The second of these two ruptures occurred four years later, on 7 July 2005 (7/7), when four British Muslim men detonated bombs across the London transport network. Three bombs exploded aboard London Underground trains on the Circle and Piccadilly lines and a fourth exploded on a double-decker bus in Tavistock Square, Bloomsbury. Fifty-six people, including the four suicide bombers, died, and over seven hundred more were injured. The bombers' stated motivation for the 7/7 terrorist attacks, recorded on videotape and broadcast across media and internet channels, was the avenging of atrocities committed upon Muslims by Western democratic states and, specifically, the UK's ongoing involvement in the Iraq war. The week in which Stephens wrote *Motortown* was the week of the London bombings – a week that would provide the pretext for Stephens's next play, *Pornography*, discussed later in this chapter. 'England has changed', Stephens wrote for the Greek newspaper *Eleftherotypia* in 2007, ahead of *Motortown*'s premiere in Athens:

> It has been changed by 9/11. It was changed by 7/7. It was changed by the [Iraq] war. It has become more scared. It has become more fractured. It has become more alienated. There are stronger currents of racism. There are higher levels of paranoia and surveillance and secrecy. These two phenomena exacerbate one another. I wanted to dramatize this moral chaos.[6]

Motortown's eight tightly-contained episodes ricochet from one pivotal event to another. When the play begins, Danny has bought himself out of the army and is staying with his brother, Lee, in Dagenham. Any hope Danny has for a fresh start with his ex-girlfriend, Marley, is instantly dispelled by Lee's opening line: 'She doesn't want to see you. She told me to tell you' (Stephens 2009: 143).[7] Danny visits Marley anyway, who tells him she wants nothing to do with him. Danny buys a replica gun, goes to London to get it converted, and pays Marley another visit.

> **Danny:** I've got something for you. I went out, into town, up London, this afternoon and got a present for you. I've not decided whether you're gonna get it yet. (177)

Danny doesn't shoot Marley. He abducts the black teenage girlfriend of Paul, the fixer who converted his P99. He takes her to Foulness Island, where he tortures and shoots her. On his way back to Dagenham he stops off for a drink at a hotel bar in Southend, where he is propositioned by a married couple of swingers. The play ends with Danny back at Lee's flat; Lee knows what Danny did, and a question mark hangs over whether he will turn Danny over to the police.

While many critics were content to read *Motortown* – and specifically the murderous violence of its protagonist, Danny – as a standard critique of the dehumanizing effects of war, Stephens is clear that any criticism espoused by the play is directed less towards the army than the culture of which it is an extension:

> I think it is easy to imagine the military as being hermetically sealed and separate from our culture, to view military atrocities as being something that are not our fault [. . .] but it is a myth. If those boys are violent, chaotic or morally insecure, it's because they are a product of a violent, chaotic and morally insecure culture. It's inaccurate to dismiss them as being part of something else. (qtd in Abrahams 2006: online)

England's 'violent, chaotic and morally insecure culture' is succinctly, if bleakly, summed up by the character of Paul: 'God. Law. Money. The left. The right. The Church. The state. All of them lie in tatters. Wouldn't you be frightened?' (171). When Danny visits Paul, he is verbally held hostage by the casually sociopathic patter of this character, whose insistence that life is valueless segues into increasingly baroque pronouncements about the amorality, futility and vapidity of the contemporary world. Paul's nihilism is articulated in his opening speech:

> To ask about the meaning of life is about as philosophically interesting as asking about the meaning of wood or the meaning of grass. There is no meaning. [. . .] There is no solidity, Only the perception of solidity. There is no substance. Only the perception of substance. There is no space. Only the perception of space. This is a freeing thing, in many ways, Danny. It means I can be anywhere. At any time. I can do anything. I just need to really try. (164)

The logical extension of Paul's worldview is that if people possess no intrinsic value, there is little to stop you from using them as instruments of your own ego; a theme that Stephens will return to in *Pornography*. This is an especially dangerous conceit to relate to a character that has difficulties in locating and reconciling actual and projected realities, as evidenced by Danny's habitual and compulsive lying. This is a vulnerability that Paul detects and uses to goad

Danny: 'You see, when you can't tell the difference any more between what is real and what is a fantasy. That's frightening, I think' (169). Paul's extended musings on the nature of space and time, however, are also an ontologically accurate description of the medium specificity of theatre, as Ramin Gray, who directed the premiere at the Royal Court, observes:

> Paul [has] a speech where he talks about [. . .] there is no space, only a perception of space; there is no time, only a perception of time. I thought that was a really good speech because it also applies absolutely to the theatre. Space and time collapse in the theatre and they expand and we can be anywhere, any time, any place. (2010).

Gray directed the premiere of *Motortown* on a spare stage that exposed the Royal Court's Theatre Downstairs' imposing brick wall. Starkly lit by an overhead bank of bright white lights, a square of white tape on a grey dance floor demarcated 'onstage' and 'offstage'. As often directed in Stephens's plays, actors remained visible throughout the play; when not engaged in a scene they sat around the edges of the square, watching the play unfold. The set consisted merely of a dozen plastic chairs, the choreographic rearrangement of which was used to indicate different locations. Gray's production created a *non-identity* between stage (reality) and fiction (fantasy) which, in place of mimetic representation, instead foregrounded the work of metaphor within the performance.

In his insightful examination of the workings of theatrical representation, Dan Rebellato suggests that, in metaphor, 'we are invited to see (or think about) one thing in terms of another thing [. . .] when we see a piece of theatre we are invited to think of the fictional world through this particular representation' (2009: 25). When, for example, the audience is invited to see (or think about) the fictional locations of *Motortown*, a non-identity of stage and fiction is in process: we see four chairs placed in a particular arrangement and engage in 'seeing' Lee's flat, Paul's high-rise apartment or the Northview bar. The relation between the chairs and location they represent is not mimetic but metaphorical; there is a vast aesthetic distance between the material reality of these chairs and the fictional reality they gesture towards. Extending this logic, we can say that, in the theatre, actors serve as 'metaphors' for characters: the actor Daniel Mays, for example, was a *metaphor* for the character of Danny. In productions such as Gray's *Motortown*, however, in which actors were cast closely to character type (indeed, the character of Danny was written by Stephens for Mays to play [Stephens 2009: xvi–xvii]) this relationship between actor and character might be better described as *metonymic*. The aesthetic distance between the 'thing we see' (signifier, actor) and the 'thing we are invited to think about' (signified, character) is very slight; the former successfully substitutes for the latter, and vice versa. As Stephens frequently attests, he is 'fascinated' by the 'directness between an actor and performance and the character' (2010a).[8] In performance, the striking *non-identity* between stage and fiction in terms of design threw into sharp relief a posited *identity* between character and actor, a dynamic which concentrated and consolidated the psychological realism of the actors' performances.

The implied proximity of 'actor' to 'character' sustained in performance was particularly exploited in *Motortown*'s graphic depiction of torture, as the production conspired to make the race and gender of the actors playing Danny and Jade profoundly and inescapably 'present'. As the audience watched a white male threaten a black female, stage reality seemed fleetingly to *vie* with dramatic fiction to terrible affect: watching 'Danny' abuse 'Jade' uncomfortably approximated to watching 'a Daniel Mays' abuse 'an Ony Uhiara'. The text itself slyly references this terrifying entanglement of actual and projected realities:

> **Danny**: Now here's a question for you. Is this really petrol or is it water?
> *He opens the canister. Holds it open, under her nose, for her to sniff.*
> What do you think? Jade? What do you think? Answer me.
> **Jade:** I don't know.
> **Danny**: No, I know. But have a guess. What do you reckon?
> **Jade:** I think it's petrol.
> **Danny:** Do yer?
> **Jade:** It smells like petrol.
> **Danny:** Are you sure that's not just your imagination?
> **Jade:** No. I don't know.
> **Danny**: Your imagination plays terrible fucking tricks on you
> in situations like this. (187)

Of course the canister contains water. As the performance of *Motortown* pressurized perceptual distinctions between actor and character, 'reality' and 'fantasy', however, such distinctions became strangely, productively, difficult to sustain. As reviewer Matt Wolf noted:

Gray blurred the boundaries between art and life to such a disturbing extent that audiences at the end had to pause a moment before applauding. On opening night the leading man, Daniel Mays, even spun himself quickly around before taking his bow, as if that action might in an instant shed the scar tissue in which so scary a play is steeped. (2006)

'Theatre exists exactly in that limbo of what's fake and what's real', attests Gray (2010). It is perhaps appropriate, then, that Stephens's work during this period – a time when the distortion and falsification of evidence was legitimized in order to prosecute a 'War on Terror' – should preoccupy itself, formally and thematically, with exploring the contradictions latent within this 'limbo'.

Pornography

Stephens's first commission from a theatre outside England, *Pornography* was written for Sebastian Nübling and received its world premiere in a translation by Barbara Christ in a co-production with Festival Theaterformen and the Schauspiel Hannover. The play's crystalline structure is built around seven parts, each inspired by one of the 'Seven Ages of Man' articulated by Jaques in *As You Like It*. It comprises four monologues, two duologues and a numbered list offering short descriptions of the fifty-two commuters killed in the 7/7 London bombings. The play situates itself within the real events that took place in London during this tumultuous week: on 2 July, the rock concert Live 8 was held in Hyde Park with simultaneous concerts held globally; on 6 July, London succeeded in its 2012 Olympic bid; on 7 July, four British Muslim men coordinated suicide attacks across the London transport network. While these terrorist attacks assume a thematic and structural centrality in *Pornography*, to describe the play as simply or exclusively 'about' the London 7/7 bombings is to overlook the complexity and nuance of its dramatic texture, as private dramas are forced into collision with a public crisis. The events *Pornography* describes may be anchored in the first week of July 2005, but the play is animated less by the reproduction of historical fact than by the observation, imaginative engagement and analytical dissection of some of the pressures, motivations and behaviours of disparate individuals living in a Western democracy during the first decade of the 2000s.[9]

A sense of stark isolation pervades *Pornography*, given varied and eloquent expression by nameless individuals cocooned in solipsistic narratives. Each of *Pornography*'s seven scenes presents 'a story of transgression' (Stephens 2009: xviii): a woman leaks a confidential report to her company's competitor; a schoolboy attacks a teacher; a brother and sister initiate a sexual relationship; a man boards a tube train with a bomb in his rucksack; a university professor attempts sexual relations with a former student; an elderly woman knocks on the door of a stranger; and, in a wryly self-referential twist, information about the victims of the London bombings is lifted from a BBC website and used as material for a play. *Pornography*'s provocation is to suggest that any distinction between these acts lies not in the category or classification of performed violation – what the act consists of – but in their order of magnitude only: 'the transgression of suicidal mass murder', Stephens writes, 'sits in the same spectrum, albeit on a far more extreme position on that spectrum, as do the others in the play' (2009: xviii). Stephens here draws not a moral but rather a symbolic equivalence between these acts. These 'stories of transgression' operate on a dual level: as autonomous narrative fictions on the one hand and, on the other hand, as metaphors for purposive acts which *irreversibly change* the co-ordinates of a situation. The businesswoman cannot un-send her fax; the schoolboy cannot un-burn his teacher; the siblings cannot un-fuck one another; the university professor cannot retract his sexual advances; the elderly widow cannot silence her knock and the terrorist cannot reverse the carnage he has wrought. These transgressions are suggestive of a dangerous estrangement from lived reality, as well as an inarticulate desire to transform it.

Pornography emerges from, and is underpinned by, a peculiarly alert sensitivity to the ways in which values and lexicons forged in the crucible of consumer capitalism infiltrate domestic as well as corporate spheres, co-opting everyday relations into miniature narratives of transaction and exploitation. The circulation of consumer goods and global brands constitutes perhaps the strongest connection across the landscape of *Pornography*: Blue Jamaican Coffee, the English rock band Pink Floyd, Upper Crust croissants and the music of Coldplay range freely across the otherwise self-contained narratives, while the individuals who consume them remain oblivious to one another's existence. The ubiquity of the iPod – 'the tube is full of people and nearly all of them nowadays have iPods' (Stephens 2009: 218)[10] – uncouples human connection from human co-presence, substituting private auditory narratives in place of a collective public experience. Business interests intervene between husband and wife:

'The Triford report is nearly finished [. . .] We actually did have to sign a contract that forbade us to speak even to our spouses about what was going on. It's a legally binding contract' (218). Exploitative television formulas hold images of the weeping bereaved 'in our gaze for a good twenty seconds before the cut' (232). Repeated references to Live 8, the Olympics and the *Metro* newspaper serve as artistic motifs, demonstrating not only the ubiquitous presence and reach of diverse media markets but also their ability to saturate public discourse and construct a mediatized collective consciousness. The internet hums and throbs under the action of each scene. Characters are isolated within their family, exploited for personal gain, alienated from their own bodies. They observe, rather than inhabit, their actions, and repeatedly fail to recognize if someone is laughing or crying. *This* is the culture of dislocation and disaffection, Stephens's text seems to suggest, from which transgressive actions ensue. In this reading, *Pornography*'s title refers less to sexually explicit material per se than to the underlying suppression of empathy which enables its consumption: it is the inability, or refusal, to imagine what it is like to be 'the other' which enables individuals to commit acts of sexual, physical, emotional or economic violence.

With at times unnerving clarity, *Pornography* dramatizes the devaluation and insidious erosion of those qualities, such as tolerance, trust, generosity and, crucially, *empathy*, which resist or exceed quantification or instrumentalization. At the same time, however, the landscape of alienation, anxiety and fear depicted by the text advances its own critique of the atomized society engendered by the monopoly of global capitalism, a critique consolidated and embodied in the play's acts of 'senseless protest', a term taken from Jean Baudrillard's illuminating collection of essays, *The Spirit of Terrorism* (2002). In these essays, Baudrillard reads al-Qaeda's attacks on the Twin Towers of the World Trade Centre in September 2001 as an attempt to destroy a 'global superpower' (2002a: 4). He contends, moreover, that this global superpower – by which he means the dominant economic order of global capitalism – has, 'by its unbearable power' *itself* 'fomented all this violence which is endemic throughout the world, and hence that (unwittingly) terroristic imagination which dwells in all of us' (2002a: 5). He posits that any power, or order, that has become hegemonic to this degree cannot be withstood: 'very logically – and inexorably – the increase in the power of power heightens the will to destroy it' (2002a: 6–7). The will to destroy the technocratic apparatus of global capitalism is the 'terror' which the West has declared war on, *but it is the West which produced this very apparatus*: 'it was the system itself which created the objective conditions for this brutal retaliation' (2002a: 9). Significantly, Baudrillard locates this 'hatred for the dominant world power' not solely or simply 'among the disinherited and the exploited, among those who have ended up on the wrong side of the global power'; even those 'who share in the advantages of that order have this malicious desire in their hearts' (2002a: 6). Terrorism then, 'like viruses, is everywhere [. . .] we can no longer draw a demarcation line around it. It is at the very heart of the culture which combats it' (2002a: 10). From this, Baudrillard concludes that the 'War on Terror' is 'not, then, a clash of civilizations or religions, and it reaches far beyond Islam and America' (2002a: 11). The War on Terror may instead be regarded as an arena in which we can witness *'triumphant globalization battling against itself'* (ibid., original emphasis).

The social and historical context of the 7/7 bombings would suggest that we are to identify the bomber in Scene Four as belonging to a 'dedicated vanguard' of Islamists willing to sacrifice their lives as part of a global movement to restore a purified *umma*. It is significant, however, that *Pornography* directs the rage and murderous violence of the terrorist towards emblems of a society stupefied by its desire and ability to consume.

> Disused Jet garage forecourts sit side by side with double driveways. Here there are food-makers and the food they make is chemical. It fattens the teenage and soaks up the pre-teen. Nine-year-old children all dazzled up in boob tubes and mini-skirts and spangly eyeliner as fat as little pigs stare out of the windows of family estate cars. In the sunshine of mid-morning in the suburbs of the South Midlands heroin has never tasted so good. Internet sex pages have never seemed more alluring. Nine hundred television channels have never seemed more urgent. And everybody needs an iPod. And nobody can ever get a *Metro* any more.
> If I had the power I would take a bomb to all this. (252–3)

The bomber's description of commuters as 'suited and smart and elegant and crisp. Weary-eyed and bloated [. . .] lugging their laptops. Clicking their heels. Pulling their shirt cuffs. Pressing their phones' (250), evinces the modern entrepreneurial culture produced under a global economic order in which people are driven not by such 'unproductive' forces as love, altruism or intellectual curiosity but by the eviscerating demands of 'R&D. Their attention to detail and the R&D is breathtaking' (ibid.). Significant also is the text's emphasis upon the bomber's own psychic territory as crisscrossed by needs, wants and desires to be fulfilled through the consumption of Western products: coffee from Upper Crust, bottled mineral water, almond croissants, the music of Pink Floyd, chewing gum and the 'sports pages of a national newspaper' (253). The bomber is thoroughly Westernized, but this does not alter his determination to attack England's capital city.

Applying Baudrillard's analysis of 'the spirit of terrorism' to the stories of transgression depicted in *Pornography*, we are, perhaps, better able to evaluate the spectrum on which Stephens claims these stories each sit. That is, we may read these transgressive acts as metaphors for what Baudrillard terms 'terroristic situational transfers' (2002a: 9): actions – in themselves singular, random, counterproductive, irrational – that enact a fundamental rejection of the values, judgements, identities and behaviours wrought by the hegemonic, suffocating rationality of a single global economic order to which Western society has submitted itself. As destructive gestures of defiance against the routinized, standardized, commodified experiences of the everyday, these transgressions constitute the very opposite of the useful and productive behaviour produced by the rational, entrepreneurial actors that neoliberalism demands and constructs. These acts of transgression do not in themselves offer alternative courses of positive action; they cannot be united or allied to a particular set of values or a coherent social agenda, and they do not command respect or approbation. In their very form as 'senseless protest', however, they do serve as unsettling 'signs of the fracture and disarray' at the heart of our contemporary socio-economic order (Baudrillard 2002b: 74). By refusing to pass authorial judgement upon the acts of sexual, physical, emotional or economic violence committed by its characters, moreover, *Pornography* stages its own defiant gesture, 'forcing us to feel and understand the complexities of each character – even if they're a suicide bomber who we would rather not know about' (Holmes 2010). In performance, this empathetic impulse can interrupt a condemnation of the play's transgressors, forming transient associations between character and spectator in which difference can be evaluated alongside unexpected and perhaps unwanted commonalities.

Pornography fractures the dramaturgical convention of a linear, unified plot. The play-text instead presents seven fragmented narratives which, the prefatory stage directions inform us, can be performed in any order *and* 'by any number of actors' (214): not only are there no pre-digestible 'characters' to organize and signpost meaning but the eight protagonists of the six dramatic scenes need not necessarily map directly onto eight individual actors. The authorial evocation of character which typically anchors readers is absent from *Pornography*; the scenes consist of unassigned text to be spoken by unnamed characters to be played by an unknown number of performers. In the case of Scene One – a numbered list offering brief biographical descriptions of the fifty-two people killed in the 7/7 bombings – it is not certain even that the text is to be spoken. Stage directions are scarce and, where they do appear, do not perform the typical function of providing hints or clarification as to how the characters behave, how the text should be delivered or how the play should be staged. If anything, as with the repeated stage direction '*Images of hell. They are silent*', they create even greater obscurity.

Interestingly, however, and by Stephens's own admission, the construction of character in *Pornography* does conform to dramaturgical convention: the speaking figures are 'characters in pursuit of objectives who learn something about themselves or fail to' (Stephens 2010a). Unlike the 'postdramatic' plays of Martin Crimp and Sarah Kane, for example, where scepticism of a sovereign self as locus and origin of human agency translates into the deconstruction, or refusal, of individualized characters, *Pornography* retains a faith in the basic dramatic function of character. Nonetheless, the decision to absent character names from *Pornography* serves to problematize the relationship between the 'speaking subject' and 'the language spoken' in ways that reverberate with the play's thematic concerns. When reading the play, the text to be spoken seems to *precede* the speaking subject, who is only subsequently lodged as 'a character' within the play. In conventional play-texts, where speech is assigned to named characters, we are often seduced into reading the dialogue as language that somehow belongs to, or is produced by, 'a character'. On the page at least, *Pornography* inverts this, using language to produce characters. These characters speak themselves into existence and, by so doing, generate the present-tense 'action' of the scene. The ways in which these characters observe and articulate their experience of being immersed in the physical, tangible, day-to-day world creates a psychological interiority which is otherwise difficult to achieve in theatre; a sense of solipsistic self-certification which contributes to the play's exploration of atomization and isolation.

The play-text of *Pornography* crystallizes some of the contrasting approaches to staging dramatic texts which prevail in English and German-language theatre cultures. Conscious of and inspired by the fact that 'writing for Sebastian would likely involve him intervening in the text', Stephens decided:

to create a text that allowed intervention rather than discouraged it, to produce a text that he could really take apart and interrogate and reinvent. And cut! Which is something that seems completely counterintuitive for any English playwright who operates in a theatre culture where the play is everything. (2010a)

In rehearsals, Nübling and his creative team approached the play-text of *Pornography* as a *point of departure* for performance. His production reordered some of the text within scenes, partially rewrote Scene Three and changed the gender of one of the characters (the story of brother and sister became one of two brothers). In the original staging, a male character was played as a male by a female actor; elsewhere in the play a female character was played as female by a male actor. Unlike the 2008 British premiere, a Caucasian actor played the role of the terrorist, a decision that was anticipated and accepted by Stephens: 'it moved the world of the play away from any realistic assessment of contemporary acts of Islamist-inspired terrorism [. . .] it made it more metaphorical' (2012). The set was designed by Nübling's long-term collaborator Muriel Gerstner and comprised half a dozen tables and chairs set before an enormous, half-finished, metal mosaic depicting Brueghel's sixteenth-century painting, *The Tower of Babel*. All eight actors remained onstage throughout, imbuing the play's fictional landscape with physical and vocal texture by assuming characters involved in subtle, interpersonal dynamics unanticipated by Stephens's writing. Furthermore, when not directly involved in the action, these 'actor/characters' engaged in the overarching 'narrative' of trying to complete the mosaic. Stephens attests that 'it was the best design I'd ever had [. . .] the necessity and impossibility of completing the mosaic seemed, to me, to be thematically relevant' (2010a).

'When a play is produced in English theatre', Stephens states in 'Skydiving Blindfolded', 'a theatre culture with the playwright at its heart, the process of rehearsal tends to involve standing the original conception of the writer as described in the text on its feet' (2011b: online). Working with Nübling on *Pornography* in Hamburg and Hannover in 2006, however, Stephens recalls that he 'started to realise the limitations of this process':

> The British director's commitment to the writer's imagination is at one and the same time its greatest strength and its greatest flaw [. . .] I couldn't have imagined the extraordinary design of Muriel Gerstner [. . .] I couldn't have seen that the cast could interweave with one

> another, doubling and trebling their roles without excavating the emotional interior of their characters. [. . .] And this excavation, this imagination, wasn't imposed onto my play but dug out from its heart. Sebastian and his actors and creative team read my play with ferocious clarity and then, in a way I've never experienced in the UK, re-imagined it. (Ibid.)

'I went home' Stephens continues, 'realising that theatre practise [sic] is not simply about staging the imagination of a playwright but a multi-authored process of collaboration, conflict, intervention and exploration. It led me to re-imagine how I write' (ibid.). Nübling's production (see Mireia Aragay's essay in this volume for an extended discussion of both this and the French premiere by Laurent Gutmann) was a major critical success, winning an invitation to the prestigious Berliner Theatertreffen.

In 2006/7, however, the open structure of *Pornography*, its refusal to delineate characters and its deliberate appeal to directorial intervention were choices which, according to Stephens, 'seemed to bewilder many readers in England' (2009: xix).

> I couldn't believe how difficult it was to get that play placed in an English theatre [. . .] I remember talking to Nick Hytner [then Artistic Director of the National Theatre] about that play and he said to me 'I couldn't really read it. There are no character names or stage directions – it's not really a play is it?' Sebastian Born [then Literary Manager] at the National said exactly the same thing. He couldn't read it. (Stephens 2010a)

Without character names to nominally 'define' its speakers, *Pornography*'s mixture of narrated and enacted action may initially appear confusing on the page, yet this blending of modes is not so radically different from Stephens's earlier play, *One Minute* (2003); indeed, as discussed later in this chapter, the degree to which form dramatizes content in both *One Minute* and *Pornography* is striking. Nevertheless, 'bewildered and frustrated by people's reluctance to produce [*Pornography*]', Stephens drafted another version of the script in an attempt to 'seduce some English theatres into producing it' (ibid.). None of the text itself was altered: Stephens simply inserted character names before the dialogue and spliced the episodes to form a new sequence of scenes which formed a chronologically linear narrative. When the director Sean Holmes – baffled by the 'weird reluctance' of his peers to produce the play (2010) – directed *Pornography* (in a co-production between the Traverse Theatre, Edinburgh, and the Birmingham Rep), this was the script that was taken into rehearsals. After encountering some difficulties with this revised version, however, Holmes decided to create his own adaptation – a decision that he affirms ran counter to his usual practice as a director: 'that was new for me, this thing of inventing, having to invent [a structure] – I'd never normally be so presumptuous to think that my structure could be better than the writer's' (ibid.). Holmes's experience of directing *Pornography* would instigate the next creative phase of his career, following his appointment in 2009 as Artistic Director at the Lyric Hammersmith, London. Sharing Stephens's enthusiasm for the challenge to conventions posed by practices of theatre-making in mainland Europe, over the next nine years Holmes oversaw a programme of work that responded to these provocations, as the following two chapters will discuss in more detail. Before that, however, it is useful to briefly dart back to an earlier point in Stephens's career, and his work with the former Artistic Director of Actors' Touring Company, Gordon Anderson.

One Minute

Commissioned and directed by Anderson, *One Minute* premiered at the Crucible Theatre, Sheffield, in June 2003. Anderson's commission set Stephens the challenge of writing a play in which individual scenes 'contrasted and juxtaposed with one another in a way that was organized but not necessarily defined by narrative cogency' (Stephens 2010a). The resulting play-text takes the genre of detective fiction – a genre Stephens would return to in *Three Kingdoms* (2011) – and turns it inside out, jettisoning the plot-driven 'hero's journey' of a Raymond Chandler novel and relocating the process of 'detecting' from within the play's fiction to the dynamic between performance and audience.

Touched by the abduction and murder of schoolgirl Milly Dowler in March 2002, *One Minute* is in part the story of a police search for a missing child.[11] Set in London, the play depicts DI Gary Burroughs and his assistant DC Robert Evans investigating the disappearance of Daisy Schults, daughter of Dr Anne Schults. Beginning in January, the play spans an eleven-month period: in April the search is scaled back, in August a body is found, and in November Gary, Robert and Anne visit London Zoo together to say their goodbyes. Orbiting and, at times, colliding with the police investigation are Catherine Denham and Marie Louise Burdett. Marie Louise contacts the police claiming to have seen Daisy two days after she disappeared; this sighting, it transpires, is Marie Louise's invention. In a manner befitting the play's 'sense of the city, its randomness [and] its parallel worlds' (Gardner 2003), despite Catherine's friendship with Gary – he is a frequent visitor to the bar where she works – she never finds out that he is investigating the Schults case; nor does Gary ever learn that Catherine flat-shares with Marie Louise. A meditation upon loss, grief and consolation, the doubled absence at the heart of *One Minute* – a missing girl whose image is never seen – is complemented by a dramaturgy which withholds the depiction of key narrative events, shifting these potentially climatic scenes to the periphery of the play in performance.

A conventional conflict-driven narrative might be expected to dramatize the pursuit of a suspect, the identification of a body, the interrogation scene; it might be expected to examine the strained relationship between Anne and her husband, or the fantasist aspects of Marie Louise's character. Instead, as Dan Rebellato describes, Stephens allows an 'emotional space and light into the structure of the text', by positioning these significant incidents and relationships 'around the edges' of the drama, in the gaps *between* scenes (2005: 175). By avoiding explicit depiction, the pain, emptiness and confusion which suffuse the story of *One Minute* appear not so much as fixed, quantifiable, known emotions as dynamic, amorphous, unutterable experiences. The underlying sense of helplessness, or impotence, which differently inhabits each character in *One Minute* finds its counterpart in a recurring sense that we, the audience, have arrived on the scene 'too late': scenes begin with half-finished conversations, or shortly after some sort of confrontation has occurred; when Gary tells Anne that her daughter's body has been found, for example, we enter the scene only *after* Anne '*has stopped crying*' (Stephens 2009: 56).[12] A sense of 'the vast unresolvedness of things' (Kingston 2003) similarly infuses scenes which evade conclusion by ending abruptly, by ending on a question or by simply trailing off into silence: 'All right. This is what happened to me today:' (22); 'Tonight, Gary. You coming or what?' (28); 'I understand, you know? People get . . .' (39). It is typical of the play's open-endedness that even as Anne ends her communication with Gary and Robert, the police investigation is ongoing.

A mixed critical reception greeted *One Minute*'s experiment with narrative cogency. While welcomed and praised by critics such as Jeremy Kingston, Ian Shuttleworth and Benedict Nightingale, Patrick Marmion declared that Stephens's 'short, oblique scenes' were 'no substitute for direct conflict and robust characterization' (2004), and Charles Spencer pronounced that Stephens 'seems willfully to have thrown away potentially powerful dramatic material' (2004a). Spencer accused Stephens of failing to 'do justice to the visceral terror of his theme' and proceeded to speculate upon the playwright's personal life: 'I may be wrong about this, but I have a strong hunch that Stephens has no children of his own, for I cannot believe that any loving parent could write with such arty attenuation on so harrowing a subject' (ibid.).[13] Spencer here equates what he identifies as Stephens's waste of 'powerful' material with a failure to stage the 'visceral terror of his theme', and attributes both flaws to an apparent lack of understanding, experience and empathy on behalf of the playwright (ibid.).

The remarks of these critics provide an interesting meta-commentary on conventions of playwriting and spectating, raising questions as to how writers 'credibly' represent the experience of extreme emotion as well as how audiences experience the representation of extreme emotion as 'credible'. It might be that Stephens's alleged waste of material is better described as a refusal to exploit for the sake of dramatic expediency the 'harrowing anxiety' which attends real-life abductions. Rather than calcify these emotions in a particular representation, the fragmentary nature of the narrative structure, its gaps and silences, 'allow these feelings to situate themselves *beyond* the world depicted by the play' (Rebellato 2005: 175). *One Minute* asks of its audiences an active engagement which goes beyond a fixed empirics of dramatic representation, and towards a liberated dynamic in which, in the words of Ian Shuttleworth, the play's 'absences and misconnections *are* the meaning, which we inhabit in our own ways as the characters do in theirs' (2004).

Anderson first encountered Stephens's work at the Royal Court, directing *Bluebird* (1998) and *Country Music* (2004) during his time as an assistant director at the theatre. Anderson's interests lay in European theatre and, during his time at the Gate Theatre, London, as well as at ATC, he directed plays by Peter Handke, Wolfgang Borchert, Franz Xaver Kroetz, Rainald Goetz and Roland Schimmelpfennig. Thinking that these playwrights 'might tickle' Stephens, Anderson introduced him to their plays; 'he was much more open to it than I thought he might be', the director recalls. 'He was really [. . .] excited that you could do things in different ways [in order] to realize your voice in different ways, and I think he found that freeing' (2010). 'This was before I had work produced in Germany', Stephens affirms, 'and these were plays unlike any other that I'd ever read in my life before. The gesture of that was really provocative' (2010a).

It is possible to read *One Minute* as a precursor to the experimental narrative structure later employed by Stephens in *Pornography*. The structure of the play was inspired by Schnitzler's *La Ronde* (1897) – a diary entry in late 2001 expresses an admiration for 'the way in which the stories touch each other ever so slightly, [. . .] the way the scenes remain so resolutely in the present tense', and the way that 'through the creation of gaps between the scenes we are able to imagine whole worlds'.[14] In 2010, Anderson expressed his admiration for the playwright's ability to 'look at small things between people in the face of bigger things happening in the world':

> He's doing that in a bolder way than he has previously. It's risky doing things that are so in the news unless you can do something really, really new and not journalistic – and that's what he's done. He's a proper theatre animal in that he does things that you can't do in other mediums. And he does them with a boldness now.

In the preface to his first collected volume of plays, Stephens sets down his 'nervous[ness]' towards plays which 'seem to place too high a value on questionable notions of authenticity and undervalue the power of metaphorical truth' (2005a: xii). While indeed tackling a subject 'in the news', Stephens's next commission for the National Theatre would deliberately refute journalistic reportage in order to explore the 'metaphorical truths' of thoughts and behaviours repressed within individuals and societies.

Harper Regan

Harper Regan was commissioned by the National Theatre in 2005, the year that *On the Shore of the Wide World* won the Olivier Award for Best New Play. For *On the Shore*, the National Theatre's then Artistic Director, Nicholas Hytner, had suggested that Stephens read the plays of American playwright Eugene O'Neill; for this commission Hytner suggested Stephens turn to one of O'Neill's own sources of inspiration, the works of Euripides. Stephens read fifteen plays by the Ancient Greek playwright and by the end of two weeks had settled upon three things:

> I wanted to write about a quest. I wanted to write a play which was dominated by a heroic central protagonist. And I wanted to write a

play in which a transgression within a family had cursed that family and the quest was an attempt to solve that curse; or to ease it; or to heal it. (qtd in Sierz 2008: online)

Drawn to 'the emotionally wrought family dramas playing out awful transgressions under the whims of the gods', Stephens's response to these 2,500-year-old texts was 'to make a play in which a similarly wrought family transgression played out under the absence of a God' (Stephens 2011a: xiii).

Seth Regan, as originally conceived by Stephens, was a play 'about somebody on the borderlines of the Sex Offenders' Register', a man ambiguously involved with online pornographic images of children (ibid.). In his introduction to *Plays: 3*, Stephens cites being 'haunted by the moral hysteria surrounding crimes of paedophilia' in the decade which preceded the writing of this play (ibid.). Public hysteria reached its height in the summer of 2000 when, following the highly publicized investigation into the abduction and murder of eight-year-old Sarah Payne,[15] the redtop *News of the World* launched its highly controversial 'Name and Shame' campaign. Over a period of two weeks the newspaper printed the pictures and names of 100 convicted paedophiles and advertised its intention to reveal thousands more. A string of riots, death threats and mob vigilante attacks on the men named, as well as men mistakenly identified as those named by the newspaper's campaign, promptly followed in the wake of the newspaper's actions. A month later the campaign was suspended in the face of severe criticism from police and child protection agencies. As a meditation upon this media-fuelled moral panic, the writing of *Seth Regan* was motivated not, as Stephens states, by 'an attempt to justify the crime so much as a sense of being troubled by moral hysteria in any form [. . .] I wanted to write about paedophilia if not with sympathy then at least with empathy' (ibid.).

Stephens had already conceived of the play's plot, characters and scenic structure when, at a script meeting, Hytner asked why it was that no contemporary playwrights were writing substantial roles for actresses in their forties and fifties. 'I was annoyed by his comment', Stephens relates:

> I remember listening to him and thinking 'well, that's the sort of thing the Artistic Director of the National ought to be angry about *but* it's built on an absolute misconception of how people conceive plays'. 'You can't impose that on somebody', I thought to myself. 'For example, if I worked through the scenic structure of *Seth Regan*', the play I was writing about this big heroic central actor, 'and I reconceived that first

scene so that it *wasn't* a man it was a *woman*, it would be . . .' And I realized that it would be much, much more interesting. And I worked through each scene that I'd imagined for Seth and re-imagined it as a woman and, to my astonishment, discovered the play. (qtd in Sierz 2008: online)

While Seth's transgression – the taking of purportedly pornographic photographs of children playing in a park – remained at the centre of the dramatic narrative, 'the play quickly became a play about his wife, whom I christened Harper' (Stephens 2011a: xiii). As with *On the Shore*, Stephens decided to write about three generations of one family; instead of three generations of sons, however, *Harper Regan* explores its subject through three generations of daughters.

When the play opens, Harper's father is in hospital, dying. Refused compassionate leave by her boss, one Monday evening Harper takes flight from both her job and her family in Uxbridge to visit Stepping Hill hospital in her home town of Stockport. Risking the family's only source of income, and having told neither her teenage daughter, Sarah, nor her husband where she is going, Harper arrives too late to tell her father she loves him. Over the next forty-eight hours, Harper experiences a series of emotionally wrought and, at times, physically fraught encounters. Summoning the courage to visit her estranged mother, Alison, Harper learns a bitter truth about her father. Devastated by the revelation, the experiences of grief, disillusionment, desire and guilt that Harper confronts and endures on her two-day journey metamorphose into a form of self-knowledge; a bruised but clear-sighted wisdom that returns her to her family, and to her marriage, prepared for the necessity of speaking the truth, withstanding failure and placing faith in forgiveness.

With *Harper Regan*, directed by Marianne Elliott in the Cottesloe Theatre in April 2008, Stephens's dramaturgy once again displaces key narrative events, or climactic scenes, from the centre to the periphery, shifting dramatic focus from the 'central crisis' to the social and emotional reverberations caused by it. The play is not about the headline-grabbing issue of paedophilia as prurient deviance; the drama that unfolds might more accurately be described as an empathetic exploration of the sexual drives which, consciously and unconsciously, influence behaviour. Echoes of the singular transgression at the heart of the narrative pulse throughout the play. It is no coincidence, for example, that Alison's second husband is, at fifty years of age, her 'toy boy' (Stephens 2011a: 282);[16] that Elwood, Harper's boss, takes particular interest in Sarah and her 'remarkable clothes'

(208); or that Harper, a white, middle-aged married woman, initiates a physical encounter with Tobias, a black teenage boy (292), and has sex with a man old enough to ask if his age 'bothers' her (265). To differing degrees, each one these circumstances tests social orthodoxy, a theme introduced by the opening scene between Harper and Elwood:

> **Elwood:** If you go, I don't think you should come back.
> *A terribly long pause. As long as they can get away with. They stand incredibly still.*
> **Harper:** I don't know what to say.
> **Elwood:** No. (205)

By themselves, these opening lines – including the torturous pause – are arguably more reminiscent of definitive break-up between lovers than a request for time off work. They certainly give little indication as to the nature of Elwood and Harper's relationship as employer and employee respectively; indeed, it is eight lines later, when Harper informs Elwood that she has not yet taken a single day off, before their social roles and relations begin to crystallize for the spectator. Once established, however, the scene appears to make some very odd digressions; for a play named after its female protagonist, the manner in which Elwood dominates this opening scene appears to throw the drama off balance. What we witness is an abuse of the circumscribed social contracts which, as her employer and as a heterosexual man, in this situation confer power to Elwood.

> **Elwood**: [. . .] It's your own fault, you know? Do you have the slightest idea how good you are at your job? You've become invaluable.
> [. . .] You have a charming smile Harper. When you answer the telephones, do you smile like that?
> **Harper:** I don't know.
> **Elwood**: I bet you do.
> **Harper**: I –
> **Elwood**: I imagine it has a remarkable impact. It must be why all these contracts keep pouring in. [. . .] Stay there. Stay exactly there. Stand exactly like that.
> **Harper**: You're unnerving me a little, Mr Barnes, I have to say.
> **Elwood**: Yes. Now.
> *Silence. For thirty seconds.*
> Do you feel any better? (209)

Harper's apparent function is to provide a blank canvas for Elwood to project his thoughts onto. When she does not comply with this effacement of her subjectivity, by stating a preference not to call her boss by his first name, or offering that she likes the punk band The Slits, she is met with '*completely mystified*' silence (210).

The subjects of Elwood's diatribes in this scene introduce another key dynamic of the play: the tension created when fear and fascination collide. The intellectual 'vacancy' of 'our young', for example, both frightens and intrigues Elwood: 'I see them all the time. [. . .] Making unusual noises to one another. Talking with their iPods still in. How do they do that?' (207). The internet, in particular, contributes to the contemporary social malaise diagnosed by Elwood; its power to absorb all human activity both shocks and entrances him:

> All of my shopping I do online. All of my reading I do online. All of my news I get online. All of my television I watch online. All of my radio I listen to online. I'm perpetually on YouTube [. . .] I am obsessed with sports news [. . .] I watch a measured amount of porn. Did you know that people can arrange illicit sexual encounters online nowadays? Honestly Harper. You can go to these places. You can look at these things. This is actually happening [. . .] I can't get enough of the things. I find them absolutely fascinating. (210–11)

The tension created by convergences of disgust and desire crackles throughout *Harper Regan*. In his first meeting with Harper, Tobias expresses his revulsion towards 'women all dressed up in their clothes and their skirts and their make-up [. . .] you ought to be ashamed of yourselves' (220); moments later, however, he admits that 'the idea of an older white woman is almost like a kind of dream to me' (221). Mickey is 'fascinated' by online 'surveillance', declaring that this covert monitoring doesn't bother him and that 'people should just be a bit more honest' about their internet activity:

> They should go on radio phone-ins and just fucking say 'I like porn! I look at it all the time! There's nothing I like more than watching images of twenty-year-old mid-western girls fucking older men. Humping them until they come their heads off. That's what I like and that's what I want to spend my free time looking at'. (254)

Mickey runs out of steam after this enthusiastic outburst in praise of online pornography and a few moments later morosely reflects: 'Sometime I think

I prefer porn to actually having sex. Do you ever worry about that?' (255). The currents of attraction and guilt which course through the play connect, ultimately, to Seth's ambiguous transgression, itself a symbolic expression of the 'catastrophe of sexual desire' (Stephens 2011a: xiii).

To accept that human behaviour is conditioned by unconscious drives is to admit that our self-knowledge can only ever be partial and imperfect, that we can never fully know what we are capable of doing to ourselves, or to others. Harper's actions in the play, which escalate from 'daring' to talk a boy she finds 'completely beautiful' (270), to crushing a wine glass into a man's neck, to having sex with a stranger she finds online, confront her with the fact that she is, in fact, capable of betrayal and violence; that she too, can consciously and wilfully transgress: 'Sometimes we step outside ourselves and we look at ourselves for a bit and ask ourselves "Am I actually doing this?" and we tell ourselves, "Yes, I actually am". And carry on doing it' (299). Harper's journey to Stockport and back may be described as a voyage of self-discovery; what is 'discovered', however, is the absence, the loss or erosion, of abiding teleological structures which explain and make sense of the world. Harper, for instance, does not simply lose her father to death: when her mother, Alison, reveals that, contrary to what Harper believed, it was *he* who believed Seth guilty of the crimes for which he was convicted, her personal mythology in which her father was idealized as a 'hero' is destroyed (261). The epistemological tremor experienced by Harper finds expression elsewhere in the play. Elwood confidently pronounces on the 'absolute absence' of morality among the young (208), and Alison voices her disdain for what she perceives as moral relativism of contemporary society: 'You can't even draw a line. You can't even say, "This is wrong, what is happening here is wrong"' – a sentiment with which it would be easier to sympathize were it not preceded by her racial slur against 'blacks' (284). In their first meeting, Tobias appeals to Harper: 'Nobody believes in God round here [. . .] If you don't believe in God, then how are you meant to know how to live? You don't. I think that must be terrible' (220). Tobias's horror at the decaying of moral certitudes is contrasted by Mickey's disavowal of journalism as an enlightened moral authority: 'They're getting rid of journalists [. . .] I don't blame them. They can Google all the news they need. Cut and paste it' (253).

Given its central role within the dramatic narrative of *Harper Regan*, the play seems to suggest that the internet has in some way worked to fill, or at least distract from, a moral or spiritual void at the heart of existence. Stephens has reflected that 'the perception of the internet' changes through his plays of the early 2000s 'from something benign to something darker', as though 'there was an realisation that the internet was an insubstantial and distractive kind of liberation' (2011a: xvi–xvii). The notion of the internet as insidiously corrupting recurs throughout the play: it inspires myopic obsession in Elwood; it spoils the appeal of sex with real women for Mickey; it facilitates, with startlingly simplicity, Harper's act of infidelity and it is the gateway to millions of pages of pornographic images, including, the play does not let us forget, images of children.

Part of the sophistication of *Harper Regan* lies in its refusal to definitively establish whether Seth is in fact guilty of his conviction. The play is careful to note that when Seth was charged, he was told 'that if he pleaded guilty then his trial wouldn't have to go to jury'; Harper tells us that Seth did this because he 'decided that that would be fairer to me and to Sarah' (266). Harper, initially, doesn't believe that the photographs of children taken in their local park were pornographic, because 'they were outside' (ibid.). 'You can't even take photographs any more' she exclaims. 'What kind of a world? What does that . . .?' (267). Harper doesn't finish her sentence. The play invites us to consider – and perhaps mourn – how, in a society traumatized by highly publicized accounts of acts of paedophilia, an appreciation of the gorgeousness of young children has become more difficult to read as unequivocally innocent. How do we conceive of or understand intimacy with children, even, or particularly, our own? Alison says to Harper, 'You had these little hands and these little fingers and skin which frankly you'd have been a fool *not* to want to take a bite out of it looked so good', and the emphasis on '*not*' seems oddly charged (284). Seth's declaration in the play's final scene that he 'like[s] the smell of my daughter's neck [. . .] and the way her hair falls down over her face when I kiss her neck' (305), is made during an otherwise restorative moment for the Regan family, yet similarly retains the potential to unsettle and disturb as much as comfort and reunite.

The premiere of Harper's 'northern odyssey' (Billington 2008) was enthusiastically received by theatre critics, who were unanimous in their praise of the actor Lesley Sharp as Harper. While Michael Billington disputed the plausibility of some of Stephens's characters (particularly the 'coke-snorting, rabidly antisemitic reporter', Mickey), he nevertheless praised Stephens as one of only a few modern playwrights capable of writing 'star parts', describing the role of Harper as a 'stunning' opportunity for Sharp to display her 'abundant emotional range' (ibid.). Paul Taylor also acknowledged the 'terrific central role' created by Stephens and credited Sharp with a 'superb performance that runs the full emotional gamut'

(Taylor 2008). Michael Coveney observed Sharp's 'rare knack' of 'making you feel exactly what the character is thinking without spelling it out' (2008) and Fiona Mountford wrote of how Sharp's 'detached style of delivery, one turn of the dial away from naturalistic, beautifully suggests a woman surveying her existence from a great distance and finding it suddenly incomprehensible' (2008). Several critics drew attention to the structural similarities between *Harper Regan* and *Motortown*; where Coveney described both plays as studies of 'the geography of a soul in torment, a spiritual odyssey as well as a physical one' (2008), Heather Neill perceived the 'beautifully structured' *Harper Regan* as a 'deliberate counterpoint to the "male" *Motortown*' (2008). Interestingly, the play's final scene was read by many of the play's (predominantly male) critics as unequivocally affirming. For David Benedict, 'this beautifully fragile final scene' suggested 'that desperation might be assuaged by hope', leading him to declare that *Harper Regan* was 'Stephens's most mature play yet' (2008).

Sea Wall

Questions of belief, faith and how one lives 'in the absence of God' also sit directly under Stephens's short play, *Sea Wall* (2008). A monologue for a male actor, *Sea Wall* weaves an intimate story of family tragedy from the recollections and reflections of its lone protagonist. It also provides a demonstration of what Cathy Turner and Synne Behrndt, discussing dramaturgies that 'make us aware [. . .] of the artificial construction of imaginary (real) worlds even while we are moved and engaged with them', have identified as 'the inadequacy of looking at the script as a discrete object, a closed system, without reference to the event of its performance' (2008: 193). As this volume explores, Stephens is a playwright inspired by the challenge of writing for specific actors and into specific theatre spaces. *Sea Wall* offers an exemplary instance of how Stephens can manipulate and exploit empirical givens in order to conjure compelling fictions.

Sea Wall was commissioned by director Josie Rourke for the Bush Theatre, London, for their Broken Space season in October 2008. Leaks in the roof of the theatre earlier that year had made the theatre's lighting grid unsafe to use, so a host of short plays were commissioned to take place in either natural light or pitch dark. The stage directions for *Sea Wall* state: '*this monologue should be performed as far as possible on a bare stage, as far as possible in natural light, and as far as possible without sound effects. Alex addresses the audience directly*' (Stephens 2009: 284).[17] As the play takes place within a designated theatre space, the expectation that a work of fiction is to take place necessarily precedes the performance and anticipates its effects. Yet, within the spectator's visual field, there is nothing else that announces itself as fictional: this *is* a stage, this *is* natural light, this *is* the grain of the actor's voice addressing the spectator(s) directly. In the 2008 premiere directed by George Perrin, the actor Andrew Scott – as yet unknown to film and television audiences – stood before an audience, dressed in what may (as well) have been his own clothes (jeans, jumper, trainers), speaking words written specifically for 'his voice' by a playwright that 'saw [Scott's] face and body when I imagined the play'.[18] There was in this situation, as Ramin Gray describes in his interview with Andrew Haydon for this volume, 'an infinitesimal amount of [fictional] material between the actor and the audience' (see p. 211).

The text of *Sea Wall*, therefore, not only anticipates but actively invests in a productive tension between the material, empirical, reality of the stage/actor and the fictional world of the story/character. The playfully dialogic interaction achieved in performance is inscribed within the written text itself:

> **Alex:** [. . .] And she says she really likes this bit.
> *He shows the area at the top of his arm.*
> This bit is one of the best bits of a man, she says. (287)

What we are literally seeing, of course, is the arm of Andrew Scott (or that of the actor in performance) but, in that moment, it both *is* and *is not* Scott's arm: it *is* and *is not* Alex's arm. To return to Rebellato's meditation on representational strategies discussed earlier, Scott's arm is a *metaphor* for Alex's arm, a metaphor in which we are invited to invest: sizing up Alex/Scott's arm is perhaps something to take pleasure in for a moment. This moment condenses and foregrounds what is always already happening within representational theatre: the 'seeing' of Scott and Alex simultaneously. The actor presents a particular, concrete example of a general, metaphysical idea; a movement from the particular to the general which, again, is wryly foregrounded within the text: Helen's affection for that bit of the arm is not in fact specific to Alex, but applies to any man.

Something peculiar happens, however, when 'Alex' delivers this speech:

> I want to acknowledge something. And it's embarrassing because
> I know it's something that you will have noticed. There's a hole

running through the centre of my stomach. You must have all felt a bit awkward because you can probably see it. Even in this light. Most people choose not to talk about it. Some people tell me that they're sorry but that, yes, they can see my hole. 'What's that, Alex?' they say. 'You appear to have a great big hole running right through the middle of you'. (291)

On a stage otherwise devoid of metaphor, the force of Alex's words inheres in the bizarrely plausible notion that *he is not speaking metaphorically*. In this moment, a 'great big hole' is torn in the actor's otherwise flawlessly mimetic performance as the *non-identity* of Scott's body collides with Alex's words. The spectacle of Scott's intact body contradicts Alex's words and, peculiarly, it is the intactness of his body – not the meaning of his words – which seems somehow untrue.

Woven throughout the play are questions regarding the existence of God and the possibility of religious faith. Mid-way through the play, Alex recounts a conversation he had with his father-in-law, Arthur: 'I say to him, "if you can't tell me what He looks like and He doesn't look like anything, then how do you know He isn't anything more than just an idea? Just something you've made up?"' (290). Alex, a photographer, dismisses God as a fiction on the grounds that there is no empirical, physical proof of his existence. Arthur responds to Alex with a string of beautiful metaphors: 'He's in the feeling of water [...] He's in the way some people move. He's the light falling over a city at the start of an evening. He's in the space between two numbers' (293). In the closing moments of *Sea Wall*, the spectacle we are confronted with is a man consumed by grief, bereaved of a daughter and unable to work because, he explains:

> There's a lie at the heart of photography that I've always cherished. When you take a photograph what you do is you freeze something that's actually alive. To do this properly you need, more than anything, to believe in life. (296)

He viciously spits: 'You see people when they say to you that they can't imagine not believing in anything because it would be just too depressing. I think there's something sick about that. The level of cowardice in that is just unbearable to me' (ibid.). Alex believes that God is a fiction, that He is 'made up', and those people who need to believe in something 'made up' to make sense of and give meaning to their lives are cowardly. Paradoxically, however, if the monologue has worked on us – if we have been moved by Alex's story – then the performance itself testifies to the power and importance of dramatic story-telling, the truths revealed by metaphor, even as we know, rationally, that it is all, all of it, just 'made up' (Stephens 2009: xvi). In common with many of Stephens's plays, though in a particularly pure and condensed form here, *Sea Wall* demonstrates how a playwright can consciously exploit the *dramaturgy of representation* in order to destabilize the theatrical articulation of a realist narrative and, in so doing, move and engage spectators through the creation of (real) imaginary worlds.

Punk Rock

Punk Rock is set in the library of a sixth-form fee-paying grammar school in Stockport and depicts the lives of seven students studying for their mock A-Level exams. The play opens with the arrival of a new girl, Lilly. She is welcomed by William, who is instantly besotted with her. Bennett, the boyfriend of Cissy, bullies Chadwick, in whose defence Tanya often speaks out. Lilly starts sleeping with Nicholas. In the sixth of seven scenes, William brings a gun to school and shoots dead Bennett, Cissy and Nicholas. The seventh scene is set in Suttons Manor Hospital, Romford, Essex, a specialist low-secure unit offering rehabilitation for men with mental health needs.

The above outline is deliberately blank; this is not to suggest a flatness or abstraction in either the plot or characterization of *Punk Rock* but rather to respect the way in which the play questions precisely those processes by which we read, interpret and make psychological inferences about characters – and, by extension, other human beings – from what they do and say. As the play's London reviewers demonstrated, attaching adjectives to these characters – Lilly is 'cool, cruel and self-harming' (Brown 2009), William 'intellectually curious and sensually undernourished' (Hitchings 2009), Bennett 'suavely vicious' (Shuttlesworth 2009), Cissy 'ambitious, quirky and malicious' (Hart 2009), Chadwick 'a brilliant nerd' (Hitchings 2009), Tanya 'teacher-besotted' (Billington 2009b) and Nicholas 'decent, honourable, slightly dull' (Hart 2009) – is apparently not difficult. Yet the readiness of reviewers to pronounce such pithy epithets, pinning them onto characters like press-stud badges (bearing a school motto, or punk slogan perhaps), sits at odds with the nexus of concerns explored by *Punk Rock*.

Looking back to the 1999 Columbine High School shooting (in which two white male teenagers shot thirteen students dead before killing themselves), but written in the immediate aftermath of the 2007 shooting at Virginia Tech, in which a white male student killed thirty-two of his peers before also committing suicide, *Punk Rock* confronts the uncomfortable truth that the contemporary phenomenon of mass shootings in the United States eludes explanation. Faced with the inscrutable, mainstream media coverage has sought to contrive explanatory frameworks which posit easily digestible cause-and-effect links between a perpetrator's lifestyle and their actions. In the case of Columbine, for example, 'speculation abounded that Harris and Klebold were exacting revenge for being bullied, or that they were Nazi-worshipping racists', or that they were influenced by the music of the controversial musician Marilyn Manson (Love 2016b: 1). Conceiving of these massacres as events attributable to, or motivated by, specific social and cultural phenomena, however, does little to explain why – in contrast to an overall decline in violent crime (including gun crime) in the United States since the 1990s – this form of violence is, in the words of activist Richard Seymour, increasing in regularity, as if it's '"gone viral"' (Seymour 2018: online). Attempts to extrapolate 'motivation' from a composite appraisal of an individual's alleged influences, preferences and dispositions has so far proved unsuccessful in providing legible rationales to account for the phenomenon; indeed, these attempts have better revealed the prejudices and inadequacies of mainstream journalistic discourse (and, perhaps, certain psychiatric practices). The readiness with which Western societies move to 'diagnose' the psychological profile of individuals from a necessarily selective assessment of upbringing, environment and lifestyle – and, further, to utilize this diagnosis as a predictor of future behaviour – is revealed as a deep source of unease within *Punk Rock*. The fallibility of such an approach is baldly foregrounded in the play's final scene between William and his assigned psychologist:

> **William:** [. . .] See, the main question people have been asking me is why I did it.
> Why do people keep asking me that?
> **Dr Harvey:** I think people are concerned about you.
> **William:** 'Why did you do it, William? What did you do it for? Why did you do that? Why did you do this?' [. . .] I don't know. I don't care. It's a pointless question. It's a stupid question. It's a boring question. Next question please [. . .] Was it because of my mum? No. Was it because of my dad? No. Was it because of my brother? No. Was it because of my school? No. Was it because of the teachers? No.

> Was it because of Lilly? No. Was it the music I was listening to? No. Was it the films I saw? No. Was it the books I read? No. Was it the things I saw on the internet? No. [. . .]
> I did it because I could. (Stephens 2011: 408)[19]

The decision to set *Punk Rock* within the affluent middle-classes was a deliberate choice by Stephens, as he outlined in rehearsal notes to the cast and creative team of the 2010 production in Hamburg:

> There is often an equation made between violence and poverty. [. . .] To me there is something in the metabolism of English culture of the last decade which means that it's not out of the question that such atrocious violence can happen to the rich, to the educated, to the affluent and the supported, to people whose parents love them, to people whose environment is built around them. Even there, in that world [there] is the possibility of a break, of a nightmarish break, in the metabolism of this culture.[20]

Punk Rock depicts this 'nightmarish break' through a dramaturgy that breaks with or suspends some of the foundational 'rules', or established conventions, of playwriting. While, once again, character remains paramount – notes written by Stephens for the play remind him to 'make sure that [. . .] each of the individual characters has a journey, an arc and a conclusion' – and time is carefully plotted – 'make sure that you are absolutely aware [. . .] how long has passed in between each scene and what has happened in that passing of time'[21] – other elements of dramatic craft are playfully manipulated. Character backstory, for example, is not so much delicately revealed through careful exposition as weaponized, as in the opening scene where William fires question after question at Lilly. While it is Lilly who is being interrogated, William's questions – 'How did you get here? [. . .] What mode of transport did you use?' (312) – work to reveal more about him than they do her. His piercing enquiries also pre-empt and deflate the potential for subtext: 'It must be slightly disorientating having to adjust to a new town in such a short space of time, is it?' (311). Writing 'a big liar' into a play – a proclivity William shares with Danny from *Motortown* and Marie Louise in *One Minute* – complicates the audience's relationship to the fiction, putting them in what Stephens describes as an 'innately unstable' position to the drama.[22] How *do* we know when a character is telling the truth? Or, more precisely, how do we know when an actor is telling a truth, or a lie, about their character? What do we have at our disposal to separate out the 'lies' from the 'truth'? William may be a fantasist, inventing stories about his family, but Lilly also doesn't always tell the whole truth. 'There's a lot about you which is a lie', William says to her in Scene Five. 'The way you tie your tie is a lie' (384) he says, and there is something about the statement which is perhaps designed to point to the *actor*'s failure to knot their tie in a fashion 'true' to the character of Lilly.

Other aspects of realist dramaturgy are also taken hostage: almost all of Chadwick's entrances into and exits out of the library, for example, appear entirely unmotivated. Indeed, the immediate environment itself has no bearing on either character or plot: the library is never used as a library and such is the irrelevance of this location that the stage directions of the published script place Scenes Two to Four in the '*the common room*' (329, 342, 365) – a typo remaining from an earlier draft of the play. Indeed, Scene Six just refers to 'the stage' (390). William's linguistically precise but eccentric description of the library as 'completely hermetically sealed from the rest of the school' (313) makes more sense as a comment *upon* the fiction than as a description *within* it: within the fiction it serves as a somewhat limp explanation for the absence of other students or teachers using what is, after all, a communal space; as a meta-theatrical statement, however, it draws attention to both the status of dramatic literature *and* the conditions of the performance taking place within a theatre auditorium (hermetically sealed from the rest of the city).

While interpersonal dialogue and social interaction between characters remain the primary means by which the story unfolds, the personalities and individual traits of these characters ultimately possess no bearing on the plot, or the play's denouement. In an ironic subversion of 'Chekov's gun', aspects of character that seem carefully placed, aren't: Lilly's self-harming is neither explained nor explored (although it does provide William with an opportunity to demonstrate some humanity); Tanya's purported obsession with Mr Anderson has no consequences; and Cissy's implied eating disorder is passed over without comment. Furthermore, the cardinal question of dramatic craft – 'whose story is it?' – is wilfully disregarded for five of the seven scenes. No single protagonist clearly emerges from the play until, we might say, too late: instead, the opening scenes set up a number of possible narratives: Lilly as new girl: how will she get on? William loves Lilly: how will that relationship develop? Is Bennett bi- or homosexual? And how will they all do in their mock-exams? Not one of these possible narratives survives beyond Scene Six; and, indeed, William's actions work retrospectively to expose the smallness, and perhaps pettiness, of these concerns.

The insignificance of everyday tribulations within the context of impending political, economic and environmental catastrophe has by that point in the play already been voiced by Chadwick:

> Human beings are pathetic. [. . .] We've been around one hundred thousand years. We'll have died out before the next two hundred. You know what we've got to look forward to? You know what will define the next two hundred years? Religions will become brutalized; crime rates will become hysterical; everybody will become addicted to internet sex; suicide will become fashionable; there'll be famine; there'll be floods; there'll be fires in the major cities of the Western world [. . .] It's happening already. It's happening now. [. . .] Species will vanish forever. Including ours. So if you think I'm worried by you calling me names, Bennett, you little, little boy, you are fucking kidding yourself. (376–7)

It is significant that it is *not* Chadwick – the boy who is bullied, whose intelligence isolates him, who courts nihilism as a form of protection – who carries out the shooting. Nor is it the 'casually sadistic' Bennett, even though his behaviour, as dramatized in this bizarre sixth-form library, repeatedly evinces and contributes to what Seymour describes as 'the general atmosphere of social sadism and official detachment, callousness and nihilism' (2018: online) pervading Western society. It is not only Bennett's tormenting of Chadwick that manifests these social st(r)ains: talking to Nicholas in Scene Six about spitting in Tanya's face, Bennett concedes that 'it was stupid' but explains that he 'just really wanted to': 'I wanted to know what it would feel like' (391). The action and explanation together comprise a gesture illustrative of, in the words of Stuart Young, 'an age of exalted individualism that requires only minimal concessions to morality in interactions with others' (2017: 22). Placing *Punk Rock* alongside *Pornography*, we might read the actions of spitting and shooting as transgressions sitting on a shared spectrum of nihilistic narcissism, accompanied, perhaps, by a third:

> **William** *goes to shoot himself. He holds his gun in his mouth. After a short while he retracts it.*

> I'm sorry. I really need a piss. Should I do it on the floor? Should I do it in my trousers, Tanya? If I do it in my trousers will you tell?
> **Tanya:** No.
> **William:** Do you think it'd be alright?
> *She nods.*
> *He pisses in his trousers, down his trouser leg, onto the floor of the common room* [sic].
> My God. The relief. (401–2)

Punk Rock exposes the incompleteness of the logic that drives people to search for a specific cause or motivation for extreme violence by problematizing both the readability and reliability of outward 'signs' to accurately diagnose and predict human behaviour. As Seymour notes, even as psychologists strive to compile psychological profiles of mass shooters – 'replete with "red flags" to look out for' – they simultaneously concede that, in the words of Tia Ghose, '"it is maddeningly difficult to separate the next school shooter from the millions of other disaffected students who may never go on to kill"' (2018: online). The form and the content of the play perform a more complex, and less accessible, hermeneutics than that discerned through superficially sociological analyses (or, indeed, portrayed via orthodox naturalism), depicting a cultural malaise that does not precisely transcend class and environment, but which cannot be reduced to deterministic, cause-and-effect models of their influence.

Conclusion

In notes made during a workshop at the Royal Court in July 2000, Stephens records that he and the other participants 'talked about the nature of political theatre', and specifically 'the way in which our contemporaries are dramatizing an absence. An absence of trust in any form of political truth. A dwelling on the symptoms of the disease'.[23] Noting that Graham Whybrow, the then Literary Manager, 'expressed reservations about the limited aspirations of this generation', Stephens pushes back: 'I think that as long as the focus is concentrated, intelligent, considered enough then there is huge political redolence in the smallest of stories'.[24] The plays examined in this chapter stage a 'response to and critique of what it means to be living at a particular time, in a particular social formation', though with a focus less on the 'particular political and legal structures and institutions' that occupied the more self-consciously 'political' British playwrights of previous generations (Reinelt 2007: 371) (see Chapter 3 for further discussion of this). Stephens instead, as Anderson suggested in 2010, focuses rather on the *interpersonal* relations, predations and dissociations engendered by a world in seeming moral and ecological collapse. As Stephens puts it in an article on one of his playwriting heroes, Robert Holman, 'the oddity of the actual stuff that people do to one another often renders political agendas imprecise' (2015b: online).

These works may be read as critiques of a culture in which acts of violence should be understood as the symptoms, not causes, of a Western liberal society in economic, political, cultural and ecological chaos. As such, these plays might be accused of 'dwelling on the symptoms of disease', and indeed, the playwright Edward Bond, in a 2012 keynote address for the German Society for Contemporary Drama in English, decried British theatre, and certain of Stephens's plays in particular, as no better than 'a theatre of symptoms' (Bond 2012: online). The contention of this chapter, however, is that these plays might more accurately be described as being creatively preoccupied by a perceived *dislocation* between 'causes' and 'effects' in the empirical world. This dislocation infuses the dramaturgy of Stephens's plays during this period, manifesting subtly in an altered attitude towards character biography and behaviour. Socio-psychological causation within a naturalist framework, for example, becomes a concept to query: Stephens's early notes for *One Minute* state that 'characters [in this play] will not have their motivation plundered in a linear causal way',[25] suggesting, perhaps, an emerging dissatisfaction with deterministic psychological paradigms. Similarly, and in a decisive rejection of the sentimentality for which earlier plays were sometimes criticized, notes for *Motortown* read: 'put an amoral character at the heart of a play. [. . .] Not excused by economic circumstances, past trauma, abuse, anything. [. . .] A malevolent shit revelling in the misery of others'.[26] In each of these plays, biographical detail – more specifically, the influence of biographical detail upon the action of the story – diminishes or recedes, as Stephens presents us instead with snapshots of characters within the limits of a scene fragment. In plays such as *Motortown*, *Pornography*, *Harper Regan* and *Punk Rock*, the imperative to conjure and communicate psychological detail produces characters who divulge, often unprompted, a degree of personal information – opinions, predilections, beliefs and prejudices – which in ordinary conversation would be bizarre. The function of dialogue in these plays (and in distinction to his earlier works) is increasingly not to harness and reflect the typical rhythms, cadences and phrases of everyday conversation in the service of creating characters who seem like 'real people' but rather to stake out physical, emotional and intellectual territory between characters, and to intimidate, unsettle and tease spectators. In this way, pressure is placed on the concept of character, and particularly on the idea of a character's 'voice' as being something idiosyncratic and distinct. From *Pornography* onwards, the 'liberal humanist concept of character, which represents humans as fully developed individuals' (Ilter 2015: 249), appears to cede way to an idea of character more in keeping with the idea of 'cipher' or 'figure', until in *Punk Rock* there is a curious sameness of idiolect across all seven characters.

As readers and spectators, we are in turn entreated to retrain our focus not on what the dialogue is saying but on what it is *doing*: 'playwriting is *not* a linguistic profession, it's a behaviourial profession', Stephens insists. 'My subject isn't what people *say* to each other; it's what people *do* to each other that interests me' (2010a). To return to his 2011 keynote, 'Skydiving Blindfolded', Stephens expresses here his frustration with the way in which UK theatre critics remain 'obsessed with words', concerning themselves 'almost wholly with a consideration of the things that characters say to one another' at the expense of reading 'physical imagery' (2011b: online). Wresting the locus of meaning and signification from language to imagery – or, more precisely, to an (at times ironic) juxtaposition of statement with action – creates collisions and contradictions within and between characters from which meaning sparks. To return to the lessons learned by Stephens from Nübling: theatre is physical, language is noise and the performance event is multi-authored – these are axioms that will impact not only Stephens's future writing but also his working relationships with British directors, as Chapters 3 and 4 explore.

CHAPTER 3
JUXTAPOSITION
WASTWATER (2011) · *THE TRIAL OF UBU* (2010) · *THREE KINGDOMS* (2011)

In discussing the theatre of Simon Stephens so far, this volume has worked within some neat divides and distinctions: between 2000 and 2005, the plays shuttled between London and Manchester before, from the middle of the decade onwards, hopping back and forth across the Channel. During this latter phase, the techniques of playwriting and conventions of staging that Stephens learned within the cultures and discourses of English, building-based, subsidised, producing theatres were confronted by European approaches to the writing and staging of dramatic texts which challenged these familiar practices. Through the figure of Stephens, a UK theatre culture that enshrines the playwright's vision butted up against a German-language theatre culture animated not by the attempt to realize the playwright's 'intended area of meaning' (Hare 2005: 106) in some definitive manner but rather by the search for what a play-text *might be capable of saying* when brought into contact with other elements of live performance: bodies, space, rhythm, light, sound. By 2011, as he attests in 'Skydiving Blindfolded', Stephens's collaborations with Sebastian Nübling had transformed not only his 'perception of what plays could be' but also his 'understanding of the relationship between a writer and a director' (2011b: online).

There are, inevitably, gaps, silences and omissions in this narrative. Plays by Stephens were also produced in Sheffield (*One Minute*), Brighton (*Christmas*) and Edinburgh (*Pornography*) during this period; other important collaborations were established (with the American singer-songwriter Mark Eitzel on *Marine Parade* [2010], for example, as well as with British playwrights David Eldridge and Robert Holman for *A Thousand Stars Explode in the Sky* [2010]); and it was the British director Gordon Anderson who, long before Stephens met Nübling, first introduced Stephens to the canon of German playwriting. Furthermore, while an interrogation of his creative practices certainly enriched Stephens's understanding of the cultural specificity of theatrical convention, this did not lead to a wholesale rejection of these techniques in his work. While plays such as *Pornography* and, later, *Carmen Disruption* (2015) and *Nuclear War* (2017) indicate a break from the 'default mimetic realism' that Stephens identifies as the predominant dramaturgical mode in English playwriting (2013a), texts such as *Blindsided* (2014) and *Heisenberg* (2017) continue to derive their emotional and intellectual force from a carefully observed naturalistic rationality. Most importantly, and as this chapter and Chapter Four will address, the next five of Stephens's original plays were staged by creative teams whose professional training and aesthetic inclinations somewhat complicate the strict delineation between 'English' and 'German-language' theatre cultures outlined in the previous chapter. It is important to tease out the nuances and possible contradictions of this narrative, not least because doing so affords greater insight into a particularly lively period of contact and collaboration between artists working in building-based producing theatres across the UK and mainland Europe. Stephens was by no means the only major figure in the mainstream of British subsidised theatre to be looking across the Channel during the 2000s; David Lan, for example, then Artistic Director of the Young Vic, London, worked with the Goethe Institut throughout the decade to send emerging directors to Berlin, in order to 'thoroughly unsettle them and shake them up with the discovery of what extraordinary things it is possible to do on a stage' (Lan 2012: online). Nevertheless, despite – or perhaps because of – an increasing level of communication and burgeoning cross-fertilization across cultures, it is useful to recognize the distinctions and differences, in practice and attitude, which continued to nuance the production and reception of Stephens's plays in England and mainland Europe during this period.

A key figure within this discussion is the British theatre director Katie Mitchell, who directed Stephens's *Wastwater* at the Royal Court in 2011 and *The Trial of Ubu* at the Hampstead Theatre, London, in 2012. Mitchell, who studied English at Oxford University and began her career as an assistant director at the Royal Shakespeare Company, departed from an otherwise conventional trajectory in British theatre when in 1989 she left England to observe directors training in Poland, Russia, Georgia and Lithuania. Recognized as 'the most internationally minded' of all her contemporaries (Whitely qtd in Rebellato 2010: 320), Mitchell has attracted both the admiration and the ire of British critics for productions of canonical classics by writers such as Chekov, Strindberg, Ibsen and Euripides. In these productions, text is often boldly cut, abridged, repositioned or interrupted by sequences of (mediated) images, dance and music in order to create what critic Lyn Gardner has described as 'austere but visually ravishing shows of almost religious intensity' (qtd in Rebellato 2010: 318). For sections of the English critical establishment, however, these interventions into – or liberties taken with – canonical texts have earned Mitchell the pejorative moniker of 'auteur'. 'Once she was content to realise an author's text', sighs Michael Billington in his review of Mitchell's *Women of Troy*, for example, 'now she has become an auteur whose signature is on every moment of a production' (2007b: online). Mitchell's posited error, or 'overweening arrogance', as Charles Spencer puts it, lies in her purported departure from a director's 'primary aim', which should be – Spencer counsels – 'to serve the dead author' (2007: online). The 'danger' of this kind of 'director's theatre', as Billington writes in his article 'Don't let auteurs take over in theatre', is that 'the interpreter becomes bigger than the thing interpreted. Or, to put it more bluntly, the director takes precedence over the writer' (2009a: online).

As Dan Rebellato has dryly noted, Mitchell is simply 'too European for some British tastes' (2010: 319). Mitchell has stated that what attracted her to the work of Russian directors such as Dodin and Vassiliev was that 'they didn't see performance as being about text; they saw it as being about *behaviour* [. . .] the visual metaphors were so powerful [. . .] their visual discipline was so rigorous' (qtd in Rebellato 2010: 321). As Rebellato relays, the term Mitchell 'uses repeatedly to describe the textual level she is trying to uncover is [. . .] the "idea structure" of a play' (2010: 331). Once this 'idea structure' is arrived at, the director may respond to it in whatever way s/he wishes, including, for example, the 'discarding' of 'less fundamental' aspects of the text in order to better serve the director's vision for the production (ibid.). Mitchell rightly does not accept the charge of 'vandalism' in her work, describing it as 'confusing that people have a picture of me smashing things up for the sake of it. That isn't the case. The first step I take is careful consideration and detailed study of the material, then I work out how to communicate it now' (qtd in Rebellato 2010: 333). Mitchell's sentiments echo those of Stephens in several ways: in the latter's insistence on playwriting as a study of behaviour, not language; in his respect for 'formal boldness' in theatre that 'values the metaphorical and the visual' (Stephens 2009: xix); and in his appreciation of the historicity of plays, engendered in part by his work producing new versions of play-texts by Ibsen (*A Doll's House*) and Chekov (*The Cherry Orchard*). However, in exploring how these shared 'European' sensibilities and affinities united on productions of

Wastwater and *The Trial of Ubu*, it is possible to detect finer variations and, indeed, deviations, in working practices between director and playwright. Identifying these variances not only helps to illuminate Mitchell's working processes more precisely but also underscores the diversity of directorial approaches in Europe that are too often, and too schematically, bundled under the sniffy invocation of 'auteur'.

An equally important figure in this discussion of UK/European dialogue is the British director Sean Holmes, who first worked with Stephens when he directed the UK premiere of *Pornography* in 2008. The previous chapter noted how the openness of Stephens's text encouraged Holmes to work in a way that ran counter to his usual practice, an approach that the director was keen to further explore. As Chapter 4 will elaborate, when Holmes was appointed Artistic Director of the Lyric Hammersmith, London, in spring 2009, he appointed Stephens as an Artistic Associate, along with the lighting designer Paule Constable and Ferdy Roberts, then Artistic Director of theatre company Filter, as a means of surrounding himself with 'artistic provocations' (Holmes 2013b). Holmes recalls that at that time, both he and Stephens were

> stumbling towards something which you can see in *Pornography,* both in the play and the production – a feeling that there are other ways of approaching new writing. [*Pornography*] drew me to [this new approach], because it felt a truer way to deal with those events [7/7] than something that was more naturalistic or narrative-driven. (ibid.)

Holmes had seen Nübling's 2007 production of *Pornographie*, as well as his German-language premiere of *Punk Rock* (2009) staged in 2010 with the Jungestheater, Basel. On being appointed Artistic Director, one of Holmes's first actions was to fly to Germany to discuss the possibility of co-producing what would become *Three Kingdoms*, a detective thriller written by Stephens to be directed by Nübling. The resulting collaboration between the Lyric Hammersmith, Munich Kammerspiele and Teater No99 – an Estonian theatre company based in Tallinn[1] – drew together actors from England, Germany and Estonia in a tri-lingual production which premiered in Munich and played in Tallinn before opening in London in May 2012. Stephens is beguilingly unequivocal about the significance of this production:

> I may have written better plays than this, I might go on to write better plays than this but I don't think I'll have a bigger single impact upon

British theatre than bringing *Three Kingdoms* to London [. . .] that, *that's* the biggest thing I'll do in British theatre history, is bring that show over here. (2013a)

As this chapter will discuss, the rehearsal process for *Three Kingdoms* was a fractious experience, with difficulties arising from contrasting and often conflicting sets of expectations and assumptions brought to rehearsals by its cast of English, German and Estonian actors. Competing attitudes towards the role and function of the play-text within the production – including its role in structuring spectators' responses to the play – were brought into sharp focus, underscoring the cultural specificity of theatre practices in a way that productively interacted with the play's own disquisition on globalization and its social and psychological affects. Chapter 4 discusses in more detail the profound impact of this production upon Holmes and Stephens, an impact which informed Holmes's 2012 production of Stephens's *Morning* (and later, although it falls outside the scope of this book, his 2016 revival of Stephens's 2001 play *Herons*), as well the founding of a temporary resident ensemble at the Lyric Hammersmith, Secret Theatre.

The third British director to bring into this discussion of 'English' and 'German-language' cultures of theatre direction is Stephens's long-standing collaborator, Marianne Elliott, who in 2012 directed Stephens's adaptation of Mark Haddon's 2003 best-selling novel, *The Curious Incident of the Dog in the Night-Time* for the National Theatre. Chapter 4 draws upon interviews with several of the cast and creatives of this production to detail its significance as not only one of the National Theatre's most critically and commercially successful shows to date (see also Elliott's previous global smash hit, *War Horse* [2007]) but also an unexpected example of the sort of European *Regietheater* to which, for decades, 'the English theatre has closed its eyes – or, more accurately perhaps, held its nose' (Lan 2012: online). Written specifically for the choreographic interventions of Scott Graham and Steven Hoggett of physical theatre company Frantic Assembly, Stephens's stage adaptation of *The Curious Incident of the Dog in the Night-Time* was widely acclaimed for its 'phenomenal combination of storytelling and spectacle' (Maxwell 2013) and remains, as the playwright attests, 'structurally [as] inventive as anything else that I've written' (Stephens 2015f).

From the late 2000s onwards, Stephens's recalibration and even rejection of a 'playwright-artist/director-interpreter' model of theatre-making (discussed in the introduction to this volume) in favour of a creatively responsive attitude towards a director's vision and working methods, has led to artistic collaborations in which a more inclusive notion of 'text', as well as a more nuanced approach to 'authorship', has been trialled. Stephens's work with these directors and creative teams has foregrounded – perhaps enacted is the better term – W. B. Worthen's observation that the ways in which dramatic play-texts may be read and interpreted – and, therefore, staged – are not governed simply by the play-text itself, but by 'the interplay between the text and conventions and practices of reading we bring to it' (2009: xv). This and the following chapter attend to the 'conventions and practices of reading' brought to the play-texts by different directors working within different theatre cultures, in order to reflect upon the differences in *status* and *function* thereby accorded the dramatic-text-in-performance.

Wastwater

Wastwater began life in 2008 as *Lullaby Burn*. Originally a triptych of scenes that could be performed in any of three orders specified by Stephens, only the third episode survived the re-drafting process intact. Part One (originally intended as 'a piece for dance') became the monologue *T5* and Part Two, which was to feature six groups of characters in either the 'noodle bar' or 'departures lounge' of 'Heathrow Terminal 5', was entirely cut and replaced.[2] While the play's title refers to the deepest lake in England, located in the Lake District, the global hub of Heathrow Terminal 5 remains pivotal to the play, a juxtaposition of geographical and, in a sense, temporal reference points which Stephens would also deploy in the two other plays explored in this chapter (the Théâtre de l'Œuvre in late-nineteenth-century Paris and the International Criminal Court in the Hague, Netherlands, for *The Trial of Ubu*, and London, Hamburg, and Tallinn for *Three Kingdoms*).

All three parts of *Wastwater* take place on the peripheries of Heathrow Terminal 5 and over the same half-hour period. The first tells a story of departure, as a young man bids farewell to his foster mother; the second depicts a sexual exchange between strangers in one of the airport's corporate hotels; and the third imagines a scenario in which a young Filipino girl is trafficked into the country. In a manner similar to *Pornography*, albeit with greater investment in interlacing narrative, the fiction is anchored by time and place while cultural motifs (the humming of 'Habanera' from *Carmen* [1875], for example) and coincidences of encounter forge connections that surge and break beyond the edges of these distinct episodes. Harry, foster son to Frieda, is leaving England to work at an ecological centre in Canada, haunted still by the death of his friend, Gavin, in a car crash for which he feels partly responsible. In the next episode, it emerges that Mark, whose online contact with Lisa has led to an extra-marital sexual assignation, taught Gavin at school, and remains deeply affected by the death of his 'best student' driving into a wall when drunk (Stephens 2011c: 34).[3] In the final episode, it emerges that Sian, who has planned and overseen the trafficking operation which has brought Dalisay to Jonathan, was also fostered by Frieda. In the first episode Frieda tells Harry that she is no longer in touch with Sian, to which Harry replies: 'You better not be, Frieda [. . .] The things she did to you' (8–9). The final episode appears to contradict this, however: Sian describes her former foster mum as 'lovely' (51) and claims that she still rings her every night (57).

References to water, the earth and the sky recur throughout *Wastwater*, an environmental trope first introduced by Harry's rumination on the ruinous consequences of mankind's transition from hunter-gatherers to an agrarian society:

> **Harry:** [. . .] You start draining your natural resources. You divert the water supply. You pollute the atmosphere. You develop social hierarchies that had never existed before. You start to feed the section of the population that has the highest economic or physical strength to the point where they actually over-feed and became [*sic*] obese. And you let another section of the population starve. This never happens when you hunt bison and gather berries. None of the catastrophes of human history would have happened if we'd not decided to farm. (14)

The strength of feeling in *Wastwater*'s first monologue, framed by the sounds of airplanes which intermittently interrupt or underscore the triptych of scenes, affords an interpretation of the play as a warning against the ecological fallout of rapacious economic 'progress'. Characteristically, however, Stephens's play favours ambivalence over didacticism in its attempts to address one of the defining contradictions of late capitalist society.

This is a contradiction captured in the thesis of 'cynical reason', advanced by the German philosopher Peter Sloterdijk in *The Critique of Cynical Reason* (1983) and taken up by Slavoj Žižek in his *The Sublime Object of Ideology* (1989). Sloterdijk observes that the workings of social ideology in liberal Western democracies can no longer be contained within the standard Marxian model of false consciousness: 'they do not know it, but they are doing it' (1987: 3–9). He suggests instead, as Žižek glosses, that the dominant mode of ideology must now properly be formulated as: 'they know very well what they are doing, but still, they are doing it' (1989: 25). Cynical reason, writes Žižek, 'is a paradox of an enlightened false consciousness: one knows the falsehood very well, one is well aware of a particular interest hidden behind an ideological universality, but still one does not renounce it' (25–6). In relation to the nexus of concerns explored in *Wastwater* – but also *Motortown* (2006), *Pornography* (2008) and *Three Kingdoms* (2011) – we may reframe this as: we know what we do, *and* the deleterious consequences of this, *but we do it anyway*. 'We know', Stephens relays in a searching interview by Ariane de Waal in 2014:

> that which distinguishes my generation [of theatre-makers] from Edward [Bond] or Nicholas Kent's generation is that *we know*. [. . .] We know completely what is happening in the Congo because of coltan wars, or what's happening in the factories of Southeast China run by Apple, but we continue to use [the consumer goods produced] because they are so convenient. The impulse [to write plays comes from] a need to dramatize and articulate not just the uncertainty, but the culpability for catastrophe.[4]

In *Wastwater*, Heathrow Terminal 5 serves as a totemic symbol of cynical reason, of what Stephens describes in notes for a blog post as 'the fundamental contradiction between what we know and how we live'.[5] It is one of Stephens's 'favourite buildings in the world':

> It seems to be both brilliantly utilitarian and aesthetically elegant. I love the speed of check in there [. . .] I love the calibre of shopping and food retail outlets available in the Departure area. I love the idea of having poached eggs at the Gordon Ramsay Brasserie and the range of coffee I can enjoy on offer. I love that all of the gates are within five minutes' walk of the main eating areas. [. . .] It is sleek and exciting and elegant.[6]

'It is also', Stephens writes, 'charged with the sense of catastrophe':

> The fragility of the ecological conditions that allow human society to thrive is widely acknowledged. We understand the imminent climate

crisis with unsettling confidence. We know we are in danger [. . .] I am fascinated by the way in which we can suspend our understanding of how much danger we are in and continue to relish the sensory joy of the lifestyle that is bringing that danger ever closer to its actualisation. We know we shouldn't fly as much as we do. But the temptation is acute and our newer airports are so seductive.[7]

Only moments after Harry has thoroughly ventilated his feelings regarding the devastation wreaked by agricultural society (with a vehemence that hints, perhaps, at a certain naivete), he expresses the 'hope' that 'they flipping do build the runway' (14) – a reference to the contentious proposal to build a third runway at Heathrow airport, first mooted by a Labour government in 2006. 'Oh, everybody gets very upset about it and agitated and they [. . .] sign all manner of electronic petitions', he says dismissively, 'but you try telling somebody nowadays that they're going to live in the same place all their life and never leave it or go on holiday or anything like that and they'd look at you with a look of just horror. That would be their idea of hell' (ibid.). It is not that we can describe Harry's attitude here as, strictly speaking, immoral (or incorrect) but rather that 'cynical reason' recasts moral probity and integrity as pathetically superfluous or extraneous to the situation. 'Thousands and thousands of years ago', Harry maintains, 'we made a terrible, terrible mistake. And it's sat under everything we've done since. And it will sit under everything we ever do. And we can't change it' (ibid.). Ecological disaster provides the pretext for *Wastwater* but the play is concerned less with the phenomenon itself than how a particular demographic of human society (here the affluent, mobile, middle-classes) perceives and lives with(in) it: *Wastwater* is a play 'about fear [. . .] about how we are drawn to that that destroys us'.[8]

Katie Mitchell received the script of *Wastwater* in the spring of 2010. As noted earlier, with the exception of plays by British playwright Martin Crimp[9] Mitchell had heretofore largely focused on revisionist productions of canonical classics. *The Director's Craft*, which Mitchell published in 2009, provides a detailed inventory of her directorial practice, offering key insights into the distinctive conventions and practices of reading that she brings to the dramatic play-text. When read in conjunction with documents residing in Stephens's archives, *The Director's Craft* both illuminates the director's approach to *Wastwater* and suggests points of productive divergence between Stephens's and Mitchell's working processes.

An Artistic Associate at the Royal Court in the 1990s, Mitchell observes what the playwright David Hare identifies as 'the Royal Court ideal': that 'one should direct new plays as if they were classics and classics as if they were new plays' (2005: 107). Plays are regarded primarily as historical documents from which information is extracted: precisely what information should be drawn out from the text, and how, is extensively detailed in the first and longest section of *The Director's Craft*. The methodological approach that Mitchell outlines is designed to 'encourage [. . .] an objective relationship to the material [that] inhibits premature attempts to interpret the play' and can be applied irrespective of the play's age or structural composition (2009: 11, 2). The director's first task is to closely read the text for the information and impressions it yields regarding place, character biographies, immediate circumstances, events, intentions and relationships. Discoveries and responses to the play-text should be organized in the form of two lists: 'facts', which are 'non-negotiable elements of the text', and 'questions', which 'provide a way of notating the areas of the text that are less clear' (2009: 11). The director should then conduct research into the period in which the play is set in order to find satisfactory answers to these questions; that is, to 'map the physical, geographical and temporal certainties of the play' (2009: 12). To do so, Mitchell recommends consulting 'reliable printed sources', photographs, paintings and, where possible, taking field trips to the places where the action is set (2009: 16, 18). The function of these lists and accompanying research is to build a densely matrixed picture of 'everything that exists or has happened before the action of the of play begins' – the 'back history' of the play – so that 'the actors have clear pictures of what happened in the past from which to build their character and relationships' (2009: 12, 19). A 'sketch biography' of each character, again based on lists of facts and questions, provides the basis of the director's work with actors in the rehearsal room: 'working out what has happened in the past is [. . .] the first step you take towards directing the action of the play' (2009: 28, 24). To complement and enhance this close textual and contextual analysis, Mitchell advises that the director also 'find out the basic facts about the author and ask "how do these facts shed light on the play?"' (2009: 44). The writer's biography should be mined 'for any details [. . .] that talk specifically to the play' (real people on which characters are based, for example, or real events which recur in the play), because research into 'what was happening in the writer's life at the time when they wrote the play [. . .] can give you an idea about why the play was written' (2009: 45–6). This research forms an integral aspect of a director's pre-rehearsal preparation:

> Remember that the attempt to create some sort of picture of the person who wrote the play – and why they wrote it – is essential, even if, like Shakespeare, very little factual information is known about the writer. Just spending an hour or so thinking about the tiny fragments of information known about a long-dead writer can shed light on the text. If no information exists at all, imagining the person who could have written the play and where their passions lay, will not be time wasted. (Mitchell 2009: 46)

Mitchell is careful to acknowledge at the outset of *The Director's Craft* that she 'works mainly on plays by dead writers' and that the relationship between a director and a living writer lies beyond the scope of her book (2009: 1). When discussing research into a playwright's life, Mitchell states that 'there is obviously a huge difference between undertaking research about a dead writer and working with a living writer' and warns that while 'you can ask living writers questions about the relationship between life and the action of the play' the director 'should be prepared not to receive a direct answer – or any answer at all' (2009: 46). Setting aside the impression that this approach intimates a situation in which a director's working relationship with a living writer might remain more opaque than with one who is dead, the primary purpose of the textual and contextual analysis recommended by Mitchell is to identify 'the ideas that underpin the text' – the intellectual structure which 'determine[s] everything that is said and done during the action of the play' (2009: 47). 'If you diagnose the ideas correctly', Mitchell states, 'the process takes you deep inside the writer's head and it is crucial to honour these ideas – however else you may interpret the material' (2009: 49).

While branded an 'auteur' for apparently usurping the authority of the playwright, the reading practice Mitchell brings to her study of play-texts hews closely to what Catherine Belsey theorises as the 'commonsense view of literature' (1980: 2).[10] 'Common sense', Belsey explains,

> assumes that valuable literary texts tell truths – about the period which produced them, about the world in general or about human nature – and that in doing so they express the particular perceptions, the individual insights, of their authors. (Ibid.)

Key notions within this reading practice are the 'authenticity of experience', 'autonomy of the artist' and the 'transparency of discourse' (ibid). These are the structuring principles of 'expressive realism': the 'theory that literature reflects the reality of experience as it is perceived by one (especially gifted) individual, who expresses it in a discourse which enables other individuals to recognize it as true' (ibid.). For the reading practices of expressive realism, to interpret a play-text is to attend sensitively to what is 'there' in the text, *pre-given* (consciously or otherwise) by the playwright. However else the material may be interpreted, the figure of the 'Author', to borrow from Roland Barthes, 'who exists before [her work], thinks, suffers, lives for it' (1977: 145), remains a significant source of consultation, preparation and legitimization.

Among Stephens's working notes for *Wastwater* are three documents, dated between May and October 2010, comprising lists of facts and questions regarding each of the play's three sections: Part One yields 37 facts and prompts 120 questions, for example, and Part Three 69 facts and 97 questions.[11] For Part One of the play, the facts range from statements about the environmental surroundings; to interpersonal dynamics (who interacted with whom, and how); to the minutia of immediate circumstances (Frieda washed Harry's socks and left them out for him, for example).[12] The list of questions fall into three distinct categories: those that can only be answered by Stephens ('What is the writer's relationship to Wastwater?'); those that might be answered by Stephens ('What season is it?'); and those that require a factual answer arrived at by independent research ('How many airplanes fly over Sipson an hour on a normal week day?').[13] While a few questions appear to seek some kind of meta-commentary ('Is there any significance in the names of the characters?'), most aim at either more precisely imagining the fictional spaces of the play or soliciting further information regarding characters' biographies.[14]

Mitchell's approach raises interesting questions regarding the ways in which aspects of dramatic language may be decoded, interpreted and reconstructed in and for performance, as well as what a playwright ought to be expected to know about her own play. In a 2011 podcast with Ola Animashawun for the Royal Court, Stephens praises Mitchell's ability to see and release ideas in the play that he never realised were there – what he refers to in his working notes as 'her capacity to realize and stage that which is subliminal in my plays'.[15] Mitchell responds, self-deprecatingly:

> Yeah, but that's very difficult to talk about, isn't it, because it's *there* isn't it? So it would be released whoever, in a way, directs it or acts it, because it's *there*. [. . .] I think that finally, whether we discover it

in rehearsals now or whether the actors then keep running it, they would eventually get there, do you see what I mean, *because there is something to find.* (Animashawun 2011: online, emphasis added)

The scientistic vocabulary employed by Mitchell in *The Director's Craft* – the attempt to arrive at an 'objective' relationship to the text, to 'diagnose' its ideas 'correctly' and to 'map' the physical, geographical and temporal 'certainties' of the play – invests the directorial process with an empiricism which purports to anchor not only the director's relationship to the play-text but also their (anthropological) recovery of the play's 'back history' and 'biography sketches' in a veridical reality: '[i]f you get the picture of what happened in the past *right*', Mitchell writes, 'it will make what the characters do in the play more *accurate*' (2009: 24, emphasis added).

Wastwater is an interesting case study in the careers of both Stephens and Mitchell because, by the time of their collaboration, Stephens was beginning to reappraise 'common sense' ideas regarding the functionality of not only text and authorship but also character and backstory in the theatre. As the previous chapter noted, the idea that socio-psychological causation provides an adequate explanatory framework for present behaviour begins to be treated with scepticism in these later plays: the influence of backstory over present-tense action appears to diminish; the significance of subtext is increasingly re-purposed or dispensed with altogether; the play's settings become looser and sketchier; and language is employed as much for its ability to unsettle and provoke spectators as it is to communicate interpersonal dialogue between fully realized characters. In interviews from 2010 onwards, moreover, Stephens is happier to refer to himself as less the 'writer' than an 'informed reader' of his plays: 'I read them in a slightly less detached way than any other reader, but I'm still a reader of those plays as much as I'm the writer of them' (2010a). 'It's not a question of me having all the secrets to the imaginary world of *Punk Rock*', he writes to the cast of the Hamburg production in March 2010, 'it being your job to unlock [those] secrets and mine to say "yes, that's right", or "no, you're wrong"'.[16]

In this respect, it is interesting to pay attention to the third and final part of *Wastwater*, in which Jonathan, who has arranged to buy a child (ostensibly for adoption, though there is an uneasy ambiguity regarding the transaction), undergoes a bizarre interrogation by Sian. The swift and erratic shifts in topic are reminiscent of Pinter (Goldberg and McGann versus Stanley in *The Birthday Party* [1957]) but, while the intention may still be to disorientate, the means here are different: Sian's questions pointedly solicit responses to questions that, within contemporary Western actor-training systems, an actor might be expected to contemplate as they build a character biography. 'What's your favourite piece of music and why?' she asks Jonathan (54); 'Where's the furthest north you've ever travelled?' (ibid.); 'What's your earliest memory?' (58). While Sian states that Jonathan's answers 'will have a bearing on what happens next [. . .] It will help us decide if we're going to go through with the transaction' (53), this is difficult to find credible given that the questions range from 'Which part of air travel do you find most unsettling [. . .]?' to 'What was the last *Star Wars* film you watched in the cinema?' (55, 56). Instead, the exchange exhibits, peculiarly, the properties of undigested material generated by playwriting exercises grafted onto (or into) a finely wrought triptych of dramatic narratives. The exchange was present in the first draft of *Lullaby Burn* in 2008 and remains, more or less unaltered, in the final and published version of *Wastwater* in 2011. That the text draws attention to itself in this strange way – not exactly metatheatrical, but perhaps meta-artisanal? – is intriguing, all the more so given that it is possible to read this section as a playful challenging of conventional processes of recovering backstory and building character biography. Some of Stephens's replies to the questions Mitchell puts to him in her preparatory study of the play support this hypothesis (and may be one of the reasons for the director's description of Stephens in the Royal Court podcast as 'very cheeky' [Animashawun 2011: online]):

> [**KM:**] What is the genre of the play?
> [**SS:**] Slaptsic [*sic*] roustabout comedy. [. . .]
> [**KM:**] Were Fiona and Jonathan sitting opposite or next to each other on the train from Salzburg to Munich?
> [**SS:**] Yes. [. . .]
> [**KM:**] [. . .] What colour hold all is Jonathan's money in?
> [**SS:**] I don't know. But I bet you do.[17]

Many of Stephens's responses to Mitchell's questions are couched in the conditional – 'perhaps', 'might', 'I think' – and in response to questions about backstory and context – including details which have a direct bearing on the plot, such as how the group for which Sian works is able to track Jonathan's movements, or whether in fact there is a helipad close to Heathrow for Dalisay to arrive at – Stephens will also often reply 'I don't know', or 'I made that bit up'.[18] The invention, or indeed haziness, of such detail regarding the play's fictional world offers another point of comparison between dramaturgical and directorial approaches here. In the podcast with Mitchell, Stephens emphasizes the importance to him of the imaginary in his work. In response to a question about the veridical reality of the play's several locations, Stephens replies:

> I think it kind of troubles a lot of people but I just made it up. Apart from Terminal 5 I just imagined the whole thing. [. . .] It's something – the role of the imagination in writing is something that I was always really kind of nervous about. I remember talking about *Motortown* [. . .] and when that play was written, a lot of people asked me if I'd done lots of research and met lots of soldiers, and I just hadn't. I just made the whole thing up. And I was so embarrassed about that that I used to lie about it and say, 'oh, you know, the Ministry of Defence are terribly obstructive to people wanting to write about Iraq', and that was just bollocks, I just imagined the whole thing. And so it is with this play. And I think you can only really understand this play to an extent if, while embracing the reality of that area, you also acknowledge that the play takes place in an imaginary world. [. . .] And I think that's where plays happen, is in the tension between the imagined and the researched world. (Animashawun 2011: online)

Writing in 2014 about their ongoing working relationship, Stephens states that, more than any other director that he has worked with, Mitchell 'has a distinct and clear vision in her head about what her show will look like [and will] work ferociously to have her actors and her artistic team realize that vision' (2016: 245). This vision – by no means confined to mimetic representation, although this was the aesthetic adopted for *Wastwater* – is hallmarked by what Stephens perceives as Mitchell's preference to ignore 'the corrupting impact of any audience' (2016: 58). 'Katie's commitment to the imagined world of plays being a hermetically sealed actuality', he writes, 'is a startling contrast to the worlds of Nübling or even Carrie [Cracknell]' (2016: 100). While Mitchell and Nübling 'are often lumped together when my work is being discussed', Stephens observes, 'they couldn't be further apart in their attitudes towards audience' or, furthermore, 'towards the question of where the character begins and the actor ends' (2016: 58). This is not something that fazes or perturbs Stephens. In a separate podcast on *Wastwater*, also in 2011, Stephens states that the differences between his and Mitchell's approaches to making theatre is something to be fascinated by, not frustrated with, because, ultimately, 'it's her production of my play':

It is Katie Mitchell's production of a Simon Stephens play [. . .] It's not my night. It's our collaboration. And in the rehearsal room, I'm working for her. I'm her employee. And I remember telling her that before rehearsals started and I think her not quite believing me but I think it's really true. I would work with every director in the way that they [want to]. (Qtd in Campbell 2011)

Mitchell and Stephens's next project together, *The Trial of Ubu*, provides an exemplary demonstration of not only Stephens's flexibility regarding the staging of his plays but also his ongoing interrogation of what it means for play-texts to 'belong' to their authors at all.

The Trial of Ubu

Stephens was commissioned by Nübling to write *The Trial of Ubu* towards the end of 2008. As Stephens explains in his introduction to *Plays: 4*, the director wanted to pair his production of Alfred Jarry's *Ubu Roi* (1896) with a new play inspired by the original. Nübling saw in Jarry's grotesque farce, in which a tin-pot dictator slaughters the royal family of Poland, an opportunity to interrogate the 'legal complexities and vicissitudes' of the International Criminal Court (ICC) in the Hague, on which media attention had recently been trained due to the high-profile trials of the former Serbian dictator Slobodan Milošević and former Liberian President Charles Taylor (Stephens 2015a: xv).[19] Fascinated by the processes involved in such international tribunals (the legal status of which remains contested), Stephens 'tried to interrogate the dignity and absurdity of such brutal despotism on trial through the filter of unpicking the morality of Jarry's flatulent anti-hero' (ibid). The conceit of *The Trial of Ubu* is that King Ubu, the central character in Jarry's play, has been placed on trial at the Hague for crimes against humanity. In working notes for the play from March 2009, Stephens reflects that 'interrogating a figure of brutal absurdity created before the start of that most brutal and absurd of centuries from [the perspective of this twenty-first] century that seems so far to be still more absurd and still more brutal, seems appropriate somehow'.[20]

The Trial of Ubu is set '*in the Trial Room 2 of The Hague and surrounding rooms* [. . .] *in the present day*' and opens with the Registrar's reading of the indictment against Ubu (Stephens 2015a: 156).[21] Eight counts of 'serious violations of international humanitarian law' are methodically

Juxtaposition

enumerated in contemporary legalese as, for example, 'Count 1. Acts of Terrorism, a VIOLATION OF ARTICLE 3 COMMON TO THE GENEVA CONVENTIONS AND OF ADDITIONAL PROTOCOL 2, punishable under Article 3.d of the Statute' (159). Ubu refuses to accept that he has committed any crimes or to recognize the legitimacy of the court which, as he points out, only exists because new jurisdiction has had to be invented for him: 'There is no justice here', he declaims, 'This is a political court. You are politicians' (164). The cases for the Prosecution and Defence are heard and several characters from Jarry's play, including Ma Ubu, are brought forward as witnesses. In the play's penultimate scene, Ubu delivers his own statement and, here, Stephens takes advantage of the historical perspective granted by living on the other side of the twentieth century:

> Your Honour, the tenets of this tribunal are built upon the Rome Statute of 2002 which is constructed in response to the Universal Declaration of Human Rights of 1948. Your Honour the Declaration is specious.
> Not everyone is born free. Not everyone is born equal. Not everybody is born with reason. Not everybody is born with conscience. To pretend that they are is dishonest. The tenets on which the Declaration was signed are lies. The tenets on which this Court is built are lies. The tenets on which your organisation is built are lies. [...]
> Do you know what is going on in my head as I stand hear [sic] listening to you talking about talking and about honour and about law and about justice and about the things that I have done? Spion Kop 1900 [...] St Petersburg 1905. Munich 1923. [...] Tarawa 1943. [...] Algiers 1957. Saigon 1968. [...] Phnom Penh 1975. [...] Santiago 1990. [...] Grozny 2000. [...] Baghdad 2003. Gaza 2009. (193–4)

The final scene of the play sees Ubu alone in his cell, jabbering to his jailor and rocking back and forth.

The Trial of Ubu premiered in a co-production between the Schauspiel Essen and the Toneelgroep Amsterdam in 2010. A UK premiere followed, directed by Mitchell at the Hampstead Theatre in 2012.[22] In his 2016 article, '"It's Not about Fucking It up": *The Trial of Ubu*, the Text and the Director', Adam J. Ledger compares these productions in some detail, offering insights into directorial decisions regarding mise en scène, characterization and acting in his discussion of these 'two contrasting productions' (348).

Stephens's text 'was not followed closely' in Nübling's production, Ledger notes, replaced instead with opportunities to indulge in the types of 'physical clowning and verbal horseplay' that an imagined encounter with Pa Ubu would invite (2016: 346). The action took place not in a court room but 'on an almost open stage [with a] wooden backdrop and a floor covered by polythene on which actors slipped' due to paint thrown around by performers variously engaged in 'excited action painting' and 'casual violence':

> Nübling's actor's [sic] sawed off (obviously fake) legs that spurted red paint, and killed Good King Wenceslas, splattering him with yet more red paint, before the actor later got up to play his other part. Elsewhere, an actor was wrapped in brown paper and 'drilled' by an absurdly long paint mixer attachment, connected to a (real) electric drill. (2016: 353)

Observing this scene of 'inventive grotesquery', described by one critic as akin to 'a children's party that descends into a bacchanal', Ledger concludes that 'as well as Nübling's bold directorial hand, it was as if Jarry himself had been let loose on the production' (2016: 346). This is a suggestive phrase, reaching back as it does not to the authority of Stephens as author of the text but a confected idea of Alfred Jarry as the carnivalesque spirit with which the production was imbued.[23]

While Mitchell's intervention in Stephens's text was no less bold, her vision for the production, and its affect in performance, was far removed from the ludic energy, irreverent impersonation and sprawling mess suggested by Ledger's account of the German-Dutch co-production. Mitchell's production filtered the entire play through the prism of one stage direction – '*In the courtroom multiple translations are used*' (159) – tilting the axis of the production so that, instead of the mimetic recreation of a courtroom, the trial was voiced through two female interpreters, 'cocooned in their accurately recreated booth, locked in the translation and verbalisation of dialogue between parties [Ubu and the rest of the court] carefully visualised by the two actors' (Ledger 2016: 349–50). 'It's a courtroom drama', Mitchell explained to Ledger,

> telly does it so much better and also we didn't have enough money to do a full court, we didn't have all the characters that were going to be in the court, a courtroom like the ICC, that's like 40 to 50 people,

to do it credibly [. . .] An impoverished version of a courtroom [. . .] would diminish the intellectual ideas. [. . .] I couldn't animate the ideas underpinning the material and the scale, the burden of the process of a two-year trial through normal means and that [alternative rendering] would conjure it, the scale and the burden, much more efficiently, I thought. (2016: 350–1)

For Mitchell's production, Stephens co-authored with the director a parallel 'text', creating the characters of, and narratives for, each of the two female translators, giving them names and backstories, including how they had achieved fluency in Ubu's language (Ledger 2016: 354). Mitchell's production, Ledger observes, 'became, increasingly, the story of the two women': their relationship and their journey through the trial was carefully plotted, with the climax of their story being that one of the interpreters becomes unable to speak anymore (ibid.). The trial took place through its translations voiced by the actors in a cool, detached monotone; the characters of the court 'appeared' only through the eyes of the actors who imagined this reality for themselves, following Stephens's script and 'seeing' the (fictional) action 'as if watching live action or film' (Ledger 2016: 347). In a 2012 interview with Aleks Sierz, Stephens describes that what he found compelling about watching the trial of Charles Taylor at the Hague was the 'juxtaposition between the savagery and the monstrosity of the things he had been charged with doing and the dry, clinical, detached rigour of the legalese and the legal language used' (Sierz 2012: online). For Stephens, Mitchell's production took this preoccupation of his and 'pushed it one step further':

[It] seemed to cut to the quick of the way in which we, in London, the West of Europe, in the north-west of Europe, make sense of atrocity. And we make sense of it with a sense of detachment, otherwise we'd go mad [. . .] And what I thought [she] did was [. . .] [find] a theatrical language which clarified exactly that problem. (ibid.)

Stephens's praise for these starkly contrasting productions – he described Nübling's as 'remarkably bold, visually confident, theatrically physical [and] intellectually daring' (ibid.) – refutes a proprietary attitude towards authorship and the text. In his interview with Sierz, Stephens holds no compunction in acknowledging that the idea for a play set in the Hague was entirely Nübling's and that, furthermore, much of the dialogue itself was lifted from transcripts of the trial of Charles Taylor, published on the website of the United Nations Special Tribunal into Sierra Leone. In preparatory notes on the play, Stephens reminds himself to 'quote, if necessary[,] from the charges against taylor [sic] because that language is so precise and the tension between the reading and the anger was thrilling'.[24] The questions put to Stephens by Barbara Christ, his long-standing German translator, reveal the fault-lines of this curious admixture of adaptation from Jarry, borrowing from Kenneth McLeish's 1997 English translation of the text, and verbatim from Taylor (and others), fused, rewrought and elaborated upon by Stephens. The following text is reproduced here exactly as it is written in the document 'B Christ Questions UBU 191109' from Stephens's personal files:

> [BC] p.5: JUDGE: . . . 'as <u>Chamber</u> of the court' . . . – chamber in which sense? (I supposed the Chamber is a group of judges . . .)
> [SS]: I think there is a semiotic differeence between being Chamber and being judge. I don;t have a clue what it is. I may also be totally totally wrong. I just quite like the word Chamber. [. . .]
> [BC] p.40: Could you please give me a hint about the 'pokystick'?
> [SS]: Ist a Jarry phrase (from Mcleish). I think Ubu uses it to refer to his sword. [. . .]
> [BC]: Is there any model for UBU's images of hurting and torturing Ma?
> [SS]: Accusations amde against Charles Taylor and his men in the Special triubune for Siera Leone. [. . .]
> [BC] p.58: UBU'S Statement - Is there any model for this? (Just curious)
> [SS]: Ist bastardised from various places or rather inspired by various sources. Especially Saddam on trial. But also Milosovic. And Marcos. [. . .]
> [BC] p. 61: the final pre-appeal verdict - is that a specialized legal term? (Couldn't find out, sorry.)
> [SS]: No. Its a rubbish Stephens made up one.
> Sorry.[25]

Stephens's responses to Christ's questions suggest a playwright operating at some remove from the model of an author who exists before his work, 'thinks, suffers, lives for it' (Barthes 1977: 145). And while this seems to reveal artistic differences that might compromise a working relationship between Stephens and Mitchell – in *A Working Diary*, for example, Stephens is fairly bullish in his criticism of what he sees as an 'obsession in British rehearsal rooms with capturing the author's voice or realizing his imagination or getting inside her head' (2016: 229) – it is Stephens's lack of propriety over the text that is enabling in this collaboration. 'I'm really proud of the work that I've done with Katie', Stephens told Sierz: '[*The Trial of Ubu*] feels like an evening in the theatre created by the writer and director together [. . .] even more than *Wastwater* last year, this feels like an evening that we created together. And that feels experimental and it feels rich' (2012: online). Stephens speaks here as a playwright alert and responsive to the fact, as W. B. Worthen puts it, that 'performance does not so much interpret the text as rewrite it in the incommensurable idiom of the stage' (2005: 4). Stephens and Mitchell would subsequently collaborate on a version of Anton Chekov's *The Cherry Orchard*, which opened at the Young Vic in 2014. Stephens's next project with Nübling was *Three Kingdoms*.

Three Kingdoms

The previous chapter queried the extent to which Stephens might be regarded as a 'political' playwright. It suggested that while his plays do not explicitly address party politics, legal structures and institutions, or seek to promote any kind of unified political perspective or agenda, their preoccupation with, and dramatization of, the experiences of living in a late-capitalist social formation nevertheless intersect with issues of a social and political character. One of the historical touchstones most readily associated with 'political drama' within the study of British theatre remains perhaps the 'state-of-the-nation' play, as propounded by playwrights such as David Edgar, David Hare and Howard Brenton, on the main stages of large, often national, subsidised theatres in the 1970s and 1980s. While there is no established formal definition of this dramaturgical model, Dan Rebellato has suggested that these plays may be recognised as large-scale productions, the action of which takes place across a range of public (and sometimes private) settings, and over years rather than hours or days (2007: 246). Equating conservatism with (bourgeois) individualism, these plays evince broadly socialist convictions, typically through a realist aesthetic which seeks to convey, in the words of Hare, 'the undulations of history [. . .] a sense of movement, of social change' in which not individuals but whole classes of people are the protagonists (Hare qtd in Rebellato 2007: 246).

Some commentators, as Graham Saunders discusses in his introduction to *Cool Britannia? British Political Drama in the 1990s*, have equated the decline of this dramaturgical model in recent decades with a more general 'disengagement and dismantlement from recognizable forms of political engagement' (d'Monté and Saunders 2008: 3).[26] Scholars such as Rebellato (2007), Elizabeth Sakellaridou (1999) and Sarah Grochala (2017), however, have answered these critiques with the simple but penetrating argument that as 'the political context in which the state-of-the-nation play was developed has changed' so, too, 'political theatre has changed' (Rebellato 2007: 245).[27]

In his historicization of the emergence of state-of-the-nation theatre, Rebellato lingers on the conceptual coupling of 'state' and 'nation'. Where the plays of the 1970s and 1980s succeeded, he suggests, was in their ability to dramatize relations between the 'judicial generality of the state' (politics) and the 'sensuous particularity of the nation' (people) (2007: 248). By focusing on 'specific, fully realized characters' set against a 'background of the historical and social forces that carry them forward', state-of-the-nation drama looked to 'hold together the public [state] and the private [nation] in its grand visions of Britain and Britishness' (ibid.). With the rise of globalization in the 1990s and 2000s, however, the power of the nation-state as a geopolitical unit was undermined, with the result that 'nation was unbundled from state' (Rebellato 2007: 252). The consequence of this, Rebellato suggests, is that old-style dramaturgical models that seek to map 'the political onto the personal, and the general onto the particular' can no longer dramatically cohere (ibid.). The state-of-the-nation model can no longer offer audiences 'help in co-ordinating our understanding of the world with our experience of it' because the lived experience of globalization renders not only national borders, but also the distinction between 'public' and 'private', increasingly porous and permeable (Rebellato 2007: 248, 252). Rebellato's analysis of state-of-the-nation drama as a 'form whose usefulness had passed and whose purchase on contemporary reality had diminished' by the 1990s is incisive and persuasive (2007: 259). It assumes greater significance, however, when in writing about Nübling's production of *Three Kingdoms* at Lyric Hammersmith, London, in May 2012, Rebellato declares that 'Simon Stephens, Sebastian Nübling and Ene-Liis Semper [the production's Estonian designer] have revived the state-of-the-(inter)nation play' (2012: online).

Indeed, Stephens's play exhibits many of the characteristics associated with state-of-the-nation drama: it hosts a large cast of characters, features a panoramic range of settings and, in its protagonists' journey from London through Hamburg to Tallinn in search of 'the White Bird', may be called epic in its geographical if not temporal span (Stephens 2015a: 56). Its protagonists are readily identified as DS Ignatius Stone and DI Charlie Lee: the judicial apparatus of the state literally represented onstage through characters with individually realised traits (Ignatius *loves* a sausage roll [Stephens 2015a: 40]). Its social and historical backdrop is that of international sex trafficking facilitated by the erasure of barriers to free movement, the rise of communication technologies and global access to online pornography. In concert with the political ambitions of state-of-the-nation drama, the play – which depicts an investigation across Europe into the murder of a trafficked Estonian sex worker – may be described as diagnostic in its approach; writing in 2013 of his favourite film noir, *The Third Man* (1949), Stephens observes that '[a]ll the plays I write consider worlds that are built on darker, more cruel foundations than they often present as a surface [. . .] A world that has the veneer of beauty might be built on foundations of criminality, selfishness and cruelty' (Stephen 2013c: 10). Like *The Third Man*, *Three Kingdoms* inhabits the noir genre to explore 'the dependence of innocence on guilt', and does so in a social context that is not undefined or elusive: it is the 'here' of Europe, in the 'now' of the first decades of the millennium, in which, as Rebellato observes, 'the transnational movements of goods, labour and services have conspired to allow the New Global Slavery' (2012: online). In these respects, *Three Kingdoms* may be described as a state-of-the-nation drama written in and for a globalized world in which the geographical, economic and psychic structures that create and police the borders of nation-state, private-public and personal-political no longer cogently map the experience of *the experience of* living in the Global North in the twenty-first century.

But there is, of course, an irony to reading *Three Kingdoms* through this dramaturgical model, as to read this tri-lingual co-production as a 'state-of-the-(inter)nation' play places it within a singularly English dramatic tradition which obscures not only the theatre cultures for which it was written (and by which it was produced) but also the audiences to which it played in Hamburg, Tallinn and London. To understand Rebellato's claim, it is necessary to revisit his statement in full: '*If only the critics could see it* [Stephens, Nübling and Semper] have revived the state-of-the-(inter)nation play' (2012: online, emphasis added). Rebellato's project here is, in part, to rescue *Three Kingdoms* from the savaging it received from mainstream, broadsheet critics. Deplored by Quentin Letts as 'magnificently bad, laughably awful', with acting 'energetic to and past the point of gammon',

Nübling's production of *Three Kingdoms* was, according to several of these critics, 'grossly self-advertising' (Billington 2012: online) and 'self-indulgen[t]' (Hitchings 2012a: online); at best, an 'adventurous misfire' (Dominic Maxwell qtd in *WhatsonStage* 2012: online). Rebellato's alignment of the production with state-of-the-nation theatre is a performative recuperation of Nübling's directorial approach within established discourses of British theatre. Among the many misconceptions Rebellato identifies in the critical response to *Three Kingdoms* is that it 'is a departure from good old British theatre practice' (2012: online). 'No it isn't', Rebellato retorts:

> Yes, it's a departure from what we say we do, but it's not a departure from what we do. [. . .] A production must – and always does – add things that aren't in a play. It's always an interpretation. This is as true of Sebastian Nübling as it is of Max Stafford-Clark. (ibid.)

Rebellato's rebuttal is consonant with his sustained advocacy of dramatic text-based theatre as 'every bit as complex, paradoxical and supple as that of performance and the postdramatic' (2009: 27). In this instance, however, I would argue that the move to absorb (or domesticize) Nübling's production into (or within) a UK theatre establishment overlooks what might be regarded as the most productive and illuminating aspect of this tri-lingual co-production: namely, the interpersonal and artistic conflicts – palpable onstage and documented offstage[28] – generated by a fractious collision of 'English' and 'European' theatre cultures.

In *Drama: Between Poetry and Performance* (2010), W. B. Worthen includes the practices of writing, directing and acting within what he describes as 'the social technology of the theatre', where 'technology' is understood as possessing a 'public, social character' (21). Such technologies, he suggests, are '"value-driven and value-producing patterns of conduct" that create, depend on, and encode cultural relationships' (Hershock qtd in Worthen 2010: 21). While this volume has so far focused on the differentiated cultural assumptions that underpin writing and directing as 'technologies', here I will draw on the testimony of actor Nicolas Tennant,[29] who played the lead English detective in Nübling's production, to offer an account of the values, processes and principles that underpinned competing approaches to acting and, specifically, 'character' within this collaboration. In identifying differences between 'British' and 'European' theatre-making cultures, my aim is neither to collapse into a homogenous mass the diversity of practices which both theatre cultures enjoy, nor to posit that Nübling's work on this production can be held as representative of all 'European theatre'. The claim is more modest: simply that there is value in paying attention to the challenges confronted by one of the UK's most successful stage actors in the rehearsal room of one of Germany's most celebrated stage directors. Tennant's account sheds important light on the 'value-driven' and 'value-producing' aspects of theatre understood as a 'social technology', grounding generalizations of 'difference' across (European) theatre cultures in specific examples.

In a 2016 interview, Tennant spoke about the production with candour:

> If someone says to me, 'oh, you did that play about the sex trade', I say, 'look, it's incredibly disingenuous for me to say [yes to] that because that's a real thing that goes on. This play was about theatre: who does the best theatre? *Who's right?*' Now I think I'm right. And they [the German and Estonian actors] all think they're right. That animosity stayed throughout. (Tennant 2016a)

Tennant was originally cast in *Three Kingdoms* as DI Charlie Lee, sidekick to the play's protagonist, DS Ignatius Stone, a part that had been written for Paul Ritter, a British actor fluent in German (in the text of Stephens's play, Stone translates for Lee when in Germany). When Ritter turned down the part, it was offered to the actor Paul Brennan, who agreed to learn German while the production was in rehearsal. Midway through rehearsals, however, Brennan left the production and the role was offered to Tennant for him to take on *in addition to* the role he had already been rehearsing, DI Charlie Lee. As Tennant recounted:

> [Nübling] says, 'listen – maybe we only have one policeman and not two. So, from this point on, just become the part of Ignatius but keep the part of Charlie that you've done in the first act' [. . .]. And I was like – 'you what?! [. . .] isn't that weird?' And they said 'No, why?' [. . .] I said, 'but that's a different character?!' And they just thought I was being awkward. (2016a)

Nonplussed by Nübling's approach, Tennant was further confounded by the director's disregard for a foundational tenet of Anglophone method acting:

> [Nübling would say] 'I don't care about motivation. That's your business and I don't want to know'. [. . .] In one of the first rehearsals,

he said 'when you've said that line, I want you to both run out of the room, just run, really quickly'. And Ferdy [Roberts, the actor who played the second English detective] asked 'why are we running out of the room?'. And he said 'because Stanislavski has asked you what you are doing [and] you are running away from him!' (ibid.)

The preface to the published script of *Three Kingdoms*, comprised of edited interviews with Stephens, Nübling and one of the production's two dramaturgs, Eero Epner from Teater No99,[30] records 'the differences in theatrical traditions' encountered in the rehearsal room for *Three Kingdoms* (Bolton 2012b: viii). What emerges from these accounts is a conflict between 'biographical' versus 'improvisational' approaches to the staging of a dramatic text and, specifically, the text's role in mediating an actor's relationship with his or her character. Nübling's view, that 'a *character* is defined by what an *actor* does on stage' (Bolton 2012b: ix, emphasis added), is echoed by Epner's assertion that 'for us, the actor [. . .] is an artist with his or her autonomy [. . .] S/he is not dependent on the text or on the fictional-historical figure s/he embodies: s/he creates a world of his or her own' (Bolton 2012b: xiii). In Tennant's words:

> Nübling hated English acting: 'All you do is walk and talk'. [. . .] The German and the Estonian style are pretty similar, really. They never do 'one-on-one' [. . .] where you follow the text and the play exactly as it is on the page. They think that that's a ludicrous idea [. . .] 'You, you English actors, you're so fucking naïve. Do something, *do* something'. [. . .]
>
> The German guy who played the lead [German detective], Steven [Scharf], big leading man at the Kammerspiele, very well respected, really nice guy, would come and do his thing. He decided that he was going to sing a Beatles song [*Rocky Racoon*, 1968] and did it. And if we wanted to stand next to him and do our lines, that was up to us. It was optional! He was going to do that, regardless. (2016a)

'We [English actors] realized then', Tennant relates, 'that we had to show [Nübling] things [. . .] with the script, or without. [. . .] You'd have to find a thing to do and you'd do it, and he'd go "no" [. . .] while jettisoning page after page after of the script' (2016a). Instead of following the script, the actors were asked by the director to improvise around (and against) the play-text in order to generate material that may, or may not, be used in the final performance. Nübling describes this approach as 'not very easy for mainly the British actors to understand [. . .] because we seldom talked about the biography or psychology of a character' (qtd in Bolton 2012b). Tennant confirms this, but also articulates the 'incredibly competitive' streak to this improvisational approach:

> The improvising we have [in England] is not like the improvising [in Germany]. Here, improvisation is used to 'unlock' a scene that the actors are struggling with. [. . .] Playing the scene but speaking aloud character thoughts before each line, or playing the scene but not using any of the written dialogue, the actor can dig deep into emotional memory and express thoughts and feelings to discover the emotional depth the characters and the director require. [. . .] This requires a deep understanding of not only one's character but also a shared history of the relationship of the characters [. . .]
>
> The German Method of Improv [*sic*], as I experienced, was one of pulling the scene apart, breaking it down and holding the structure to account to see what else it had to offer. If a scene was about death, then 'death' would be examined both in the abstract and the theatrical. Improv went on for days. [. . .] The actor is expected to 'change' his colleague by the nature of the Action played upon him. The aim always to DO something to the other person, something unexpected, something different. This can lead to exciting developments; some dangerous (I was spat at, slapped, hit, pushed) [. . .] the aim is to change the person and thus take the situation into unexpected territory. (2016b)

This approach to improvisation was 'hard' for the English actors to engage with, Tennant admits, because 'ultimately, we spend our time in rehearsals getting rid of any problems, so that people feel safe. And that's the fundamental difference [between approaches]. If it's safe, it's not interesting: "If you feel safe, you can't show me anything that's interesting"' (2016a).

In 2012, Nübling's direction transgressed conventions particular to mainstream British theatre practice, where production choices tend to be motivated by (and justified with recourse to) the playwright's original conception, and rehearsal processes are structured to discover (uncover, recover) the meaning(s) of a play-text, its characters, actions and internal dynamics. Nübling's approach, instead of seeking to realize the play-text in some definitive manner, sought rather to 'expos[e] text to performance' in order to ascertain what it '*might be capable of saying with and through it in/as performance*' (Worthen 2010: 82, 68, original emphasis). This approach holds that 'the theatre' is less 'the site for the *representation* of a fictive narrative' than a 'scene of action defined not [exclusively] in relation to the text but as part of the larger world surrounding the stage' (Worthen 2010: 213). Such a reading practice dispenses with the idea that the playtext is an originary source of meaning to be realized in performance, and undermines the privileged position of the 'author' as a singular arbitrator of language and meaning. Stephens acknowledges that his role in Nübling's production 'was never authorial', and that his main work in rehearsals was to 'refin[e] the shape of the text' and to 'encourag[e] the British actors not to be frightened when Sebastian behaved in a way that felt counter-intuitive to their culture'. '[The actors were] so used to using the playwright's text as a bible,' Stephens states, 'Sebastian had an instinct to tear it up. I had to let them know that I was happy with that' (Bolton 2012b: vii).[31]

Nübling explains his approach to language, words and text in his foreword to Stephens's *Plays: 4*:

> I am a director who depends on text. Words are the source of all the images that occur to me in thinking and talking about a play. And words are the source of all the images that occur in the rehearsal room, which is the central space for me to develop and construct a production. (2015a: ix)

As Stephens has described, however, the director's concern does not lie 'with the minutiae of psychological action brought about by linguistic nuance'; what is taken from the text instead is 'the idea and the possibility for manifesting that idea. [. . .] He is using the language and the text as a starting point for image and action' (qtd in Radosavljević 2014: 265). Tennant confirms that conversations in the rehearsal room were 'not about motive; they were about situation' (2016a). The first act of *Three Kingdoms*, for instance, contains a scene in which the two male English detectives interrogate a female Estonian sex worker, who remains largely mute. Tennant recalled that they played this scene 'over and over', without knowing anything more than 'it just had to be strange' (ibid.). Then:

> There was an animal head [of a deer] lying around the rehearsal floor, for some reason, and [the actress] just put it on and stood there and [Nübling] went: 'yeah, that's it'. So *we* were talking about what would happen in this situation *normally*, but he wasn't interested, he wasn't bothered about any of that. [. . .] He would just say that what intrigued

him [in this instance] was two people talking to someone they hadn't seen before and that they didn't understand. How extreme could you get that position? (ibid.)

By his own account, Tennant 'dug in [his] heels' against this non-representational aesthetic: 'My job', he relates, 'was to hold onto the fucking story. I thought, "right, you can throw all this stuff at me [. . .] I'm just going to keep telling this story"' (ibid.). When the production played in Munich, an audience member at the post-show Q&A asked Tennant what he had learned by doing the play. 'And I said, "I've learned how English I am". And it got a huge laugh; they were saying, "yeah, yeah, you look really English"' (ibid.).

During its run at the Lyric Hammersmith, London, *Three Kingdoms* drew criticism for what was deemed to be the production's misogynistic portrayal *of* misogyny.[32] Citing the lack of female actors – two in a cast of thirteen – and the relative silencing of these female characters through portrayals of fear, dispossession or language barriers, as well as what was perceived as their sexual objectification through costume and gesture, for Melissa Poll and others 'the ways in which this depiction of women act[ed] as more than a reproduction of their marginalization [was] unclear' (2016: online). For Poll, what was missing from the production was 'a salient critique of sex-trafficking', which for her meant that the production necessarily defaulted into 'loitering in its salacious details' (ibid.). Objecting to a production which failed to offer any 'insight as to the realities of [. . .] sex trafficking', Poll reads its non-representational aesthetic as an abnegation of responsibility: 'Where were these women's gashes and bruises from their abusive pimps? Or the track marks and emaciated limbs associated with drug use?' (ibid.). Sophie Nield concurs with Poll's view, complaining that 'the production didn't even bother to produce an authentic image of prostituted woman' (2016: 397). In her reflection on Nübling's production, however, Diana Damian cautions against readings that impose 'cues that we associate in some ways with the representational', as well as those that 'introduc[e] a problematic Western morality to a production *that systematically attempts to call that into question*' (qtd in Tripney 2012: online, emphasis added).

For Damian, key to reading Nübling's *Three Kingdoms* was to recognize the production's inter-theatrical dialogue with established narrative conventions, most particularly those coded as noir:

On the surface, and in effect, *Three Kingdoms* works within the conventions – dramatic and narrative – of the noir genre, anchoring its audience to one character – Ignatius – and his downfall, in a rather transparent way [. . .] [T]he production grounds its gender politics in the code of theatrical noir. It plays with that sense of lawlessness which escalates, but I think it makes very clear that this is not a play about sex trafficking. It uses and abuses that score in a fictionalized manner to draw an acute and sharp portrait of contemporary Europe. (ibid.)

Daniel B. Yates concurs with Damian in his observation that *Three Kingdoms* is 'a noir thriller and can't be divorced from those constraints' (qtd in Tripney 2012: online). For Yates, as for Damian, the provocation of this production was that, 'having assimilated the baseline misogyny of the detective genre', Stephens and Nübling opted not to 'presen[t] challenges' to this misogyny – as a more mainstream, digestible narrative might have it – but rather 'plumped for amped-up accelerationist games' in the creation of 'jouissance-laden images of masculinity' (ibid.). Yates concedes that this is 'dangerous ground' but observes that the production

is thunderous in its ability to make us complicit with the worst [. . .] the libidinous investment in vileness is marked, yet the point is firm – it's this hidden economy, silent in the murky mechanisms of globalisation, that remains such. (ibid.)

In a document titled '9 Questions to Simon Stephens', the transcript of an interview Stephens gave in Kiel in May 2013, Stephens admits that *Three Kingdoms* 'is a pessimistic play [. . .] defined by a horror at the potential in heterosexual male sexuality'.[33] As a heterosexual male, what remains intractable for Stephens is the culpability of this demographic 'for perpetuating the objectification of women that sits under the sex trafficking industry'.[34] From this perspective, the perceived absence of an overt authorial commentary denouncing the 'harsh realities' of sex trafficking need not be translated into a covert or inadvertent replication of misogynistic practices and attitudes; it might instead be read more productively as a skewering of 'the false security of [a] moral high ground' claimed by the professedly liberal, democratic values of the West (Damian qtd in Tripney 2012: online).

In its circumvention of authorial 'message', in favour of an aesthetic that 'condenses its atmospheres into powerful, emotional ripples' (ibid.), Nübling's production presented a series of challenges to habitual viewing practices within Anglophone theatre cultures. With reference to the final act of the play, Catherine Love describes being 'assaulted with unfathomable image upon unfathomable image' that became 'increasingly hard to follow and digest':

> This frustrates the very British aim of getting to the bottom of what a play is 'saying', *but perhaps it is the critical approach that is at fault rather than the production*. We can be determinedly blinkered as a theatrical culture and have nurtured a sort of suspicion towards theatre that asks its audiences to feel and experience as much as it asks them to think. [. . .] Perhaps [the diverse reactions to *Three Kingdoms*] heralds the realisation that we need new ways of seeing, of experiencing, of expressing. And perhaps that isn't such a bad thing. (2012: online, emphasis added)

Andrew Haydon also admired the phantasmagorical aspects of 'a production that exists more as a series of feelings than thoughts' to suggest that it was in this very distortion – of both mimetic and liberal scripts – that the production was at its most intellectually stimulating:

> Rather than simply showing us that forced sex and violence against women is a Very Bad Thing and that Europe, still living through the traumas of its history, is riven with darkness and violence [. . .] sending us into the night saddened and a bit depressed – it instead shakes us, makes us feel something and fires up our brains in entirely unpredictable ways. (2012: online)

The critical consensus on *Three Kingdoms* was that it was not – or not only – about sex trafficking but, more expansively, a disquisition on globalization, cultural imperialism, post-colonialism and exploitation. As such, it is hard to disagree with Sophie Nield's observation that '[o]nce again, here was yet another story about men in conflict with one another – physically, morally, in terms of status, sexually (because it always is) – being played out yet again on and through the bodies of women' (2016: 397). Nield continues, however, '[p]erhaps it is time for theatre to recognise that it, too, is situated within regimes and structures of representation, and actually speaks through them in ways that cannot simply be disavowed because we are all nice people, and we mean no harm' (2016: 399). Rightfully acknowledging the respective 'regimes and structures' of the theatre cultures from which this production emerged, it might be more appropriate to read Nübling's 'polyglot' (Hitchings 2012a: online) production as rejecting a notional transparency of representation –

mimetic (or, after Belsey, expressive) realism – in order to forcibly collide differing (cultural) modes of theatrical production. This 'culture clash' served to '*dramatize the implication of theatre* – the images it constructs and our consumption of them – in the reproduction of social reality' (Worthen 2010: 213), activating the *dramaturgy of representation* itself as a productive site of meaning in dialogue with the (posited fabula of) the play-text.

More provocatively, it perhaps need not be assumed that in this endeavour Nübling, or indeed any of the male or female actors, cast themselves in the role of 'nice people' who 'mean no harm'. The term repeatedly invoked by Tennant to describe the atmosphere in Nübling's rehearsals is 'antagonistic': 'the antagonism that was in that room was really uncomfortable, and quite draining', he relates, 'it was intense and unpleasant' (2016a). Describing rehearsals in England as processes of 'solving problems', Tennant relates that in rehearsals for *Three Kingdoms*, 'problems' were identified only to be made 'bigger and bigger, because the *problem* was *real*, and the problem was physical and visceral and sensual [. . .] and that's what he wanted the audience to feel' (ibid.). At the start of Act Two, for example, when the English detectives meet their German counterpart for the first time, an actress dressed as a cleaner stood by and poured, agonizingly slowly, a bucket of water onto the floor. According to Tennant:

> [In England], many actors would go – 'is she going to do that while I'm talking? Because no one's looking at me, they're looking at that water being poured'. And then the next thing they would say is, 'look, there's a really dangerous puddle of water on the floor here, how are we going to get rid of that?' Well, that water stayed there for the rest of the show. And it *was* really dangerous. *But the audience knew it was really dangerous as well.* [. . .] And it didn't distract from the scene because how the water made you [the audience member] feel was how you distilled that rather bizarre conversation [between the detectives], and it made you think 'I don't feel good about this'. And that's what the scene was about. And we could have acted that but [Nübling] would say 'no, what about the audience?' (ibid.)

Admitting that 'the further away from the play I've got, the more excited I've become about it', Tennant concludes that:

> Nübling wants the audience to feel something real. Not for us to pretend that something is happening, which is what he felt English

acting did. [In his productions] the audience are not voyeurs. They're not looking through a fourth wall [. . .] you're not doing something that you hope they're watching: it's totally for them'. (ibid.)

In a 2005 article in *Theater der Zeit*, Hans-Thies Lehmann addresses the complex implications of the formulation 'making theatre *for* the audience' (12, original emphasis).[35] In describing relations between audiences and performances in German-language theatre, he uses the word '*treffen*', a word without English equivalent which may be translated as 'to meet socially with' but also carries connotations of 'to strike', 'to move' or 'to injure' (Lehmann 2005: 12). The term connotes an antagonistic yet *attentive* acknowledgement of spectators as participants in, rather than consumers of, a theatrical event, and aptly captures the aggressive yet energizing relationality between performance and audience cited by *Three Kingdom*'s supporters and detractors alike.

Worthen's metaphors of 'tools' and 'technologies' remind us that practices of acting, writing, directing and spectating operate 'according to learned protocols of engagement, critique [and] interpretation' (2010: 20). 'Like tools', Worthen writes, 'texts can be made to function in socially accredited ways, in illicit ways, and in ways that [. . .] require us to rethink the technology and the work it accomplishes' (2010: 21). Tennant's experiences as an actor in *Three Kingdoms* may be read as an index of how twenty-first-century 'state-of-the-(inter)nation' theatre might productively prompt a 'rethink' of stage technologies and the 'work' they seek to accomplish. Where the political certitudes of a state-of-the-nation theatre which sought to 'socialize realism' aimed at reconciling and co-ordinating (personal) experience and (political) engagement, works of theatre which respond to the disorientation engendered by clashes of values and conduct in a globalized world are, perhaps, today more politically apposite. As Rebellato concludes in his chapter on state-of-the-nation theatre:

> Where realism seemed essential, now a kind of non-realism seems so; where politics was the object, now it is ethics; where once playwrights proclaimed 'messages first' [. . .] now aesthetic experiment may be the right means to achieve an effective political response to the challenges of a consumer culture and marketized world. (2007: 259)

As a work of 'state-of-the-(inter)nation' theatre, the political significations of Nübling's *Three Kingdoms* inhered less in the drama represented than in its dramaturgy of representation, an *affective* rather than *discursive* dramaturgy which captured, held and refused to glibly resolve antagonisms and contradictions generated by conflicting patterns of (aesthetic) values and (cultural) practices.

Conclusion

In a UK theatre culture structured according to a hierarchical model of playwright-artist/director-interpreter, Stephens's advocacy of the director-as-artist works productively to disturb and dislodge literary-critical approaches to the staging of dramatic texts which privilege the individual playwright as creative genesis and source. In place of these approaches, he offers an alternative set of dramaturgies that, in form and content, circulate and disperse the work of meaning-making throughout the 'team' – a more appropriate analogy might be 'band' – of players involved in the creation of a live event of theatre, including the audience. Straining against the expectations that a play inheres in the words committed to print, Stephens writes that 'the more I work in theatre [. . .] the more I realize that the words are the least important part of any theatrical experience. [My] experience of writing is more of a crystallization of ideas found in other forms, carved out of a culture rather than imagined out of an ether' (2016: 117). What this approach offers, in the words of Nübling, is 'enough words to start the imagination [. . .] to leave space for imagination':

> Simon writes exactly enough words to leave space for the unspoken, for what is said between the lines, or underneath the lines. And in this dark and scary gap between the spoken and the unspoken, reality lives. And out of this gap images occur about fear, anger, desire and desperation. And this is what in my opinion theatre is about: words and images from the dark side. (2015: ix)

How do you stage 'ideas [. . .] carved out of a culture'? For Stephens, 'each play is a different gesture and each production of a play demands a different process':

> The only thing that's really important is a consistency of approach. Not imagining that some rules are innate but finding the right and

appropriate rules of each production of each play and committing to those with consistency. (2016: 10)

Where post-war British (London) theatre featured an extensive roll-call of playwrights who could, in the words of David Hare, 'boast a regular director as loyal and as companionable as a partner or husband' (2005: 106),[36] Stephens has consciously and consistently sought out new collaborations, forms and provocations, while simultaneously nourishing and sustaining existing relationships (it is worth noting too that, unlike the playwright-director partnerships of the twentieth century which were almost exclusively male, three of the five key directors discussed in this book are women). There is no doubt that Stephens's conception of plays as collections of ideas and gestures, rather than intellectual schemas and blueprints, has enabled him to write for and create with a range of directors whose individual practices (and, in all likelihood, politics) differ markedly from, and even contradict, one another. This openness and responsiveness to the creative contributions of others continues to both sustain a productive career and inspire and provoke those around him. Sarah Frankcom affirms Stephens's willingness to 'never say no to anything' in rehearsal:

> He will watch something and it might be a million miles away from what his initial impulse or intention was, and he will always go: 'well, maybe'! His presence enables a freedom. That probably sounds really wanky, but he never thinks that there is a wrong way or a right way, he comes from the point of view that there are a million ways to do something and we'll happen on the right way for the people that are in that room at that particular time. (Frankcom 2014)

In this context, 'wanky' is a word that speaks volumes, ghosted as it is by the long shadow of anti-intellectualism associated with British theatre cultures.[37] Perhaps Stephens's most important contribution to the industry has been the 'freedom' to take aesthetic questions seriously – through play and experiment – and to do so without fear of embarrassment or ridicule from one's peers. 'Without being wanky', offers Holmes, 'it's learning, weirdly, after decades of doing it, how to be an artist' (Holmes 2013b). The final chapter returns to Holmes's creative experiments with Stephens, both on and off stage, and addresses what might be seen as the biggest contradiction in Stephens's career to date: the sunny, uplifting, commercial success that is his stage adaptation of *The Curious Incident of the Dog in the Night-Time*.

CHAPTER 4
CONTRADICTION
MORNING (2012) · SECRET THEATRE (2013–15) · *THE CURIOUS INCIDENT OF THE DOG IN THE NIGHT-TIME* (2012)

The previous chapter described Nübling's production of *Three Kingdoms* (2011) as advancing an affective, rather than discursive, dramaturgy that held and refused to resolve antagonism and contradiction. Contradiction – together with tension, transgression and juxtaposition – is a key term within Stephens's dramaturgical lexicon, operating as both philosophical premise and structuring principle across his oeuvre. In a 2015 article Stephens wrote about the plays of British playwright Robert Holman, he contends that:

> Too much of our theatre [is] paralysed by fear at the possibility of contradiction or inarticulacy [. . .] This strikes me as profoundly ironic at a time when politically, economically, socially, sexually and culturally our world seems cut to the quick by such complication and such contradiction and such inarticulacy. (2015b: online)

The impulse to represent contradiction without need of its resolution finds parallel expression in Dick Hebdige's influential study of British punk subcultures of the early to mid-1970s, *Subculture: The Meaning of Style* (1979). Given the extent to which music – particularly rock and post-punk – has influenced Stephens's writing (see Svich in this volume; Innes 2011; Stephens 2014d), Hebdige's study presents an interesting perspective to apply to the playwright's work. In an unpublished interview from April 2006, Stephens suggests that 'most of [his] sense of dramatic structure comes from an obsession with music', citing specifically the influence of post-punk British band The Fall (1976–2018) as having a galvanizing effect upon his imagination:

> I genuinely think [The Fall are] one of the best cultural phenomena of the twentieth century, I think they're extraordinary. You listen to

that music and there's an incredible malevolence, and an incredible deliberate structural chaos, and a tonal discordance in a lot of their music that I think is completely thrilling. [. . .] An awful lot of the way I have been affected has come from music as much – if not more – than it's come from theatre. I've wanted to affect people with my plays in the same way that music's affected me.[1]

In his twenties, Stephens played bass guitar for the self-styled art-punk band the Country Teasers, founded in Edinburgh in 1993. Seeing the band play at Stephens's wedding in 2005, Ian Rickson – then Artistic Director at the Royal Court – approached the playwright and, according to Stephens, observed: 'You're in a band that is dissonant, discordant, aggressive, angry, noisy and [yet] you've never written a play that has those qualities [. . .] it might be the kind of play that I'd want to produce'.[2] The result of this conversation was *Motortown* (2006), about which Stephens recalls:

In each scene [of the play] the effect I wanted to achieve was a sense of disquiet . . . to disquiet the audience, to unsettle them, by writing scenes which were almost normal but [with] something ever-so-slightly awry in them. [. . .] So, for example, in that first scene [when Lee says]: 'See Denise Van Outen? I'd like to *be* her' – these moments just come from way out leftfield and land in the middle of the scene [. . .] You think you know where you are in the scene, and then something happens to flip it over, and that's something I think I got from The Fall.[3]

Musical influences upon Stephens's work grow more pronounced as his oeuvre develops. Where earlier plays – not only *Motortown* (Motown) but also *Country Music* (2004) and, indeed, *Punk Rock* (2009) – conspicuously reference musical genres in their titles, later plays cite specific works (Bizet's 1875 *Carmen* for *Carmen Disruption* [2014]; Patti Smith's 'Birdland' for *Birdland* [2014]), and even serve as the pretext for original music (Mark Eitzel's 'Go Where the Love Is' for *Song From Far Away* [2015], and Jarvis Cocker's 'Hymn of the North' for *Light Falls* [2019]). *Morning*, however, which followed *Three Kingdoms* in a co-commission between the Lyric Hammersmith and the Junges Theater, Basel, occupies a unique position within Stephens's back catalogue: a play conceived and structured in direct response to the 1979 album *Metal Box* by Public Image Ltd (PIL), a landmark of post-punk music released the same year as the publication of Hebdige's *Subculture: The Meaning of Style*.[4] This play, directed by Sean Holmes on the main proscenium stage of the Lyric Hammersmith, paved the way for Stephens's and Holmes's next significant project together, Secret Theatre, which this chapter will discuss before proceeding to the final play analysed in these four chapters.

The Curious Incident of the Dog in the Night-Time (henceforth *Curious Incident*) presents a significant milestone in Stephens's oeuvre, at least as this book has periodized his career. It marks the end-point achievement of an incredible professional trajectory from a debut play produced in a black-box studio as part of a new writing festival, to a multi-award-winning, globally commercial juggernaut of a production created by one of the largest and most experienced creative teams to be hosted by the National Theatre. On the surface, there seems little in Stephens's 'dark and scary' preoccupations as a playwright (Nübling 2015: ix) that prepares for, or anticipates, the joyous, uplifting, life-affirming experience offered to audiences of *Curious Incident*. And yet, in many ways *Curious Incident* also represents the culmination, and celebration, of precisely the theatrical languages, conventions, dispositions and passions adopted and propounded by a peripatetic playwright who continues to embrace working across forms, genres and theatre cultures. That Stephens's most commercially successful play to date should also be – as members of the production's creative team testify – one of the most technically inventive, formally experimental and professionally challenging of his career creates a pleasing contradiction. Ending on this note of contradiction is an apt way to conclude this volume's discussion of the first fifteen years of Stephens's career.

Morning

In *Subculture: The Meaning of Style*, Hebdige builds on Phil Cohen's definition of 'subculture' as a 'compromise solution between two contradictory needs: the need to [. . .] express autonomy and difference from parents [. . .] and the need to maintain parental identifications' (qtd in Hebdige 1979: 77), in order to offer his own Marxian interpretation. For Hebdige, 'subculture' offers a form of resistance 'in which experienced contradictions and objections to the ruling ideology are obliquely represented in style' (1979: 133). Focusing on 1970s 'punk ensembles' specifically, Hebdige identifies this resistance, or 'break [. . .] with the parent culture', as manifesting in styling practices that 'did not so much magically resolve experienced contradictions as *represent the experience of contradiction itself* through visual significations (bondage, the ripped teeshirt, safety pins, bin liners, etc.) (1979: 121). In music and dress, he writes, punks 'self-consciously mirrored' the structural subordination and social betrayal upon which bourgeois society was founded, 'parodying the alienation and emptiness which have caused sociologists so much concern [and] celebrating in mock-heroic terms the death of the community and the collapse of traditional forms of meaning' (1979: 79). Hebdige styles punk sensibility as 'essentially dislocated, ironic and self-aware' (1979: 123), a description that resonates strongly not only with the clashing pastiche of literary genres and theatrical conventions offered in Stephens and Nübling's *Three Kingdoms* but also – and most particularly – the jagged, disaffected, even 'mock-heroic' attitude struck by *Morning*.

Originally titled *Metal Box*, each one of the ten scenes which comprise *Morning* corresponds to the ten tracks on PIL's album, including three 'instrumental' scenes composed only of brief stage directions which, Stephens suggests, 'may work as stimuli to choreography'.[5] In early drafts of the play (dated August 2011), scenes bear the titles of individual tracks but the actual aural proximity of this album to the play in performance is left undetermined by Stephens's note that 'the music on the album may or may not be used in production of the play'.[6] *Morning* is not a vehicle for *Metal Box*; it might better be described as a dramatic complement to, or theatrical manifestation of, PIL's album, understood not simply as a collection of songs but as a work of creative labour. The correspondences between the text of *Morning* and the phenomenon of *Metal Box* go beyond the pairing of song titles and scenes, though placing these in parallel does shed light on interpretative riffs and dramaturgical puzzles in the published script, such as Scene Eight ('The Suit') in which a character completely redundant to the plot makes a single appearance; or Scene Ten ('Socialist') in which the play's protagonist '*writes obsessively over and over again*' Marx's famous dictum: 'The philosophers have only interpreted the world. The point, however, is to change it' (Stephens 2015a: 249).[7] As a lightning rod for the album, *Morning* also draws from what might euphemistically be called the album's 'sleeve notes'; specifically, the experiences and preoccupations of PIL's front man, John Lydon (formerly Johnny Rotten of the Sex Pistols). Two biographical details in particular structure the play's narrative blueprint: the lingering illness and drawn-out death of Lydon's mother from cancer (captured in 'Death Disco/Swan Lake'); and a news story Lydon read in the *Daily Mirror*, about a girl who was kidnapped by two men and driven to a forest where she was eventually abandoned. As Lydon relates in liner notes to PIL's *Plastic Box* compilation (1999), the men 'had a cassette machine with an unusual tune on the cassette, which they kept playing over and over. The girl remembered the song, and that, along with her recollection of the car and the men's voices, is how the police identified them' ('Poptones'). The abrasiveness of the play's central duo, Stephanie and Cat – manifested as much by their lies, cheats, affected boredom and distortion of social cues as by the play's central act of violence – further recalls PIL's original proposal, relayed in the Wikipedia entry for *Metal Box*, that the album be packaged in a kind of sandpaper, that would 'effectively ruin the sleeve art of any records shelved next to it'.

Scene One of *Morning* ('Albatross') presents us with Stephanie, a teenage girl whose best friend, Cat, is due to leave for university the following week. We learn in Scene Three ('Death Disco/Swan Lake') that Stephanie and her brother, Alex, are carers for their mum, who is dying of cancer. In Scene Four ('Poptones'), Stephanie drives her boyfriend, Stephen, and Cat out to a forest, where Stephen learns that he has been brought there 'as a kind of leaving present' for Cat (218). Through taunts and teases, kissing segueways into biting, which progresses to Cat tying Stephens's hands together with her belt. Stephanie kicks him to the ground and in the head, and Cat pins him down and uses Stephanie's scarf as a gag: Stephen *'realises they are not playing any more'* (227). At this precise moment, the scene 'flips', to use Stephens's term:

> **Stephanie**: Oh, look.
> **Cat**: What?
> **Stephanie**: My tooth's come out.
> **Cat**: When?
> **Stephanie**: Just now.
> **Cat**: How did that happen?
> **Stephanie**: I've no idea. (ibid.)

Stephanie leaves the scene and returns with a rock with which she proceeds to smash in Stephens's skull. Sometime between Scenes Five ('Careering') and Six ('No Birds'), Stephanie and Alex's mum dies. In Scene Seven ('Graveyard'), Stephen *'comes alive again and turns into an angel'* (237). The police interview Stephanie, twice, but don't find the body and no charges are brought. In Scene Nine ('Bad Baby'), Cat leaves for university; Stephanie has failed 'to stop [her] from leaving' (248). In Scene Eleven ('Chant'), Stephanie delivers a vitriolic incantation:

> All music is shit and all art is shit and all theatre is shit and all television is shit and all sport is shit and all cinema is shit. The food is shit and everything is fucking shit. [. . .] We could refuse to vote in the next election. We could all of us vote in the next election. We could burn down polling booths in the next election [. . .] We could recycle. We could refuse to recycle. None of it will change anything. There is only terror. There is no hope. (249–50)

In Scene Twelve ('Radio 4'), the play's quiet conclusion, Alex '*changes into clothes for his mother's funeral*' as '*the set for the play is in some way dismantled and made brighter*' (250).

In an echo of Stephens's earlier play, *Herons* (2001), the epigraph for *Morning* is taken from *Cries Unheard: The Untold Story of Mary Bell* (1972), Gita Sereny's account of the trial of Mary Bell who in 1968, aged eleven years old, was convicted of the manslaughter (on the grounds of diminished responsibility) of two boys aged three and four: 'What it was . . . still mostly is in my mind . . . is unconnected flashes of horror' (Sereny 1972: 199). The 'flashes of horror' which punctuate *Morning* are set against a bourgeois imaginary of Dads who set up bank accounts for their daughters (202), family holidays to Corsica (203), Mums who make their own tomato sauce for pasta (206), tuna and cucumber sandwiches (217) and first dates at the zoo (230). As with *Punk Rock*, in *Morning* Stephens looks askance at social determinism as an explanatory framework for human psychology, and is drawn instead to representing experiences of 'contradiction and confusion and behaviour that is odd, misguided and illogical' (Stephens 2005a: xii). Writing about *Punk Rock* and the 'affluent, disaffected youths' that populate that play, Stephens contends that 'the real punk spirit' – that which was responsible for producing 'some of most compelling music of my lifetime' – 'wasn't born out of class dissidence but out of existential horror' (2011a: xv). If previous of Stephens's plays have posited 'the death of community and the collapse of traditional forms of meaning' as sources of societal atomization and moral collapse – of that 'alienation and emptiness which have caused sociologists so much concern' (Hebdige 1979: 79) – *Morning* inhabits this landscape, and barely looks away from its screen. Dramaturgically, zero consequences follow from Stephen's death: Stephanie is not arrested; Cat goes to university anyway. Reflecting on the play in 2015, Stephens recalls that it was 'a new thing for me to write a play not defined by geographical specificity but it seemed to satisfy an attempt to ask whether psychopathy and despair are generated by socio-economic factors or something stranger' (2015a: xvi).

It feels apt to describe the play as 'adolescent', with all the valences this term carries in cultures where 'the teenager' is posited as both (a) juvenile and a force of latent potential. 'By the time we've reached seventeen we have dreamed everything that we will ever dream', Stephens writes in working notes for a later play, *Nuclear War*, 'After that point everything we do is an attempt to manifest that dream'.[8] Thinking of *Morning* as a play of and for adolescence – five of its six characters are seventeen – strengthens associative connections between Stephens's writing and the gestures of punk subcultures, which in turn find parallels with Stephens's own position within, or stance towards, what might be regarded as the 'parent culture' of British new writing – expressing '"autonomy and difference"' while observing '"the need to maintain parental identifications"' (Cohen qtd in Hebdige 1979: 77). *Morning* is one of four plays collected in *Plays 4* (2015) that Stephens wrote specifically for Nübling to direct, and while (as the director notes in his Foreword) these texts notionally observe the 'social/realistic genre' for which UK new writing is known, 'the reality [. . .] is pure construction' (Nübling 2015: x). Although developed with actors drawn from the Young Company at the Lyric Hammersmith, London, and the Junges Theater, Basel, *Morning* is not a documentary study of the lived experiences of contemporary teenagers; it is a meditation – perhaps even a nostalgic one – on the persisting mythos of adolescence within the Western cultural imaginary.

Although all references to *Metal Box* were removed from the final published version of the play, traces of John Lydon's lyrics linger in the play's often cryptic dialogue. The album's opening song, 'Albatross', for example, suggests a figure contemplating whether to stay or leave, and lingers on the idea of intimacy as a kind of grotesquery. Stephanie, whose reaction to Cat leaving for university is to threaten 'I'll make you stay' (205), echoes the song's lyrics both in her description of her boyfriend, Stephen, as 'unbearable', and in her moody injunction to Cat:

Stephanie: Don't go.
Stay here. You'll fucking hate it anyway. So you may as well. I know you extremely well and I know you'd hate it. (204)

This opening scene establishes the scenario (Cat's imminent departure for university) that ultimately results in Stephanie and Cat's kidnap, torture and murder of Stephen; what fascinates about the scene and its relationship to *Metal Box*, however, is its strange shifts in focus, direction, pace and subject matter. Structurally, the scene frustrates dramatic momentum, not least by studding throughout the dialogue the stage direction '*some time*' (201, 202, 204, 205, 206), which sits on the page without any discernible accompanying energy – the menace of a Pinteresque 'pause', for example, or the 'active silence' of debbie tucker green's deployment of the em dash ('–').[9] Contrasting affects grind against one another, as Stephanie professes that she 'fucking hates' her boyfriend in one breath and expresses a desire for 'ice cream' in the next (204). Metaphors distort and disgust even as they illuminate and communicate, as when Cat describes the other students she met when being interviewed for university: 'Every single last one of them had an entirely cuboid head and all their clothes were exactly the same colour and when they spoke no real words came out just a series of metallic clicks' (203). Here, the dialogue again points back to *Metal Box*, specifically to the abrasive, metallic guitar sound that was a signature of PIL's guitarist Keith Levene; an 'in-joke' that self-consciously performs the 'essentially dislocated, ironic and self-aware' sensibility that Hebdige identifies in punk (1979: 123).

The tonal quality established by the opening scene of *Morning* is one of languor and boredom; *ennui* without the implicit moral compass that grounds despair.

> **Cat**: [. . .] I'm not staying here under any circumstances. It's horrifying. The whole town stinks of sugar. The shops are all wretched. The people are mentally retarded. It's cold. You can't get any good stuff. Nothing ever happens. All my friends apart from you are boring. Including you sometimes. Including you a lot of the time. (204)

The scene's timbre – quietly but relentlessly nauseating, suffocating, dislocating – sounds throughout the play, translated visually into the disquieting image of Stephanie being unable to 'stop smiling. I feel so sad it's like I'm going to be sick' (215). Disaffection pulses through the play, affecting the incessant, repetitive, thrumming bass which underpins the tracks on *Metal Box*. In these ways, *Morning* offers a case study in Stephens's developing fascination, first outlined in his keynote 'Skydiving Blindfolded', with the idea that 'language is noise' (2011b: online). In his Foreword to

Stephens's *Plays: 4*, Nübling describes this aspect of the writing: 'When you hear Simon reading parts of his plays, he blurs the borders between characters, he leaves psychological reasoning behind, he loves to follow musical lines and he transforms text into sound' (2015: x). There is an instructive echo here between Stephens's restless, searching approach to theatre-making, his open, musical and porous texts, and Sean Albeiz's description of '*Metal Box*'s embrace of noise as purposeful message' in his analysis of the album: 'An understanding that this music was a road to somewhere [. . .] is crucial. Being here now and "no futurism" prematurely curtails utopian thinking and creativity; the consequence of existing in a hermetically-sealed present [fiction?] is atrophy' (2003: 371).

Sean Holmes's production of *Morning*, which premiered at the Traverse Theatre, Edinburgh, in August 2012 and transferred to the Lyric Hammersmith in September that year, returned to lines of creative enquiry raised during his 2008 production of *Pornography* and enlivened by Nübling's 2011 production of *Three Kingdoms*. 'We were beginning to look to Europe', Holmes reflected in 2013 about his working partnership with Stephens during this period:

> Simon's experience of that was more than mine, mine was minimal [. . .] but there was just a sense of 'there's got to be more to life than . . .', you know, 'what's your action? What's your character?'. We were reeling from the experience of *Three Kingdoms* and we weren't sure if it was as straightforward as [that] anymore. (2013b)

Holmes describes his experience of directing *Morning* as:

> probably the first time [. . .] that I was the lead artist on [a production], that I was making decisions about the play. That *I* was taking it into this territory, as opposed to 'my job is to support the writer's vision' [. . .] I thought that, well, if Sebastian can do it, I can do it! (ibid.)

Holmes's visual aesthetic for *Morning* – realized by Hyemi Shin's set and Charles Balfour's lighting design – was described by critics as akin to 'a piece of art installation' (Shore 2012), an 'electrifyingly strange' staging comprised of a large fish tank half-filled with water, a fridge, building-site lights and a plastic-sheeted structure reminiscent of a police incident tent (Basset 2012). An onstage sound technician – Michael Czepiel (also teenage) – created a 'brooding, itchy soundscape' (Hitchings 2012b) through 'deafening techno and unsettling ambient hums' (Lukowski 2012), occasionally editorializing the onstage action through comments unscripted by Stephens. Holmes's direction of Stephens's text expressed ideas and artistic (re)orientations developed in response to *Three Kingdoms*, summarized by Stephens as 'an interest in removing the artifice of mimetic mise en scène, removing the [. . .] attempt to recreate an imagined other world on the world of the stage' in order to 'celebrate the metaphorical gesture of an actor pretending to be someone else' (2013a).

Reviewers generally expressed enthusiasm for Holmes's rendering of what Henry Hitchings described as 'the nihilism of an alienated generation whose violence is abrupt and offhand' (2012b). Sarah Hemming, however, while rightly recognizing the production as a 'deliberate experiment: a theatrical laboratory set up to explore an extreme psychological state and a desensitizing environment', identified this very sense of experimentation as the source of the production's shortcomings (2012). It is sometimes instructive to reflect on what reviewers identify as those aspects of a play or performance that, in their view, prevent it from fulfilling the criteria of 'proper drama'. For Hemming, what made the production 'feel a bit like a staging post on the way to something, rather than a fully-fledged drama' was its failure to 'solve the problem of evoking sympathy for someone [Stephanie] who cannot empathise' (ibid.). Hemming's complaint that 'the alienating techniques keep you disengaged from the characters' reveals an unexamined assumption that 'good' or 'successful' drama is that which positions audience members in a relation of compassion or empathy towards its characters.[10] By short-circuiting the theatrical devices that elicit such feelings, Holmes's production of *Morning* posed a challenge to that assumption: a 'punk' gesture that he and Stephens carried forward into their next project together – not the staging of a play, but the founding of an ensemble: Secret Theatre at the Lyric Hammersmith, London.

Secret Theatre

Launched in June 2013, the Secret Theatre project was founded in part as a practical response to the closure of the Lyric Hammersmith during a multi-million pound redevelopment of the adjoining Kings Mall shopping centre: realizing that the theatre's auditorium would itself remain untouched throughout the renovations, Holmes and Stephens decided to 'make this auditorium a flexible space hosting whatever audience we could get in through back doors and goods lifts' (Holmes 2013a: online). The material and economic conditions which created this 'Secret Theatre at the heart of a building site' were consequently seized by Holmes and Stephens as an opportunity to explore and test the conditions – both aesthetic and ideological – which then prevailed in rehearsal and production processes of large-scale subsidized building-based theatres in the UK. Originally conceived as an eight-month season of classics and new plays played in repertoire by a resident ensemble of ten actors – a model which departs from the established British system of freelance actors and four-week rehearsals to move towards structures more reminiscent of the German repertoire – the company continued making and performing work together until March 2015, staging seven shows in total ranging from classics (*Woyzeck* [1837] and *A Streetcar Named Desire* [1947]) to new writing, to a piece devised by the company itself.[11]

In a speech made at the launch of the project, Holmes singled out Edward Bond's *The Chair Plays* (2012)[12] and *Three Kingdoms* as works which had recently 'challenged [the Lyric] in profound ways', raising questions and provocations that the theatre wished to explore (2013a: online). In this speech, Holmes asserts a crucial point: that structures of working directly influence aesthetics. He argues that the standard institutional structures by which work is made in this country has created a 'theatre culture that, when it approaches text, especially new writing, is rooted in literalism' because there is neither the time nor resources to 'imagine anything other than what the playwright has written down' (ibid.). This culture of literalism within producing structures has, in turn, engendered an industry which continues to duck questions – aesthetic and political – regarding diversity and representation, the cultural work achieved by theatre, and what might constitute 'success'. 'Maybe the existing structures of theatre in this country', Holmes offers, 'whilst not corrupt, are corrupting':

> I speak as someone who is absolutely part of – ingrained into – those structures. Structures forced by economic realities of course, but also by an unconscious acceptance of those structures. [. . .] I've hidden behind the literal demands of the text and avoided the really difficult questions about representations of gender and race and disability. I've pursued star casting at the expense of the right casting. And given exaggerated respect to the five star review. And I wonder if many of us feel the claustrophobia of that potential corruption more than we like to admit? (ibid.)

An attempt to 'fundamentally change the conversation in the rehearsal room', the original Secret Theatre company comprised an ethnically diverse ensemble of five male and five female actors, one of whom identifies as disabled. This composition, as Holmes averred, automatically attacked 'existing structures of literalism' which otherwise marginalize and obscure female, non-white and disabled actors (ibid.). In the company's way of working together, longer and more flexible rehearsals aimed to 'explore the *why* as well as the *what*' of theatre-making (ibid., emphasis added); a dedicated design team rehearsed technically in the theatre over a number of weeks rather than days; and four writers were commissioned to 'write for specific actors in conditions that challenge the assumption of what a new play might be' (ibid.).[13] Underpinning these endeavours was a stated 'concentration on releasing the spirit of the text whilst gleefully disregarding the letter of the text' (ibid.).

Secret Theatre was jointly conceived by Holmes and Stephens in part 'as a really clear response to meeting lots of young artists, directors and writers, who are dissatisfied and a bit bored with British theatre' (Holmes 2013b). The director Maria Aberg – who in May 2012 was one of six directors invited to a week-long workshop with Holmes, Stephens, Edward Bond and Sebastian Nübling – is a good example of a director whose work in Sweden (her home country), Germany and Britain evidences the discipline of 'always pushing against your own tradition as well as the tradition of the culture that you're in' (Aberg qtd in Hutton 2013: online). In April 2012, Aberg staged for the Royal Shakespeare Company (RSC) a radically edited version of *King John* which changed the gender of two characters, including the central character of the Bastard. Rehearsals began with the whole company engaged in two weeks of workshops which were 'very much about exploring and experimenting and to do with creating the world of the play rather than going into detail about the text' (Aberg 2012: online), a process Aberg repeated for her 2013 Glastonbury-inspired *As You Like It*, also for the RSC, for which many of the creative team who worked on *King John* were reassembled. While commending the latter production's strong ensemble work, Catherine Love also wrote of the 'joy to see Nicolas Tennant on stage again after *Three Kingdoms*, here embracing another kind of anarchy with his wryly shambolic take on Touchstone and even briefly breaking out of the text to deliver a bit of deadpan stand-up' (2013: online). In his review, Trueman also praises Tennant's 'ticking, depressive shambles' of a Touchstone: 'it's a particular pleasure', he writes, 'to glimpse the influence of *Three Kingdoms* in the way he grabs the part and shakes it, sometimes all the way out of the play itself' (2013: online). The influence of Stephens's work on a younger generation of directors and actors within British theatre has encouraged greater ownership over the notion that the seemingly immaterial 'scripts' of theatrical tradition and convention – that is to say, the material conditions and ideological precepts which structure and inform the interpretation and realization of play-texts – present a set of imperatives as cogent as the 'script' of the dramatic play-text itself. These 'scripts' are not, furthermore, equivalent to one another and, in the words of Aberg, 'being faithful to theatrical tradition is not the same as being faithful to the text' (qtd in Hutton 2013: online).

Four key artistic imperatives underpinned the project of Secret Theatre: an interest in the possibilities of ensemble and, allied to this, a renewed appreciation of the artistic agency of actors; an expectation of extended rehearsal periods in order to accommodate (and incorporate) workshopping and improvisation; an expectation that creative teams, including set, costume, lighting, sound and video designers, will be present with creative contributions within the rehearsal room; and an recognition that these roles are functions not, necessarily, individuals: an acknowledgement that professional territories need not be jealously guarded but that roles might blend and synthesise. In articulating and prioritizing these principles over other creative approaches, Secret Theatre sought consciously to emulate working practices established in German-language theatre cultures. As Chapter 3 observes, in UK theatre these practices have long been associated, disparagingly, with so-called directors' theatre, the work of which is frequently dismissed by commentators on the grounds of its 'wilful obscurity, over-the-top-stagecraft [and] auteur-ish egocentrism' (McCarter qtd Boenisch 2015: 1). It is interesting to note, then, that within Stephens's oeuvre, the production which most carefully observes these imperatives also happens to be his most commercially successful to date: Marianne Elliott's 2012 staging of *The Curious Incident of the Dog in the Night-Time*.

The Curious Incident of the Dog in the Night-Time

> *The Curious Incident of the Dog in the Night-Time* was never written with the impulse to make money, but it was written to be theatrically open. (Stephens qtd in Barnett 2016: 316)

The success of Mark Haddon's novel, *The Curious Incident of the Dog in the Night-Time*, was instant, global and extraordinary by publishing standards.

First published in 2003, it sold in millions, garnering seventeen literary awards including the UK Whitbread Book of the Year, the Silver Kiss (Holland, 2004), Yalsa Alex Award (USA, 2004), Grand Prix, Sankei Children's Book Awards (Japan, 2004) and the Premio Boccaccio (Italy, 2004) (Haddon n.d.: online). As of 2020, it has been translated into 44 languages and sold more than 5.5 million copies worldwide (The Lowry 2020: online). The novel is written from the first-person perspective of a fifteen-year-old boy, Christopher John Francis Boone, who, prompted by his teacher Siobhan, is writing a book about his attempts to identify the murderer of Wellington – his neighbour's dog – who he discovered stabbed through with a pitchfork. Though never explicitly stated, from Christopher's narration of events and his interactions with people – his hatred of being touched; his difficulties with understanding emotions; his scrupulous attention to detail; his fits of violence – the reader can intuit that Christopher is a teenager on the autistic spectrum. While the book that Christopher is writing as a school project focuses on solving the mystery of 'Who Killed Wellington', it becomes clear that the real subject of the novel is Christopher himself.

Following the book's success, Haddon received many offers from producers who wanted to adapt the book into a play, a prospect that Haddon initially rejected on the grounds that it was 'a preposterous idea': how could a book 'set entirely in the head of single character' be translated into theatre? (Haddon 2013: online) Haddon was aware of Stephens's work and, when both writers were on attachment to the National Theatre, asked the playwright if he might like to adapt the book. Stephens was familiar with the novel, having read it to help 'crystalize the character' of Lee in *Motortown*, and accepted 'on the understanding that I didn't take a commission and that I just did it as an experiment in process' (Stephens qtd in Radosavljević 2014: 257). This understanding – that by refusing a commission, Stephens was removing 'the pressure of a commissioning theatre on my neck' (ibid.) – would prove the first of several actions that created a particular set of conditions – or, to return to the phrase used by Holmes in his aims for Secret Theatre, 'structures of working' – in which the stage adaptation of *Curious Incident* was created. The sense that the project was a creative challenge, 'an experiment in process', would underpin rehearsals – not least because, as Marianne Elliott admits, 'the stakes [for this production] were particularly high' (2015). According to Katy Rudd, the show's assistant director:

> From the beginning, the [rehearsal] room had this energy of 'well, let's just try' [. . .] Everyone was out of their comfort zone. Everyone

was just trying their best. It was very protected, this production: it had a limited run in the Cottesloe [the National Theatre's smallest stage], it had big things either side of it,[14] it was very much under the radar [...] And that is what made it work. (2015)

Curious Incident premiered at the National Theatre, London, on 2 August 2012. Set design was by Bunny Christie, lighting design by Paule Constable, and choreography by Scott Graham and Steven Hoggett of Frantic Assembly. The production won seven Olivier Awards including Best New Play, Best Director and Best Actor (for Luke Treadaway's performance as Christopher) and transferred to the Apollo Theatre in London's West End in March 2013. In October 2014, the show made its debut on Broadway, New York, at the Ethel Barrymore Theatre, winning a further trove of awards, including six TONY Awards. In addition to its runs in London's West End and New York's Broadway, the National Theatre's production has completed two UK tours, a US tour and an International Tour.[15] In addition to these large-scale tours, and in collaboration with the NT's Theatre Nation Partnership, a stripped-down ninety-minute version of the production has also embarked on two Schools Tours (The Lowry 2020: online). In 2014, in collaboration with the Prince's Foundation for Children and the Arts, the Society of London Theatre and the Theatre Management Association, *Curious Incident* was the first West End production to introduce regular 'relaxed performances', in which the theatre environment 'is specifically adapted for theatregoers with autistic spectrum conditions, those with sensory, communication or learning difficulties, and anyone else who would benefit from a less formal environment' (Mottram 2015: online). At the time of writing, it is estimated that *Curious Incident* has been seen by over 5 million people worldwide (The Lowry 2020: online).

One of the most critically and commercially successful shows of the twenty-first century to date, there is a case to be made that the National Theatre's production of *Curious Incident* is also an unexpected example of the sort of European directorial practices – *Regietheater* – that this book explores in relation to Nübling's productions of *Pornographie* and *Three Kingdoms*. This kind of directing, as Patrice Pavis explains, involves '"choosing a direction, an orientation, an interpretation", while still "taking as a starting point the text's givens as unalterable"' (qtd in Boenisch 2015: 3). Peter Boenisch, who has written extensively about *Regie*, identifies this practice in approaches to play-texts which seek to transform the drama of the written text 'into an experiential economy generated through physicalization, spatialization and rhythmalization' (2008: 42). Discussing the work of German director Michael Thalheimer in particular, Boenisch glosses a practice which seeks to find the 'essence' of a play-text in order to transpose it 'onto other layers of theatrical presentation: space, rhythm and bodies':

> That 'essence' of a playtext [. . .] is not to be found by condensing it to a single meaning, nor to an assumed authorial 'intention'. He [Thalheimer] conceives of the 'essence' not as stable core, but as an animated process, as an experiential nucleus that generates, in the first instance, sensations, perceptions, and images which fashion a visceral and vital impact. (2008: 33)

For Elliott's production of *Curious Incident*, the 'essence', or 'experiential nucleus', of the drama was, simply, the character 'Christopher Boone'. Understood as an act of creative invention, 'Christopher' offers a referent simultaneously indeterminate, stable and processual: a cipher, or icon, made manifest only by an act of collective imagination. On receipt of Stephens's script, Elliott was clear that – however the show was to be made – it was to be a visual manifestation of Christopher's interiority: her work on the production was 'to fill in the visuals with the way that his brain might work [. . .] and try to get the audience to feel what he feels, emotionally' (2015). Consequently, creative decisions were governed by the extent to which they successfully conjured 'Christopher Boone' – his point of view, his imagination, his encounters with the outside world. In the words of Adrian Sutton, who composed the music for the production, the sound, lighting, images, movement – 'literally everything, every element of the stagecraft of that play' – was 'lined up like iron filings in that direction: Marianne's principle concern was that everything had to be played from Christopher's point of view' (2015). Responding to the 'givens' of Stephens's text, and taking a definite 'orientation' from it, Elliott's production drew out 'Christopher' and fixed him as the production's 'essence' from which the creative experiment cascaded: in this way, the production was *born of* the text, not *dictated by* it. 'The little catch-phrase that I and the creative team used', Sutton relates, 'was: "Christopher would have approved"' (2015).

Stephens's text was itself organized around the very particular challenge of adapting a novel 'told entirely through Christopher's perspective' for the 'three-dimensional medium of the stage' (2015f). Aside from the necessary shift from the subjective 'first-person' viewpoint of the novel to the objective 'third-person' viewpoint of the stage, Stephens's adaptation is extremely faithful to the narrative, characters and environments described in Haddon's novel. While the action is condensed for effective storytelling, Christopher remains the central protagonist and, just like the novel, the play is created from the book that he writes. For Stephens, the 'guiding idea was to make sure that everything [in the play-text] was behavioural, to make sure that everything was active' (ibid.). This is, of course, a key tenet of Stephens's playwriting practice:

> Theatre is a behavioural medium, it deals not with what people feel or think or remember or say but with what people *do*. [. . .] You can't put what Christopher 'sees' or 'thinks' onstage. It just doesn't work, because 'thinking' is undramatic. So the really hard thing was extricating the play from Christopher's mind. I needed to locate the drama and in order to locate the drama I needed to look at the things that people *do* to each other. (ibid.)

The preparation for the adaptation was a two-step process: first, Stephens simply listed all the events that happen in the book and, second – observing that 'like a playwright', Haddon 'only has people talk to one another out loud [. . .] when they're trying to affect each other quite directly' – typed out all the direct speech into the form of a script (ibid.). According to Stephens, 'the text came out of those two documents' but the problem of 'Christopher Boone' remained (ibid.). As Stephens recounts, 'you've got to have Christopher's voice [from the novel] in [the script] because otherwise you miss it. So how do you get Christopher's voice *out*?' (ibid.). Two devices – one literary, the other theatrical – were mobilized to solve this problem: the introduction of a narrator in the form of Siobhan, Christopher's schoolteacher; and an ensemble who would work as a company to manifest, visually and physically, Christopher's imagination. As Stephens explains:

> The sense I had was the way Christopher thinks, his thinking is balletic. The agility with which he moves from thought to thought is the agility of a dancer, and that lent itself to that physical kind of dance. [These ideas] were an attempt to dramatize [. . .] the interior of Christopher Boone's brain. [I wanted] to get what's *in* there *outside* in his behaviour. (qtd in Theater Talk 2014: online)

In another key action for this production, Stephens wrote his adaptation specifically with the work of Frantic Assembly in mind. Founded in

1994, Frantic Assembly creates performer-led ensemble work, often commissioning and working with writers and composers in ways that encourage a collaborative approach to writing, music, choreography and movement. While Elliott had not previously worked with its Artistic Directors, Scott Graham and Steven Hoggett – as had none of the actors involved – Stephens was committed to their involvement and wrote the script so that movement, dance and the ensemble ethos of a company of actors would be integral to the play's realization. As a result, stage directions in *Curious Incident* are used sparingly and typically offer very little information as to how a particular scene, or transition, is to be realized. As Stephens observes, like his earlier play *Pornography*, *Curious Incident* 'has hardly any stage directions. What *Curious Incident* has is problems: it has a series of problems to solve' (2015f). Key passages of the play choreographed by Graham and Hoggett include, in Part One, Christopher's routine when he comes home from school, his fantasy about being an astronaut and his memory of his mother in Polperro; and, in Part Two, the extended sequence where Christopher travels from Swindon to London. 'It would make me laugh in rehearsals some days', Treadaway recalls, 'where I'd see the section we were working on might be "Christopher walks into Paddington Station" and, you know, it's a week's work of twists and turns and lifts and things' (2015). 'What we did with Scott and Steven', he attests, 'was a huge part of the show and of its success':

> The way Frantic Assembly look at things is: 'what's the most exciting, what's the most interesting way we could tell this story?'. And if that's not the most realistic then that's great, that's even more exciting. By taking *mentally* what was going on for Christopher, him feeling like he's being crashed into, and spun round, and all the energy that he feels from a crowded place, for example, we tried to *physically* show that. [...] A lot of [the show] came just through physically working on different scenes and seeing how you get them to be the most exciting, most rich, most complex versions of each moment for Christopher. (2015)

Frantic Assembly's involvement – their first collaboration with the National Theatre – prompted another key action by which the structures of working on this production were determined: a week-long workshop with actors led by Graham, Hoggett and Elliott, with Bunny Christie, the set designer, and Katy Rudd, the assistant director, also in attendance. While not unheard of at the National Theatre, the extension of rehearsals via a pre-rehearsal workshop (implemented also for Elliott's 2007 hit *War Horse*) is not standard practice, and nor were the improvisational methods employed by Graham and Hoggett familiar to the ten actors involved. Recalling that workshop in 2015, actor Nick Sidi, a member of the show's ensemble, is unequivocal about its significance:

> To this day, that workshop was the most exciting ten days I've ever had in any rehearsal room, ever. It was totally incredible. I think by the end of the first day there was just this feeling of: we are so lucky, this is so exciting, this is golden. [. . .]
>
> With Frantic Assembly, one of the first things we did was this crazy exercise where one person walks slowly into the middle of a group of people, who each takes a piece of that person's body and collectively lifts them. So a person walks and before they know it, they're up in the air. Howard Ward, who was in the show, he's a big strong guy but it was amazing – he could walk in and just by us collectively working together at the same time – whoosh, he would be up in the air. It's amazing how it frees you up, immediately. [. . .] I've done workshops where they say they're 'going to explore themes' or something and actually you just sit around reading a draft of the play and try and finesse bits of that. This wasn't that at all. (2015)

Nicola Walker, who played Judy, Christopher's mother, echoes Sidi's articulation of a process contrary to convention:

> Sometimes workshops are about working on the script and you're asked to give your ideas and to say how well you think the script works. I mean that would have been laughable. [Stephens's] script worked absolutely beautifully as it stood that day. But then Marianne sort of pushed away from the table and said 'well, now we have to find how to stage this'. [. . .]
>
> Scott and Steven were phenomenal because they got us, straightaway, to put our scripts down. Normally in a workshop you're sat down intellectualising something but Marianne and Frantic went: 'right, we're going to move it physically and see what we can achieve'. (2015)

Given the way Stephens's script was structured – a mixture of narrated and enacted action, in which scenes rhythmically shift and dissolve into one another – the workshop was used to explore how a fictive world could be created without any set: 'we explored how we might show the routine of what he does by using physical movement, instead of props [. . .] or furniture' (Elliott 2015). As Sidi recalls:

> Marianne always had this thing of: we're going to tell this story from Christopher's point of view. So how can we show that this is a boy who obviously has rituals, who needs the security of knowing that everything is the same, who doesn't like change – what does he do when he comes home? How can we create Christopher's daily routine? How do we create his room? We were sent off in small groups to create something and we were just constantly trying things [. . .] the idea being to use your bodies, to use yourselves as people to create this room. We were doing things like sitting on the floor and pretending to be a toilet so Luke would sit on you, or he would go and open a blind and someone would be there with their hand in the air and Luke would pull something and they would move to the left. And, of course, it's really embarrassing! You're thinking 'what am I doing, some kind of mime?!' But everyone was doing it and everyone was really getting into the spirit of it and, as I say, that freedom we felt was so playful. [. . .] I don't know why, but just something happened, the chemistry of the people in the room was so brilliant. *Curious* explored *physically* what it's like to be Christopher. (2015)

As revealed by Sidi's admission of the embarrassment that, alongside the playfulness, was also present in the room, this was a way of working in which none of the ten actors were trained. 'In this country it's all about holding the script and arguing about lines and whether you feel your character would do that', states Walker. 'But we, straightaway, put the script down and just started playing [. . .]. [Scott and Steven] had to see how they could get us to work together as a group, and how far they could push us in that physical way' (2015). Walker remembers the final exercise on the final day of the workshop as, for her, crystallizing the potential of an improvised, performer-led response to text:

> It had finished, the week's workshop, and I think we were beginning to think about packing up, and Scott and Steven said 'hang on, we want to do one last exercise'. And they said, 'right, the mother and the father: you've not been allowed to touch Christopher for a week.

We're going to give you forty-five seconds: you can touch him and look at him and hold him in whatever way you choose. And the man who was doing it in the workshop, Burn [Gorman], picked Luke [Treadaway] up. And I think they were about the same height but he picked Luke up – he didn't have time to think about it – so he picked Luke up like a baby. And they just stood there for forty-five seconds with him cradling him. A big man, holding another man but Luke suddenly looked like a baby. He was just holding him, he wasn't doing any grand acting, just what he in that moment instinctively felt like doing. And I was just sobbing! I think we all were at that point.

And then they said, 'okay, Judy, you've got forty-five seconds'. And I stood with Luke and what was fascinating was that what Judy seemed to want was to be held by Christopher, rather than hold Christopher, and I think is the big difference between the mother and the father. So Judy got forty-five seconds to make Christopher hold her, embrace her. And he was doing nothing, Luke was still being Christopher so he's not actually joining in that embrace. So I'm having to hold Luke quite hard, which seemed quite true about Judy, forcing him to love me and show he loves me and physically touch me and hold me. [. . .] So at the end of the first week, you thought, 'there's definitely something in doing it this way'. (2015)

Reflecting on the process, Elliott is diplomatic: 'A lot of things [that we tried in the workshop] didn't work. A lot of the things that we thought did work, that we thought were so brilliant, didn't work ultimately [. . .] But it gave us a sort of language on which we could build the show' (2015).

The discoveries made during that workshop fed directly into Bunny Christie's set design: initial ideas had included setting the play within a school gym, but by the end of that week, Christie was determined that 'the set had to be magical [. . .] it had to be a magic box and out of this magic box must come these wonderful things. They're hidden, but he [Christopher] thinks of them and, because he thinks of them, they're there' (Elliott 2015). Christie's design for the Cottesloe theatre evoked the landscape of Christopher's ordered, methodical mind by seating the audience on four edges of a square playing space, the floor of which resembled mathematical graph paper: white lines forming a glowing grid of tiny squares on a black background. The floor was a blackboard, onto which Christopher could chalk emoticons and diagrams as he tried to deduce Wellington's killer. This space became a virtual map of Christopher's mind, revealing his inner life through lighting and video projections of whirling algebraic equations, galaxies of stars and cascading numbers and letters. Contained within this bare geometric space were trap doors, from which 'props were conjured like thoughts from his fevered imagination' (Marmion 2012), and into which were studded hundreds of LED lights, which formed 'patterns like [the] neural pathways' of Christopher's brain' (Thompson 2012). 'It's a space where Christopher can just magic or conjure the image that he wants', explains Rudd, 'and then change it straight away: it could be the school but it could also be his home, it could also be Swindon train station' (2015). Props and costume also stemmed from, or were folded into, the concept of Christopher's perception. Rudd explains how, in terms of costume design, the colours are

> all kind of grey, monotone [and in order to indicate a new character] each of the [actors] puts on something which is often quite neon and harsh, which is how Christopher sees those things. He has hypersensitivity to noise, and colour, and those people to him, the strangers he meets in the street, are very loud and garish and strange and frightening, and that's reflected in the design. (ibid.)

With the prop design, Elliott explains:

> Christopher doesn't really like eye contact and he doesn't notice the things we notice. He would talk to somebody and he would fixate on a particular object that that character might be holding, like garden shears, or like the oven glove that the woman at no. 44 has – whatever it is, that's what he fixates on. So it felt important to us that that was the only thing [of significance] that could be in the scene, and that it was a very bright colour because for him this prop is of heightened importance, it's what he's fixating on. (2015)

All of the props used in the production were set around the edge of the stage and, in the Cottesloe production, were individually labelled. 'If you've ever seen a theatre props table', Rudd explains:

> the stage management tape out each prop and have a label for exactly where it goes. We thought Christopher would love that, so each of the props should be round the edge of the space, laid out for each act and on the side ready to be used, clear for all the audience to see. (2015)

'We wanted to declare everything', states Elliott, '[so the audience were] not going to see major acts of illusion or great big sets chugging on, it's just these people telling a story' (2015).

Adrian Sutton's music design likewise looked to 'Christopher Boone' for its orientation:

> It seemed to me that a good place to start would be, okay, we know Christopher loves maths, and that he's especially obsessed with prime numbers. So I thought, let's take the first few prime numbers, 2, 3, 5, 7, 11, and let's try using them in various different ways as applied to musical parameters. So, for example, let's make a rhythm so that the rhythmic emphasis is 2, 3, 5, 7, 11. So that it goes: **1** 2, **1** 2 3, **1** 2 3 4 5, **1** 2 3 4 5 6 7, **1** 2 3 4 5 6 7 8 9 10 11, **1** 2, **1** 2 3, **1** 2 3 4 5 – so it's emphasizing the downbeats. And that's how the show opens, if you listen to the very opening cue: the lights go down and there's a kick drum that begins with that rhythm.
>
> [Another approach] is to consider the musical scale as a ladder, with steps. So let's pick the second, third, fifth, seventh, and eleventh 'step' on that ladder and just use those pitches in some way. And I thought because Christopher likes ordered things, he likes the idea of neat, ordered, non-random sequences, it seemed obvious that he would want to repeat that sequence of pitches over and over. [And now] you can combine those two ideas: you've got the rhythmic one and the pitch one, and so now you can apply the rhythmic emphasis to the pitch model. [. . .]
>
> When it came to the actual sounds themselves, the actual instruments that played these pitches and these rhythms and everything else, it seemed a pretty straightforward decision. Again, because Christopher loves computers and he loves mathematics, it seemed that all the sounds should be synthetic and computer-generated, and they pretty much are, with one or two exceptions. [. . .]
>
> We were always working in the service of what it's like to be Christopher. In his head, it's a crashing overload of 'I can't cope with this, I can't cope with all these people, all this movement all these lights, and sounds'. [The music] had to convey his feeling of terror. (2015)

'[Marianne] wanted us to all feel as though we were Christopher', affirms Rudd. 'That we were breathing the same air as him: the audience and the ensemble' (2015).

In the original National Theatre production, the ensemble of ten actors played forty-one speaking parts between them. In the words of Sidi:

> We were an ensemble company in the true meaning of the word. Usually if you're in an ensemble then it's a bit like being in a chorus: you get trotted out and you do a big crowd scene and then you're shunted off. We, however, were on stage more or less all the time. [...] You felt like you were in every moment of every beat. One minute you were sitting on the side and the next you were creating a house. Then you were on the train. Then you were in the station. And then you were being an actor, saying your lines and playing a character. And the changes, the *switches* from one moment to the next . . . it was just incredible. It was thrilling. In the Cottesloe, you could actually hear people gasp. Because [...] you were two feet away from the audience. It was thrilling to do and exciting to watch. And you were part of that machine, of this incredible company togetherness, and that is *really* what an ensemble is. We all had each other's backs – *physically*. We literally had each other's backs. (2015)

Niamh Cusack, who played Siobhan, concurs: 'although [the production] was obviously very focal on Christopher, we were a very bonded company and we knew that the whole thing wouldn't work unless we had that commitment to each other [...] I think that bondedness was really, really palpable and essential to the show' (2015). The company 'bondedness' was fostered by Frantic Assembly and Elliott in part through a rehearsal process that included what Walker, Cusack and Sidi referred to as 'Boot Camp': a strenuous workout at the beginning of each and every day which would see the company falling into the National Theatre canteen at lunchtime, 'sweating [...] and *starving*' (Sidi 2015). A company warm-up before each and every show was also, in the words of Cusack, 'non-negotiable':

> And once you had Una Stubbs [who played Mrs Alexander] saying 'okay, I accept this is non-negotiable' it was fantastic. Because if you've got the oldest person in the company saying, 'I'm going to give it a go, and I'm going to turn up at half past six [every evening], and do it' – that again, it's more than just 'doing a warmup'. It seeps into your association with the play. You cannot phone in a play where everybody is coming in at half past six to go over anything that's gone wrong, or anything that anyone's worried about, and everybody's

going to do a warm-up, everybody's going to make eye contact with each other, it just makes a difference. And that is something incredibly special. (2015)

According to Sidi, the ensemble ethos was founded in the pre-rehearsal workshop, not just among the actors – among whom 'seven or eight' went on to be cast in the original production – but, as crucially, among the creative team (2015). Reflecting on her rehearsal process, Elliott articulates an approach to direction which opts for the horizontal, non-hierarchal organization of theatre languages and skills favoured by Stephens in his collaborations:

> On a big show like [*Curious Incident*], where visuals are going to be so important, I would always have a trusted creative team around me and there would be discussion and talking constantly, as a team. [. . .] Each one of them wants their own skill or their own department to be able to enhance the story, so therefore what you're doing all the time – and it has to be with trusted people – is you're asking 'who's going to be dominant in this moment? Is it going to be lights, is it going to be projections, is it going to be sound, is it going to be the actor, is it going to be costume?' And sometimes you can find a way of working where everybody is at full tilt but the focus is still very, very clearly on one thing. (2015)

Elliott's appointment of collaborators provides perhaps the final key action that determined the structures of working for *Curious Incident*: with the exception of Graham and Hoggett, and just one of the actors, Elliott had previously worked with everyone involved in the production. In the words of Treadaway, the familiarity bred of this informal ensemble created 'an acceleration of working methodology that we could call upon' (2015). 'The genius, I think, of the show and the production', avers Sidi, 'is the combination of people that were in the [rehearsal] room, and I think Marianne has to take huge credit for bringing those people together' (2015). Indeed, Elliott's 'democratic impulse' in rehearsals (Stephens 2015f) – the mixing and levelling of disciplines and hierarchies that she achieves – is one of the reasons Stephens determined that Elliott should direct his script:

> I've talked about the way Marianne arranges the rehearsal room. At one end of the rehearsal room there will be the various designers,

she'd have the set designer and the lighting designer and the sound designer and the composer and the video designer, and I'd sit with them. We'd all get our little laptops out and we'd be sitting there watching and making notes, and I kind of thought: 'Yeah, I'm just the language designer here! That's what I am', which I quite liked, it was quite enjoyable.[16] (qtd in Radosavljević 2014: 260)

Adrian Sutton confirms Elliott's way of working, together with the efficacy of an approach that runs contrary to expectations within mainstream British theatre:

> I attended a lot of the rehearsals, which I wouldn't normally do. [. . .] And then it was just really easy for Marianne to say, 'Adrian, watch this sequence, can you try a bit of music against it?' And I'd look at it and say, 'okay, let's try this'. So you could tell immediately whether the combination of that particular piece of music and the movement that Scott and Steven were doing in that particular sequence worked, whether it had the right feeling. [. . .] It became a dialogue [. . .] it was lovely to realise that this could be a two-way dialogue. (2015)

Sutton's experience is echoed by Walker:

> What was fascinating was, [the creative team] were pretty much always present – you know, sound, design, video design, the boys [Scott and Steven], Katy – and there was never a sense of anyone judging you or anyone judging anyone else, there was just a sense of everyone wanting to serve Christopher really, really well. It was unusual to have everyone there almost all the time. [. . .]
>
> It was about opening up possibilities for lighting, opening up possibilities for music, so that you were all feeding into each other. And certainly not a feeling of us, as actors, having to fit a costume design or having to fit a lighting design or having to fit a soundscape. Whereas I have been in rehearsal rooms where you put on the costume and you think, 'well they should have cast someone else, I don't a) physically fit this costume, and b) this is isn't how I imagined [the character] at all'. And you just have to have to get on with it. And what I found amazing about Marianne is that although it is concept drama, *Curious Incident*, you never felt like you were serving a concept

because you weren't, you were serving Christopher's world. And she just kept very quietly, but really strongly, repeating that. (2015)

A key aspect of the process of making *Curious Incident* as 'concept drama' is the extent to which collective improvisation and physical play guided and informed the production. Again, there are resonances here with the ensemble-led approaches fostered by *Regietheater*, not least the process described by Tennant in his experience of *Three Kingdoms*, whereby material was generated by actors and creatives improvising against and/or in response to the text, to later be fixed (and rationalized). In Sutton's words, Elliott's directorial methods are

> very organic and, probably to an outsider, quite messy, but the important thing is that you're trying out what might be daft ideas, or ideas that you don't necessarily have much confidence in, at a very early stage. Your stagecraft instinct tells you whether or not it will end up being something that is worth going for and developing [. . .] and then in the later stages of rehearsals you fine-tune it. (2015)

Drawing from the actors' testimonies, a defining difference in the logics and logistics between the rehearsal rooms of Elliott for *Curious Incident* and Nübling for *Three Kingdoms* was the creation of an atmosphere in which a feeling of 'safety' was deliberately engendered or endangered. Sutton credits Elliott as a director 'particularly good [at] instilling the sense that the rehearsal room is a safe place' in which 'everybody, including actors, can try out ideas that might be crazy, in order to see whether they work or not' (2015). 'Her rehearsal rooms are brilliant', attests Walker:

> because she's not aiming for you to 'get it right'. You feel very free with Marianne and she won't judge you for going the wrong way; she'll pull you back and push you down a more sunlit path rather than the wrong path, but she'll let you go down it because there might be something down there that's useful and you can bring it back with you. (2015)

Cusack testifies to the director's 'rigour': 'I love someone who is driving herself and everyone else – if she wasn't driving herself that would be different but she drives herself harder than anybody else. That really permeated the whole thing' (2015). 'You are never in any doubt that Marianne is in charge', states Walker. 'She's able to say "I'm not sure how we're going to create this world of Christopher's" – but you know that she has a number of ideas of how she might do that, she just hasn't decided yet which one works best, and [your role is to] help her to find the way through to that' (2015). For Elliott, 'often, it is not the director making the decisions. The director is a leader, definitely, has to be. But the director is not the one coming up with all the ideas, [she's] the one who is harnessing and encouraging the best ideas and then trying them out' (2015). When ideas are 'tried out' in this way, collectively, open-endedly, in order to step back and critically assess the results, directing becomes an inductive process: an intervention, to return to Boenisch, 'on the level of presentation in performance [and] thus in the medium of theatre itself' (2008: 42).

'What's the point of going to a theatre', asks Elliott, in an unconscious echo of the German playwright and dramaturg Gotthold Ephraim Lessing (1729–1781):[17]

> or what's the point of killing yourself and opening your veins trying to put a show on, if it actually works better when you read it? It can fail, horrendously, and that's the risk but I suppose that's what gets me going [. . .] And hopefully it's exciting to watch because it's not necessarily what you expect. (2015)

For *Curious Incident*, that risk involved asking actors trained in a text-based, narrative-led tradition to engage in a process of physical, performance-led improvisation, turning Stephens's script over to the collaborative practice of devised theatre-making, and trusting that the contributions of all creatives would work to realize a concept born of, and belonging to, the collective imagination of the ensemble. While improvising and physical experimentation drove rehearsals – actors were requested to learn their parts before rehearsals began, so that they would not be encumbered by scripts – so too a commitment to psychological realism, character backstory and 'real' environments remained central to the actors' work; loosely Stanislavskian principles which no doubt added to the sense of 'safety', through familiarity, in the rehearsal room.[18] Walker describes the world created onstage as comprising 'realist relationships in a totally free floating, surreal environment', identifying it as a new experience for her as an actor:

> In this country we sometimes separate out [realism and physical theatre], saying 'oh, it's a conceptual piece, because there's dancing

and movement' and [it feels] more 'artistic', or more 'European' for that reason. [. . .] I suppose my fear with physical movement is that it can sometimes take over a piece and it can seem artistic, rather than grittily realistic. Not with Frantic. [Scott and Steven] are all about it being very, very real. They said, 'we'll never ask you to do anything that isn't totally real, and completely and utterly true'. [. . .]

It was a very different experience because normally, you know, the actor often looks after the physicality. They'll say to a director 'oh, I don't feel this bit's working here, maybe it's because I'm standing in the wrong place'. And a director will say 'oh, well, try and come downstage, is that better?' And that will be the extent of the physical vocabulary. And [*Curious Incident*] just blew it apart, all of those technicalities were totally irrelevant. It was a real education for me. (2015)

Interestingly, Walker credits *Curious Incident* with preparing her for working with the Belgium theatre director, Ivo van Hove, Artistic Director of the Toneelgroep Amsterdam, on his production of Arthur Miller's 1955 *A View From The Bridge* (2014, Young Vic). 'I spent quite a long time wondering how I could walk into a rehearsal room after Marianne's', Walker admits:

so to find that Ivo's rehearsal room was just as exciting as the *Curious* rehearsal room was a fabulous, endlessly surprising delight. It was really nice to walk into Ivo's rehearsal room and think, 'oh, okay, I've been here before'. Day one, Ivo wants you off book, he wants it gone, and he has this musical landscape from the beginning. And the set-up of his set was the same, this very bare box set. [. . .] I walked in and went 'oh, hello, I like this!' I'd just spent a long time on this type of set! Also, no props in Ivo's production. I'd had minimal props in *Curious* and normally, in other rehearsal rooms, I've looked for props; I've looked for teacups and sandwiches, to try to feel more real. And that flew away with *Curious*. Because there's more truth in standing and saying the words and making eye contact with the other actors than in showing an audience how clever you are by drinking a cup of tea and saying your words at the same time [. . .] if you strip away, strip away the stuff that you don't need and focus on the minutia of interaction between characters, that's much more interesting. (2015)

For Walker, Elliott 'more than anyone else has embraced the idea of making something conceptual – though she wouldn't say that she makes conceptual theatre at all' (2015). Certainly, Elliott's way of working speaks directly to Stephens's ongoing interrogation of 'the possibility of the authorial in the making of theatre' (Stephens qtd in Ue 2014: 115). As Stephens related to Tom Ue in 2014:

> in the novel, [Christopher's] voice is absolutely singular, he's a singular distillation of Mark [Haddon's] singular voice. [But] it's very difficult to tell through the staging of the play what are the decisions made by myself, what are the decisions made by Marianne [. . .] what are the decisions made by the individual actors or by Paule Constable, [. . .] Bunny Christie, [and] Frantic Assembly. You know, there isn't a singular authorial voice. (Ibid.)

Both the novel and the play have achieved canonical status, in that both have been recognized by UK GSCE exam boards: Stephens's stage adaptation has featured as an optional set text for GCSE English Literature in the syllabi offered by AQA and Eduqas/WJEC since September 2016.[19] In a compulsory education context in which the study of Drama is increasingly marginalized by government directives,[20] the play's inclusion within an English literature syllabus is significant, as fundamental to both the process and production of *Curious Incident* is a celebration of theatre and theatre-making. True to Haddon's novel – which is, in part a novel about writing a novel – Stephens's play similarly employs a metatheatrical framing device. That *Curious Incident* is a play about putting on a play is revealed at the start of Act Two, when it emerges that Christopher's school has turned his book into a play for 'everybody' to 'join in [with] and play a part in' (Stephens 2013b: 53). For Stephens:

> These little reminders that you're watching a play [such as when Christopher stops the action to redirect the actors onstage, or tells an actor he is too old to play a part] welcome you into the theatre and welcome you into an art form that's completely unique. I wanted to celebrate the essence of theatricality because I love the theatre. I think it's our best art form. (2015f)

Cusack regards *Curious Incident* as 'a great play' for young people to study:

> it's an anarchic play, ultimately, [. . .] and I think Simon is probably a bit of an anarchist too. There's an element of saying: 'Here's the play:

play' And that's a glorious gift to give to anyone who's interested in making theatre [. . .] Simon's plays are quite robust and bold, and so they can be treated with the same sort of boldness and robustness. And I think that's a marvellous gift. [. . .] [Simon] is a very courageous playwright. He's not tentative. And he dares you not to be tentative. (2015)

One of the most successful shows in the National Theatre's history, *Curious Incident* can also be regarded as a case study for a type of performance practice which enlivens sedimented conventions regarding the 'page-to-stage' dynamics of drama/text/performance through an interrogation – perhaps even redistribution – of authority invested across professional territories and hierarchies. That so much of what made *Curious Incident* a global success was, necessarily, unanticipated by Stephens's text – discovered and supplied instead by an ensemble of creatives working in the service of a 'concept' – is indicative of a growing interest within British theatre for fresh perspectives upon the relations between scripts and performance, authority and interpretation.

Conclusion

Looking back over Stephens's career from the perspective of *Curious Incident*, it is possible to trace a trajectory, plotted by productions such as *Pornographie* and *Three Kingdoms*, which sees the playwright repeatedly trouble the notion of authorship in the theatre and, in so doing, redraw the co-ordinates of established playwright–director relations. Sarah Frankcom recalls reading the first version of *Curious Incident* at the same time as reading a middle draft of *Three Kingdoms*, and offers the view that Stephens:

> wouldn't have been to do *Three Kingdoms* if he wasn't becoming interested in how you can be brave and bold with an adaptation, and how to connect with someone else's vision. I found *Three Kingdoms* very difficult to read, but it was interesting – as a director of Simon's work [my]self – to see in it some of the ways that he leaves space for the director. (qtd in Costa 2016: 389)

Admitting that there are plays of his that she doesn't like, and that some of her own productions of Stephens's work have not been liked by others of his collaborators, Frankcom pays tribute to the playwright's ability to 'create these key relationships and keep everybody happy and challenged and nourished' adding, significantly, that 'you never feel that he is compromising, he's not ever giving you anything other than all of what he thinks and feels at that particular point in time' (ibid.). To return to the article on Robert Holman cited at the start of the chapter, Stephens's tribute to this playwright inevitably captures and reflects some of his own ideals and values:

> [Holman] remains, also, determined to have faith that his actors, directors, designers and most importantly audiences are excited by the creative possibility of interpretation rather than dependent on having ideas spoon fed to them in self-explanatory speeches and that they are touched by the honesty of contradiction and metaphor rather than nervous of them. (2015b: online)

The value of contradiction as a means of seeing, feeling or experiencing something more deeply is cleaved to across the plays discussed in this volume. Caught contradicting himself in a 2010 interview, Stephens laughingly responded:

> But contradictions are good! Contradictions are very useful. They're very creative [. . .] I remember having this conversation with the Swiss director Christoph Mehler where we kind of realized that some contradictions in life disprove one another and other contradictions in life, rather than *disproving* the contradictory ideas, seem to somehow clarify or crystallize them. So the contradiction 'this shoe is black' with 'this shoe is red' [disprove] one another. But the contradiction 'I love you' and 'I hate you' seems to actually make both the love and the hate more pronounced. (2010a)

While grounded, for the most part, in a reality made legible by ideas and values held in common, the reality in Stephens's plays, as Nübling eloquently articulates, 'is pure construction', defined by 'two antagonistic terms: despair and hope' (2015: x). This is

> a point of view from which to see the world we live in which I totally share: don't ignore the fucked-up state our world is in, but fight with all you have for keeping this world as long as possible a place where people can live. (ibid.)

In this volume, I have identified tension, transgression, juxtaposition and contradiction as key energies and movements in Stephens's body of work. Following Nübling, to these we should add despair and hope, as a kind of secular Manicheanism animating Stephens's living, breathing, theatre. 'Metabolism' is another favoured word in Stephens's vocabulary: he will often talk about a certain theme, or idea, sitting 'deep in the metabolism' of his plays. Coincidentally, but correspondingly, there is in California a long-standing group of activist artists and thinkers called the Metabolic Studio. Their axiom is: 'Artists need to create at the same scale that society has the capacity to destroy' (n.d.: online). This, for me, defines the underpinning gesture of Stephens's plays. We need to fight with all that we have to keep this world a place where people can live.

* * *

There is an exercise that Stephens sometimes uses with his playwriting students, particularly if he is going to be working with them over a number of weeks or months. Writers are given a blank piece of paper and an envelope and asked to write down answers to the following questions: (1) What is your greatest strength as a writer? (2) What is your greatest weakness as a writer? (3) What one fear do you have about your writing/this course? (4) What one hope do have about your writing/this course? These answers are sealed in an envelope and returned to the students at the end of the course. When I have used this exercise myself, students have been delighted, surprised and sometimes a little dismayed to find what they wrote.

While the following was not written to such prompts and for such a purpose, I choose to end my discussion of Stephens's plays by returning to this diary entry from March 2001, just a couple of months before the premiere of his first commission for the Royal Court, *Herons*. It remains, in my view, an excellent distillation and articulation of why Stephens writes, and what he hopes to achieve with this work. After all the generosity he has shown in sharing with me his time, his thoughts, his unpublished works, private archives and nights at the theatre, I offer this as a little gift back to him, and as a potential stimulus for future playwrights.

> I write for many, many reasons. There is a whole spectrum. At one end of this spectrum is a quite singular vanity. Perhaps this is a specifically masculine phenomenon, but I think there is part of me that is attracted to the macho notion of the male writer, craggy, cut in

the granite face of literature shite and all. Also the vanity of glorying in my sensitivity.

I write to pay the mortgage. I write for fame. This is a stupid reason. Playwrights are rarely famous.

I write to scratch existential itches. [. . .] I write to make sense of an un-centred world. [. . .] To try to at least.

I write to emulate. I think implicit in the answer to the question why write, is the answer to the question why read? I write because I love to read and I have always loved to read and always been captivated by literature. [. . .]

I write to aspire to a kind of canonical status.

I write because I know that I will die. This has two effects. One is an attempt to philosophically analyse the nature of an apparently meaningless existence, an analysis that is carried out through dramatic literature through its process of interrogating humanity. The other is an attempt to survive death in some way. The permanence of the printed word surviving long after I have died.

And then it is true that I have a faith that the literary or the dramatic experience can change the world. Not through a sweeping, general political shift but by a gentle touching of the individual. I have seen plays, films, read books, poems that have changed the way that I have thought about the way in which things work. Sometimes these changes have been moral, sometimes aesthetic, sometimes political. I write in an attempt to engage in that massive process of communication and mutual exploration. To change one or two people in however slight a way. [. . .] This sounds trite but actually it is true. We enter into a dialogue.[21]

CHAPTER 5
CRITICAL PERSPECTIVES

CAN'T HELP FALLING IN LOVE: SIMON STEPHENS'S 'LATE' PLAYS (2014–19)

Caridad Svich

It seems a tad absurd to talk about Simon Stephens's 'late' plays when, given how extraordinarily prolific he is as a writer, he will likely have a much later 'late' period as a playwright than others who have built a shorter body of work as a whole. Yet, there is something in the plays that were produced between 2014 and 2019 that signal a kind of turning in his work – equal parts reflective (looking back on earlier terrain) and disruptively angsty. Call this period of writing, then, the 'unsettled' Stephens: *Blindsided* (2014), *Carmen Disruption* (2014), *Birdland* (2014), *Song from Far Away* (2015), *Heisenberg* (2015), *Rage* (2017), *Nuclear War* (2017), *Maria* (2019) and *Light Falls* (2019) represent a writer wrestling with himself and the world through characters and situations that identify and dissect states of profound loneliness and dislocation. These plays are, after all, produced on the heels of Stephens's worldwide success with his adaptation of Mark Haddon's novel *The Curious Incident of the Dog in the Night-Time* (2003), which saw not only West End transfer after the National Theatre's 2012 production but also Broadway premiere and TONY Award for Best Play, as well as multiple productions globally. For some theatregoers, especially in the United States, there was – suddenly, as if out of nowhere – this astoundingly articulate and imaginative writer named Simon Stephens! His dance card, always full, was now filled to the brim with projects and deadlines and more, as documented in his beautifully honest and discursive *Working Diary* (2016), published by Methuen Drama.

What these plays from 2014 to 2019 have in common besides the overriding subjects of loneliness and transience are an unease, and maybe even a whiff of distrust, with the form of theatre itself, as Stephens is at once catapulted to global fame through the phenomenon of *Curious Incident*. I think of these plays, in part, as Stephens's 'hotel' plays, in that they seem to arise out of the kind of jet-lagged limbo that permeates a writer's state of mind when they are juggling multiple projects and living in and out of hotel rooms. There is an edge to these plays that depict an assortment of characters and voices marked to lesser and greater degree by sudden loss and grief: addled by fame (in the cases of both *Birdland* and *Carmen Disruption*); longing for connection and human touch (*Blindsided, Heisenberg, Song from Far Away* and *Maria*); the discordant feeling of anonymity in the contemporary world (*Rage* and *Nuclear War*); and struggling to survive and connect after tragedies (*Light Falls*).

In these 'hotel' plays, the spoken text cuts and wounds, amplifies and diminishes itself, is embodied and disembodied. The voices and figures that animate and haunt these plays are moving targets, chased by the situations and circumstances constructed by Stephens in an effort to contain them. Yet, curiously, the culminative effect of these plays is that of a lack of containment – a spilling-over effect. Even in the tautest of the plays linguistically – *Blindsided* – there is a noticeably raging uncontained arena of emotion that cascades from the spoken text: an explosive subtext, as it were, that reaches outside the page and stage, that positions Stephens's dramatic project in this phase of his career on a precipice.

Given the rate of his productivity, by the time of this book's publication perhaps several new plays by, and collaborations with, Stephens will have premiered. For the purposes of this chapter, however, I would like us to imagine for a moment that 2019 were the cut-off point, and we were left looking at *Light Falls* as the last play in this series, positioned on a cliff, leaving us to wonder what would come next. Because the effect of these pieces is precisely that: we are on a cliff. Stephens has torn into the page in a feverish haze and has asked himself and us as audience and readers to meet him on the other side of this journey, and has perhaps asked us too to consider what can be made next. I almost see it as a dare to himself, as well as one to us. And the effect is thrilling, if disorientating.

Chronologically speaking, *Blindsided* begins this new phase of writing. Stephens is once again writing about his hometown of Stockport for one of his artistic homes, the Royal Exchange, Manchester, and once again collaborating with director Sarah Frankcom. Opening on 23 January 2014, *Blindsided* is about love and its cruel delusions. It focuses on the life of a young woman named Cathy Heyer and her epic, doomed affair with a man named John Connolly. Part One is set in 1979 and is comprised of fourteen scenes. Part Two is set in 1997 and comprises two scenes. We go from the era of Margaret Thatcher's Conservative government to the eve of Tony Blair's Labour election win. In the second half of the play the actor who plays Cathy's mum, Susan, now plays Cathy as an older woman, and the actor who played John Connolly now plays his son Harry. The overt theatricality of this casting requirement aside, the play moves along not unlike a conventional melodrama, and I do not mean this disparagingly. Stephens uses the conventions of melodrama and its late cousin, the soap opera script, to tell a story that feels familiar – of young, headlong, doomed teenage love: the rush of endorphins in such a love that may cause someone to go over the edge; an act of sexual and emotional betrayal (John cheats on Cathy with her best friend); and Cathy's Medea-like revenge as she kills their baby daughter. As such sad stories go, Cathy goes to jail for murder and the second act finds us with a woman who twenty years later has a new name and is living a new life, trying to put the past behind her. So, what is it about *Blindsided* that makes a reader and a spectator sit on the edge of their seat in an unconventional way?

There is a glowing and strange tenderness alive in Stephens's writing of all the characters in *Blindsided*, but especially that of Cathy, John and Susan. His renderings of these people in their bleak and difficult circumstances catches the audience off-guard, and makes us feel as blindsided as the characters are themselves. What would we do for love? How would we rage? When the economic circumstances of a character impose limits on what is possible, or what they may imagine could be possible, what choices do they think they have?

In the *Guardian* review of the play at its premiere, Lyn Gardner called *Blindsided* 'strange, haunting and hyperreal' (2014). Ian Shuttleworth in the *Financial Times* compared Stephens to Edward Bond but without the latter playwright's ideological force or theatrical moral rage. In a sense, Shuttleworth locates in Stephens's work something of an Achilles's heel: Stephens can't help but fall in love with his characters. By giving them his all – writing from inside their skins, consciousness and histories from a writerly perspective – Stephens may be getting in his own way. His compassion and sensitivity as a writer towards his characters sometimes stops him from generating a harsher sense of distance in which to view them critically. But, then again, this is tricksy, right? Because Stephens is a Romantic. Not in the Byron and Shelley sense, but in a swoony rock 'n' roll sense. His sensibility as a writer straddles both Brecht and Springsteen. As such, in Stephens's plays, there is often a strong tonal and stylistic push-pull between the adrenaline-charged, wonderstruck abandon of rock n' roll and the acerbic, mordant didacticism of Brecht. He wants us to love his characters and identify with them and, also, be shocked by the extent to which they will go for, or out of, love with love. He wants us to sit in compassion with them, to not be so quick to judge them or the world in which they live. He wants, moreover, his characters to transcend the circumstances in which they find themselves. He wants us to want that for them too, and he creates that desire in us by the manner in which he draws his characters.

The portrait of Stockport and its characters – especially its women – is unfinished, purposefully, by which I mean they are rendered ambiguously hopeful. The play may be over, but they are not. This distinguishes his work from that of Edward Bond, to use Shuttleworth's comparison, whose characters' lives, especially in the great plays of his early to middle period, are over when the play is over. Stephens's characters, especially in *Blindsided*, feel as if they are about to start new lives. The journey for Cathy and Harry respectively, for instance, is far from over. In the play's final stage direction, they '*look out over the horizon*' (Stephens 2014a: 103): a portal of potentiality and possibility, suggestive of life beyond. Stephens asks his audience to consider the future lives of his characters beyond the horizon's limits and towards the unknowable, spiritual journeys where they may discover a greater or more fulfilled sense of themselves.

On the ashes of an opera, a play arises. Or is it an opera-play? *Carmen Disruption* premiered at the Deutsches Schauspielhaus, Hamburg, in March 2014, directed by another of Stephens's long-time collaborators, Sebastian Nübling. The play, true to its title, is a disruption of Bizet's *Carmen* (1875). A singer – inspired by interviews with and played by (in the Hamburg premiere) the mezzo-soprano Rinat Shaham – arrives in a city ready to play the title role. Instead of seeing her play Carmen, we meet her as she leaves the opera house for the world outside. Her entrance is an exit, in other words, into the real world. Her inner and outer life intersects with characters called Micaëla, a female Don José; Escamillo, a male Carmen; and a Chorus that may also be the spirit of the character of Carmen. Is the Singer encountering these figures or dreaming them? The play slips and slides through a series of interlocking monologues and mini-scenes that reverb and echo off Bizet's famous score, seizing and turning inside out the characters originally found in Prosper Merimee's 1845 novella, and later Henri Meilhac and Ludovic Halevy's libretto. If, as an audience, we believe that the singer leaves the opera house, the play feels as if the world outside has come crashing into the opera itself.

The figures re-imagined by Stephens live in a contemporary world ridden with armatures of excess but each, in their own way, longs to be stripped of the material shackles that bind them. Here Carmen is a preening rent-boy; Micaëla is a suicidal young woman; Escamillo is a futures trader; and the female Don José is a driver working for a powerful unnamed man to whom they owe a debt that must be paid. They are all stars, circling around each other; sometimes half-meeting, at others, merely acknowledging a glance. The spoken language of the play swirls and cascades and juts up against moments of pain, sadness and longing. The play is as much a desire carnival as Bizet's opera is but splintered and shot through the lens of a contemporary-scape of social media anomie, and seemingly futile gestures of Romantic yearning, in a world that makes grand passions fodder for reality TV shows, anonymous Grindr hook-ups and empty trade. Everyone in the play knows they are merely seen as commodities, ready to be bought and sold. As such, the play makes these figures not only avatars for Bizet's characters but also shimmering icons emblematic of late-twentieth-century neoliberal market capitalism and its tidal waves of despair. Here we are on the shore, Stephens seems to say, broken before we are born, coming into a world where the grand gestures of the past, the grand narratives, have lost their meanings, despite our desire to reclaim them. It's no use, my friends. The world has become a hollowed-out marketplace and true human connection is barely possible. All we have left is a way to look and try to remember what real feeling must have been like.

The nearly stream-of-consciousness text flows from one character to another, cutting into their interior landscapes cinematically. The effect of being inside the piece as a reader is heady and exhilarating. Fierce and swoony, the text contains allusive riffs to the music of Daft Punk, Sonic Youth and Kraftwerk.[1] The tempo is both stately and staccato. Long phrases turn and break into short declamatory statements. Each plane of text is like a pane of glass or a bar of music, illuminating what will come next, but never quite giving up its secrets. The Singer is a celebrity and, as we will see in *Birdland*, the play that follows *Carmen Disruption*, fame will burn through a person and leave them staggering in a pool of blood.

In its Hamburg premiere, Nübling staged the text with his characteristically cool yet hot energy in a mostly neon-lit world that emphasized the desolation and emptiness of the figures that move through Stephens's play. Elements of the scenography evoked a contemporary train station or airline terminal. Sleek efficient portals at the rear of the stage served as ominous void-like apertures from which the figures emerged onto a cold barren stage space. Static group tableaux alternated with sections of explosive physical movement, mimicking the manner in which Stephens's text swerves between singular, vertical columns and dense textual planes, and from cinematic wide shots to intense close-ups. The production proved something of a mixed affair critically. That said, Andrew Haydon in the *Guardian* thought the Nübling staging brought out the play's strengths in a 'counterintuitive' manner by starting the piece with a chorus of 'forty non-professional extras streaming from the auditorium into the large onstage replica of the Deustches Schauspielhaus, before which all the action takes place', noting that the play switched from 'intimate to epic with startling ease' (2014a).

If the Nübling production was lauded for its bold yet cool approach to the text, Michael Longhurst's UK premiere of the play at the Almeida, London, in April 2015 approached the play with a fiery and immersive sensibility. The audience entered through backstage, glimpsing the opera singer applying makeup at her dressing room table before walking across the stage itself in order to take their seats. Lizzie Clachan's set featured the carcass of an enormous dead bull, and the performers swirled and even danced at moments to live instrumentation. Longhurst, working with an exceptionally strong design team, choreographer Imogen Knight, and composer Simon Slater, fore-fronted the play's sense of emotional dislocation and chaos by taking a sharp, visceral approach to the material. Reviews in the *Guardian*, *Telegraph* and *Exeunt* by and large commended Longhurst's staging, praising the play for its existential critique of a technology-addled contemporary world dispossessed of the rooted carnality of Bizet's *Carmen*.

The 'catharsis of imagined experience', which Stephens has said gives theatre one of its unique charges (qtd in Thompson 2014: online), is fully at play in *Birdland*, a play inspired, as James Hudson writes elsewhere in this volume, by Brecht's *Baal* (1923). Premiering at another of his artistic homes, the Royal Court, London, in a splashy production starring Andrew Scott and directed by Carrie Cracknell, *Birdland* traces the last week of a rock star's international tour with key stops in Moscow, Berlin and Paris. The habitual rock 'n' roll lifestyle markers – sex, drugs, alcohol and excess – are on full display in a script that charts the star's inevitable meltdown the closer the tour draws to an end. This meltdown is exacerbated, similarly to the one in *Blindsided*, by an act of sexual betrayal. In *Birdland*, rock star Paul sleeps with his bandmate's girlfriend, causing a rift in their relationship and eventually leading to the woman's suicide. Setting aside for a moment the troubling dramaturgical aspects of a woman's death serving as a potentially quasi-redemptive force in a cis male's narrative, *Birdland* is written with a caustic eye towards the downside of glamour and the costs of fame.

Complex and irreverent, Stephens uses a familiar structure – the rise and rise and questionable fall of a rock star that has made a Faustian pact with the devil – to immerse its audience in a world riven with fear, distrust and paranoia.

Destabilized by celebrity and its trappings, Paul is a compelling figure at the centre of this densely wrought play: by turns, charming and disgusting. He is an attractive and simultaneously repellent force, and if the trajectory of the play is familiar, the hurt inside it is genuine. Who is Paul beyond his celebrity image? Someone propped up to serve another god, the god of late capitalism and a music industry interested in churning out product at the expense of the human. Stephens acknowledges that 'the rock star becomes a puppet for our cultural collective imagination' (qtd in Thompson 2014: online), and what Stephens sees in a figure like Paul is an emblem for a brand of toxic masculinity, a raging ego and a culture that will allow someone to get away with murder. Rather than lean into what would be a sentimentally redemptive ending for Paul, the play makes him face us, the spectators of his spectacle, squarely in the eye. He tells us he's going to 'live for years and years and years' (Stephens 2014c: 122). The resolute hedonism of the 'pornographic age' is here to stay (Stephens qtd in Thompson 2014: online). Can we stop it? Or are we so enamoured of the media circus and its product line of 'stars' that we will accept anything from them and, in turn, ourselves?

The reviews for *Birdland* were positive to mixed. Cracknell's vivid, exuberant staging was heralded, as was Andrew Scott's blistering lead performance. Scott's star power draw – even prior to his role as the 'hot priest' in the televisual adaptation of Phoebe Waller-Bridge's *Fleabag* (BBC, 2016) – stemmed, in great part, from his successful turn as the entertainingly show-boating villain Moriarty in the BBC series *Sherlock Holmes* (2010) starring Benedict Cumberbatch. There was, for audiences and reviewers alike, something satisfyingly surreal about having a star play a star, notwithstanding Scott's close relationship with Stephens's writing (his hour-length monologue *Sea Wall* [2008] was written for Scott in both its stage and filmed versions). Michael Billington in the *Guardian* praised the play and production's ceaseless inventiveness in dealing with a time-honoured theme and narrative, and noted the play's reference to Patti Smith's 1975 song 'Birdland' (2014). Smith's song explores a son's longing for his father and, indeed, in one of the play's most poignant scenes, Paul has an emotionally stunted backstage encounter with his father that exposes the son's fear and vulnerability. Other critics, including Paul Taylor at the *Independent* and Charles Spencer at the *Telegraph*, inveighed vitriolically against the play, reading the play's relentlessly bleak atmosphere and time-worn narrative as faults, rather than strengths, though there was praise for Cracknell and Scott.

I would like to take a moment here to talk about the 'bleak' nature of Stephens's writing, and how I think his work may be misconstrued by many critics. Perhaps because of the sunny appeal of his adaptation of *The Curious Incident of the Dog in the Night-Time*, critics and audiences unfamiliar with his work prior to and after this production may be surprised at the dark aspect to Stephens's writing for the stage. I don't think the weight in Stephens's writing goes against his natural strengths as a playwright, which include the compassion with which he renders all manner of characters and situations, the care and control he takes with spoken language, and his willingness to go where the play leads him. There is a recklessness and abandon in Stephens's work that carries dark rock 'n' roll energy, and his passion for music is evident in all of his work for theatre. As such, audiences should not walk into a play by Stephens expecting an artfully constructed Taylor Swift-like pop confection, but rather – as Jacqueline Bolton writes in Chapter 4 – the atmospheric, fraught musical world of, for example, post-punk band The Fall.

Because Stephens's musical tastes are wide, his work dips into different styles and musical genres for inspiration. He is upfront about how he plays with musical sources as atmospheric blueprints for his textual scores for the stage, and about his own stint in a rock band, the Country Teasers. If Stephens lingers in the dark too much for some critics' liking, it may have something to do with his moral outrage at cycles of damage and destruction in society. Writers who lean dark, as I call it, often struggle with capturing the light, because the juice of the writing comes from entangled places of darkness. If your imaginary is fired up by fire, brimstone and the devil, to paraphrase the singer-songwriter Nick Cave, then better to own it than lose yourself. Nonetheless, what is true of Stephens's writing, especially in this 'hotel' period, is that the texts circle again and again around issues of despair, loneliness and pending personal and global catastrophe in ways that feel as if Stephens is wrestling with the core of the modern condition, and cannot see even a utopian, or post-utopian, way forward.

In *Song from Far Away*, for which Stephens shares the writing credit with lyricist/composer Mark Eitzel of the indie rock band American Music Club, a 34-year-old male banker named Willem receives a phone call from his mother with the news that his brother has died. The ensuing play is composed of a series of letters to the late brother, Paul, as Willem tries to reconcile and move through sudden stages of grief and a reunion, of thorny sorts, with his estranged family. Produced by Dutch theatre company Toneelgroep Amsterdam in a co-production with Mostra Internacional de Teatro de São Paulo, *Song from Far Away* received its UK premiere at the Young Vic, London, on 2 September 2015, directed by Ivo van Hove. The play was written for, and performed by, Eelco Smits, a company member of Toneelgroep Amsterdam. Like *Carmen Disruption*, and to some extent *Birdland*, we follow a protagonist moving through the financially elite spaces of the contemporary world, detached and aching for connection of any kind. It is a familiar trope: that of the wandering, aching figure lost in a wasteland of their own making – or, perhaps, one in which they are complicit. The restless anomie of the protagonist is measured in sharp declarative sentences that lay out the events of his days with a seeming order when there is rolling chaos underneath. In the production, van Hove and his long-time designer Jan Versweyveld situated the play in a white box set, the main feature of which was a tall window behind which snow fell. Smits performed most the monologue naked, and critics praised his brave, dedicated work. Running at about eighty minutes, the play serves as a potential mirror to Stephens's *Sea Wall*, which also focuses on a grieving man. But where *Sea Wall* exposes its reveal mid-stream, *Song from Far Away* tells us what we are in for right away. This is an elegy. One that will not find respite, even if the letters are meant as solace. They are about someone lost in himself and at the same time shattered by the loss of his brother. Eitzel's song, written specifically for the play, 'Go Where the Love Is' becomes, ultimately, the play's destination point. Where will Willem go after he has written all these letters? Where he can find love. While this may seem sappy, there is such delicacy and near astringency in Stephens's writing that the song's sentiment does the neat trick of countering the reserve in which Stephens has held his protagonist for most of the play. The song is the release. Music may free this character. If only for a little while.

Written on commission from Manhattan Theatre Club (MTC), New York, *Heisenberg* premiered in 2015 under Mark Brokaw's direction and received its UK premiere, directed by Marianne Elliott, in the West End in 2017, where the surtitle *The Uncertainty Principle* was added. A two-hander, the play is a 'meet-cute' play about a volatile 42-year-old woman named Georgie and a reserved, 75-year-old man named Alex. These two strangers meet in a crowded train station and sparks of the romantic kind fly between this seemingly ill-matched May–December couple. What attracts them to one another? Is this love or just a magnetic pull between what appear to be opposites? In rare tragicomic mode, Stephens has written the kind of 'brief encounter' play that used to be seen earlier in the twentieth century, and especially in Britain; the kind of play where the small glances and odd quirks of and between characters speak of unrequited longings and misspent loves. But inside that template, Stephens pulls off a play about entanglement and estrangement. Georgie – wild, sexual, funny, voracious – may be the play's driving force but it is Alex who holds its centre, the man held in, aching for connection and slowly allowing himself to fall for this unusual stranger.

The carnal ardour that Alex feels for Georgie is presented with ambivalence and candour by Stephens. Alex is thirty-three years older than Georgie and the substantial age difference between the characters generates considerable tension. While the politically problematic older man to younger woman romantic trope is deployed regularly in film and television, it is more rarely seen on stage. Stephens dances around built-in audience expectations regarding the representation of such a relationship, and asks spectators to see it in a new light. Georgie is doing the chasing in the play; Alex is the object of her pursuit. By flipping the expected narrative, Stephens goes a long way to revitalize the tiredness of the trope. At heart, his thesis is centred around the uncertainty and, yes, the unpredictability, the unruliness, of desire. There are no clear vector points. A person cannot predict to whom they will be attracted and in whom they will find compatibility. As it turns out, both characters are bruised and battered by life, and both are seeking redemption. During six encounters (across six scenes), the play shows how this couple, or couple-to-be, dances the wary dance of desire. Alex is hesitant yet firm. Georgie is goading but possibly emotionally untethered, and potentially dangerous to herself and to them both. Yet somehow, unlike in other of these 'late' plays, the world doesn't entirely fall apart. Instead, Alex and Georgie come to a tentative agreement at the end, and Alex's last words to Georgie in the play are: 'Thank you' (Stephens 2015h: 60).

In Brokaw's original production, Georgie was played by Mary-Louise Parker and Alex was played by Dennis Arndt. Parker's wild card energy and unique delivery made her the focus of reviews and of the production, but Arndt delivered an exceptional and unfussy performance that held its own against Parker's starry wattage. Stephens stresses in the play's stage directions that the theatre-ness of the space should be revealed – lighting rig, props, walls, and so on – and that the stage should be bare. Brokaw's production was true to his intention, but the play itself does not hold up to the theatre-ness of the authorial intent. In fact, in production, especially in

New York, the 'exposed' theatricality only heightened the naturalism of the play's dialogue. I am sure that the tension between such 'exposure' and the fairly clipped, yet slice-of-life, dialogue is one of the goals of this directive by Stephens but this is an instance where the directive may be at odds with the content; in performance, at least in the New York production, the conceit felt imposed rather than organic to the piece. Nonetheless, the tension between the exposed theatricality of mise en scène and the psychologically rooted, naturalized dialogue is a device worth noting here, as it is one that occurs in other texts by Stephens. On the one hand, the device heightens the realism of the language and dramatic situations, forcing them into the light without interference from a world of objects and photo-realistic scenographic choices. On the other hand, the device draws attention to the disjunction between the spoken text's behavioural realism and the self-aware theatricality of its staging. I would posit that the stage directions also function as a safeguard against future theatre companies staging the play as if it were photo-realism, and perhaps too as a reaction against the MTC's tendency to stage works with a stylistic fidelity to realism, or what I would call 'default realism' as a mode. Interestingly though, in the global field of theatre, and specifically in Europe and Russia, treating this play through a photo-realistic lens would hardly be the default mode by theatre companies and the *Regietheater* 'school' of directors. Given that Stephens makes work in the UK and in Europe, and is staged internationally, it is worth noting the specificity of his prescriptive stage directions in the case of *Heisenberg*, and also, as discussed in earlier chapters in this volume, in *Sea Wall* and *Motortown* (2006).

Still, in regard to *Heisenberg* as a play, there is no denying the appeal of these sharply drawn characters and the tenderness and lonely hearts beauty of the piece. It is no surprise that the play found itself on Broadway after the original run and has been one of Stephens's most produced plays in the regional circuit in the United States, outside of *Curious Incident*. When I met Stephens in 2015 at a preview of *Heisenberg*, he said to me that, just as he would with any theatre, he wanted to write something that the commissioning theatre would actually produce. In this instance, he wrote an MTC play for MTC. Nothing if not deft, Stephens can be a master at shape-shifting technically as a writer and yet still retain his core concerns, which in *Heisenberg* continue to be themes of loneliness and the difficulty of human connection in the modern world.

Premiering in the autumn of 2016 at the Thalia Theater, Hamburg, under Sebastian Nübling's direction, Stephens's next play, *Rage*, was commissioned and presented as a counterpoint text to Elfriede Jelinek's *Wut* (2016). The play is comprised of thirty-one short scenes all set on New Year's Eve 2015 in the city centre of Manchester. These scenes are in turn based on a picture gallery of photographs taken by freelance news photographer Joel Goodman, originally published on the *Manchester Evening News* website (Ramsey 2016: online). One in particular of Goodman's shots – of revellers on Wells Street – went viral on social media, lauded as worthy as a Renaissance masterpiece in its compositional artistry (Safi 2016: online). The photograph depicted a policeman wrestling a man in the foreground while a crowd watches in the background, while another man in the mid-field of the image lies drunken on the street, reaching for a bottle of beer. Goodman's work as a street photographer, evidenced from this particular series, is characterized by an uncanny attention to the potency of the everyday gestural vocabulary of the people he captures. The human figures in his frames are caught in moments of seeming contradiction, both elated and angry, full of life and dejected, defiant and seeking comfort in the arms of potential self-destruction through excessive drinking or other means. The photographs are colourful, sharp and crisp (almost hyperreal) and register his subjects' pain and beauty with finesse and vivid humanity. Each image brims with narrative potential and, as such, it is easy to see what attracted Stephens to this photo series.

Veering drastically from the measured cadences of *Heisenberg*, *Rage*, as befits its title, explodes onto the stage in a kind of delirium of excess: a carnival (in spirit) play that lets loose demons of anxiety, fear, loneliness and violence as the myriad characters depicted wrestle with desires that oscillate on the twin axis between Eros and Thanatos on this precipitous turn towards a new year. It is a play that feels, as with the other pieces Stephens has written for Nübling, fearless in its exploration of discordancy, fluid in its possibilities for staging and liberated from social realist constraints, even though the root of every action is grounded in 'the real'. Echoing Goodman's photographs, the scenes in *Rage* are realistically drawn, rooted in the specifics of their situations: snapshots of humanity magnified by Goodman's camera and reimagined by Stephens on stage. Travelling through the New Year's Eve revels on a cold Manchester night, the play depicts a time-fluid collage that juxtaposes scenes of violence with ones of tenderness, scenes of bonding with ones of dissolution. Surprisingly, for all its dark exuberance the play was not seen in the UK until 2018, in a production at the Royal Welsh College of Music and Drama. At the time of this writing, the play has yet to receive a professional production in the UK.

On less certain ground, possibly because of its difficult development history, *Nuclear War* finds Stephens back in the monologic, stream-of-consciousness terrain seen in *Carmen Disruption*. A meditation on desire and death and the vagaries of time, the play is a text for dance, and was originally developed alongside director Ramin Gray and choreographer Hofesh Schechter for Actors Touring Company (ATC). After an on-and-off-again gestation and exploration period with ATC, the project landed at the Royal Court, where it premiered at the Jerwood Theatre Upstairs on 19 April 2017. *Nuclear War* was directed by choreographer Imogen Knight, designed by Chloe Lamford and scored by electronic musician and composer Elizabeth Bernholz – aka Gazelle Twin. If *Heisenberg* was a formally certain play about the uncertainty principle, *Nuclear War* is an uncertain play about the certainty of death. I do not say this disparagingly. I find the uncertainty of *Nuclear War* thrilling: its instability as a text radiates a mercurial vulnerability. It feels like an exposed nerve. Raw and written in angular bursts of language, the piece feels as if it is on the brink of collapse. There is a vulnerability at work in this text that is close to the one exhibited in *Carmen Disruption* but standing on less known ground (of deconstructed adaptation).

With its undifferentiated text – possibly for one woman but maybe for more – *Nuclear War* recalls Martin Crimp and Sarah Kane's work in this vein: the seminal *Attempts on Her Life* (1997) and *4.48 Psychosis* (2000), both of which also premiered at the Theatre Upstairs. Prefaced in the published edition by a manifesto of sorts by Stephens on the nature of theatre and its provocations, and his belief in the form as one that is irrevocably live, *Nuclear War* is, as he admits in the preface, a 'return to his teenage self' and the songwriter he wanted to be (Stephens 2017b: 6–9). The text suggests a narrative of a person being watched by – or imagining that they are being watched by – a figure of loss. This figure may be interpreted variously. In the text as written, the ostensible narrative is of a woman grieving the loss of a lover, depicting a day in her life as she reckons with the darkly erotic, destructive nature of their relationship. But this narrative shifts prismatically as the play moves forward. At times, it feels as if it could be Stephens himself grieving the loss of his teenage self. The writer that was once meeting the writer that is now. If seen from this angle, the text takes on a fascinating aspect in relationship to Stephens's trajectory as a writer during this 'late' period. The piece becomes one of mourning a former self, yet also longing for that self to be put to rest. Yet, this reading of the text is one of many potential readings. Given the open-ended nature of the piece, and the fact that it is composed in shards and slivers of images and actions, the piece's meanings are decidedly unstable.

Its strengths as a score for theatre rest in its evocation of mood and atmosphere. By turns sinister and tender, the play feels like an angsty, punk-romantic song that bears a trace of the Police's 'Every Breath You Take' (1983). In the play, the grieving woman keeps seeing a person watching her on the tube, on the street, in their bedroom. By a shift in perception, the person multiplies into a crowd – Stephens deploys here a cinematic effect. The speaker sees an image and the image blows up, becoming magnified and distorted. The person that is doing the watching – the dark self, the dead lover – becomes an all-seeing eye, as if his eyes were those of a surveillant city-state. The lines blur between reality and fictive life, between what the figure mired in grief understands to be true and what their mind alters. Desire overwhelms, burns, makes the speaker possibly disassociate from themselves and their environment, pulled apart by the torrents of their grief. The atomized particles of selves – the grieving lover, the haunted woman, the object of the phantom's desire – splinter through time and, in the end, the speaker is left counting down to a possible . . . ending: the ending of her mourning after doing battle with the demons of their past and the residue of trauma.

In terms of critical reception, *Nuclear War* proved to be confounding to most. Sitting uneasily in a theatre like the Royal Court, which remains most readily associated with narrative-led drama, *Nuclear War* may have had a better reception at venues such as the Battersea Arts Centre, LIFT Festival, Gate Theatre in Notting Hill or even at the Yard in Hackney Wick, where audiences have been habituated to enjoy the plasticity of performance through exposure to dance, music and spoken word, and to accept that such works can function unproblematically as experiments. Certainly, *Nuclear War* seems to be a piece that need live in this kind of artistic environment, given that Stephens did not originally conceive it for the Royal Court and, indeed, wrote it for a yet-to-be-determined venue. Be that as it may, the piece did find some love and attention from Holly Williams in the online theatre magazine *Exeunt*. She found Knight's production 'sensuously rich' and remarked at the occasional disjunction between the text and the staging – Knight emphasized the sections that evoke tenderness, but elided the coarser sexual descriptions contained within the text (Williams 2017: online). One of the things that Stephens articulates, particularly in the italicized sections of the play-text, are moments of emotional difficulty and instability which arousal and desire naturally evoke. The woman at the play's centre wants to tie the man to the bed, and the unnamed male figure wants to make love to his partner while her elderly mother is in the room next door (Stephens 2017b: 19). The Dionysian impulses that activate and unmoor humans in the erotic realm confront us sometimes with darker and troubling aspects of our unconscious. Stephens is truthful about this, and if Knight elided it in production, then it should also be understood that the production is Knight's and not Stephens's. The dark nuclear internal war ended, in Knight's hands, with a golden, rapturous dance of hope instead of a disappearance into the void.

Premiering in 2019 at the Thalia Theater, Hamburg, and once again written for Nübling to direct, *Maria* might be regarded as a sister play to *Light Falls*. It is also, perhaps, a nod to Stephens's first breakthrough play, *Port*. In *Maria*, an eighteen-year-old woman named Maria, but called Ria by all, is pregnant. The father of the child is absent. Her own parents are gone, and she only has a sickly grandmother for whom she cares. The play follows Maria through to the end of her pregnancy, the birth of her daughter and the eventual end-of-life situation with her grandmother. In what is clearly a conscious evocation of the Virgin Mary, this modern-day Maria/Ria is a single mother trying to find her place in a world that asks much of her but never sees her for who she really is. Objectified by men at the dock in the port town where she lives, and by those she meets online in an (eerily prescient) world without touch, she is alone with her own curiosity and will to survive against all odds. She is the kind of central character often seen in the films of the Dardenne Brothers – a 'insignificant' cog in the societal machine – figures stuck in the lower classes that do menial or servile work and are underpaid for their physical and emotional labour. Ria thus withstands cruel, leering taunts by the male dock workers she walks by in the street, and is equally subjected to monologues of male isolation and desolation by the men that chat her up in the online world in which she works. Although she is 'subjected' by others, she is never made abject by Stephens. It is one of the gifts of this play, and Stephens's delicate hand as a writer within it, that Ria nominally escapes the traps of being a female Woyzeck, preyed upon by others until she is crushed by society's machinery. Instead, Stephens walks with her as a character, as if he were taking her hand as viewers visit each station along her spiritual journey.

The play is structured in three panels – the Town, the Screen and the Body. Although Stephens does not use the term 'panels', I am using it here instead of 'acts', because the triptych structure of the play evokes three-panel religious paintings or altarpieces. The first panel locates Maria in the empirically deterministic world of the port town, where she is presented by Stephens as a mercurial and resilient female heroine. In this first panel, we see Maria in everyday, 'slice-of-life' interactions with the dockworkers, her grandmother, her doctor, her priest, her neighbour and so on. The interactions are for the most part realistically portrayed in the manner of mid-century American theatrical realism of the kind made popular by Clifford Odets and Tennessee Williams. If viewed through the frame of Williams, whose own theatrical works mined symbolic Christian iconography to great effect, the encounters witnessed in the scenes in *Maria* function like stations in the Stations of the Cross, except here the viewer is not being asked to witness Ria's journey towards crucifixion but towards a kind of enlightenment. Thus, we are privy to encounters on Maria's everyday pilgrimage towards possible holiness through life. In contrast, the Screen panel is located entirely in the world of cyberspace. Here Maria is figuratively hired to tell stories to 'callers' that 'book' her in an unspecified cyber portal that functions somewhat like a chat room. But really what she does is hold conversations with a series of mostly lonely men of various ages and life experiences. The effect of this second movement of the play is a little like watching in reverse the famous peepshow scene from Wim Wenders and Sam Shepard's *Paris, Texas* (1984). Instead of the desired female spilling her story of trauma to the silent, aching man, here men spill their stories to a captive yet defiant woman for some comfort in a landscape devoid of human touch and feeling. The Body shows Maria back in the grounded world, in hospital, with her dying grandmother. In this panel the grandmother is mostly silent as Maria narrates her days to her last known kin. It is a heartbreaking scene and the ending, while gently nodding to a kind of human beatification of Ria – an everyday saint in the modern world – also resists burdening Ria with such. She is an ordinary woman getting by and, maybe just for tonight, on this stage before us, she can be herself, without anyone asking anything of her. *Maria* is a morality tale about contemporary morals or lack thereof. It is about a person trying to live a decent life during 'indecent' and rapacious times. A haunting and mesmerizing play, it is uniquely positioned in Stephens's late plays both by the sheer clarity of its vision and the formal elegance of its execution on the page.

Parsing through the distinct yet thematically connected stories in Stephens's last play from this 'late' period brings us around full circle. In *Light Falls*, which premiered at the Royal Exchange, Manchester, in October 2019, directed by Sarah Frankcom and with music by British rock and electronic popular music figurehead Jarvis Cocker, a woman named Christine narrates her death from a brain haemorrhage in a supermarket in Heaton Moor, Stockport. In the series of discrete and funny scenes that follow, we meet her three grown children – Jess, Steven and Ashe – and we also meet her husband, Bernard, who during the course of the play has a mistress named Michaela and a friend, Emma, with whom he has a threesome. The play follows the exasperated, confused, mixed-up lives of these characters, their lovers and friends, in the wake of Christine's death. By the play's end, the audience is at her funeral. So, what the audience sees is what happens in the aftermath of Christine's death, before returning in flash back to the day of her funeral. It is a play about a lost mother retrieved through storytelling by those she left behind. It is also a play about the mythic character of the towns in the north of England – Stockport, Blackpool, Durham, Doncaster and Ulverston. Stephens, although working in a realistic vein in the play, deliberately positions the piece as a hymn of, and to, 'The North', a region historically portrayed in British popular culture as rife with uncouth, ornery, parochial people.

Epic in scale, expansive in performance (running at nearly two and a half hours), but tender and bittersweet in affect, *Light Falls* showers its forlorn characters with love and shows Stephens working with a decidedly light touch as a writer. His fifth collaboration with director Frankcom, and her last production as Artistic Director of the Royal Exchange, *Light Falls* picks up on the themes of sexual betrayal; loneliness; desire for human connection; the elusive nature of time; the powerful state and stages of grief; and the alienating nature of modern life evident in the prior eight plays from this period, and spins them into an elegant and grounded 'panorama' play of the kind rarely written anymore.[2] For all its strife and trouble, one could even call *Light Falls* something of a tragicomedy in its warmth and reflective light. *Light Falls* ends this period of Stephens's 'late' plays with a feeling of both resolve (a chapter is closing, as it were) and thrilling ambiguity. The desolate exhilaration and wandering of the plays from this period have come to an end, perhaps signalling new beginnings for Stephens in theatre and film. While I suspect that he will always be a writer chasing after his own sense of wanderlust, I think the restlessness and anxiety evidenced in these 'late' plays may transform into a stage of his writing that is even more probing, slower in its tempo and cadences, and perhaps more grounded, while he continues in his dedicated pursuit of unsettling audiences.

So, what is it that we see in these nine plays, besides Stephens's passion for writing and remarkable gift for diving into his work with heart and soul? I think we see the journey of loss itself, and what I mean by this is a loss of 'firsts'. During this 'late' period of his career, Stephens saw his first Broadway premiere, for one, and was catapulted into worldwide fame with the international success of *The Curious Incident of the Dog in the Night-Time*. After a hard-won career building a reputation as one of Britain's leading voices and playwriting mentors, he was suddenly, by dint of *Curious Incident*, a 'known quantity'. He was no longer the 'newish kid on the block', which means that his capacity to reinvent himself as a writer, especially in the eyes of the global theatre industry, became much harder. It is no wonder that a sense of dislocation is central to these 'hotel' plays. Stephens is grieving a side of himself as a writer – the one that shows up in *Nuclear War*, the teenage self – as he searches for connections to a spiritual sense of home, while moving through fame and the discordant tribulations of contemporary life, and its increasing sense of isolation. It is, like a great deal of writing, an elusive and existential search. Inside of this quest, we witness a writer pulling and tugging at the skin of theatre – at what it can do, and how far he can push himself through exploration. In my view, *Carmen Disruption* is the apex of the exploratory period and the plays that follow pull from its gloriously dense, searching language for, and towards, their own centres. Caught between the text-based tradition of British playwriting and the performance and live art worlds where some of his contemporaries like Chris Thorpe and Chris Goode live, Stephens straddles ways of thinking about and making text, and moves with fluency between the, shall we say, dramatic and post-dramatic traditions. He also sits between generations: older than Lucy Prebble, Lucy Kirkwood and Alice Birch, and slightly younger than Mark Ravenhill and David Greig. In this, he serves perhaps as a kind of bridging figure, wrapping his long arms around the breadth and depth of British writing with startling ease and deep love, and paving the way for the next generation, some of whom he mentored at the Royal Court. What these nine plays evidence is that his questing path is rich, varied and – thankfully for us – relentlessly restless. Never settling. Even when you think he has.

PORNOGRAPHY'S EUROPEAN DIRECTIONS: GERMANY AND FRANCE

Mireia Aragay

To a large extent, both Stephens's biography and his playwriting career are defined by travel. Born in 1971 in Stockport, he has often reflected on the significance and implications of the journey that took him from the place he would, 'instinctively', still call his 'hometown' (2015d: online), to the University of York, Edinburgh, and eventually London, where he has been living for over twenty years. Likewise, his plays have travelled far and wide, from London, Manchester and elsewhere in Britain to Australia, Belgium, Brazil, Canada, France, Germany, Ireland, Japan, the Netherlands, New Zealand, Spain and the United States, among many other places. Journeys, both physical and emotional, are also a recurring motif in his plays, from his stage debut *Bluebird* (Royal Court, 1998) to *Fatherland* (Royal Exchange, 2017; co-authored with Frantic Assembly's Scott Graham [also director] and Underworld's Karl Hyde [also composer]) and *Light Falls* (Royal Exchange, 2019). It is therefore hardly surprising that as *The Funfair* (2015), Stephens's version of Ödön von Horváth's *Kasimir and Karoline* (1932), opened at Manchester's then new arts centre HOME, he should ponder 'the curious contradiction in an arts centre having the name "Home"', given that 'one of the most important functions of art – cinematic, theatrical, visual – [is] to take people out of their homes [...] to unsettle and trouble, to provoke and excite, to alarm and inspire' (2015d: online). In this essay, I take as a starting point the way in which Stephens has also refused to 'stay at home' in his role as a playwright by increasingly moving away from Britain's predominantly writer-centric theatre culture, where the 'individual playwright is at the centre of the theatre-making process' (Sierz 2011: 50) and creative teams (directors, designers, actors) and performances are perceived as serving the demands of playwrights and their texts.[3] Instead, Stephens has demonstrated a growing 'receptiveness to radically different productions of his texts' (Love 2016a: 320), gravitating towards a range of forms of collaborative authorship, as exemplified by several of his 'late plays' discussed by Caridad Svich in this volume.

In 'Exit the Author', Dan Rebellato notices a pattern of dramaturgical and theatrical experimentation with authorship in British theatre since the start of the twenty-first century, with playwrights such as Sarah

Kane, Martin Crimp, Tim Crouch or, indeed, Stephens himself 'variously absenting themselves from their plays' (2013: 11). As Rebellato notes, these are plays written in what Roland Barthes would describe as a 'writerly' (*scriptible*) fashion: 'the writerly text is *ourselves writing*, before the infinite play of the world [. . .] is traversed, intersected, stopped, plasticized by some singular system (Ideology, Genus, Criticism) which reduces the plurality of entrances, the opening of networks, the infinity of languages' (1974: 5, original emphasis). The published script of *Nuclear War*, for example, starts with a stage direction that in its openness immediately creates that sense of a multiplicity of potential points of access: '*A series of suggestions for a piece of theatre. All of these words may be spoken by the performers but none of them need to be*' (Stephens 2017b: 12). This openness is reinforced by the absence of character names, the blurrings (of character and action, stage directions and utterances, image and utterance prompts, spoken and sung language) and the uncertainty as to the number of (speaking or singing) voices at any given point in the play-text. While this allows Stephens to reflect on *Nuclear War* as an investigation of how words and movement/dance might 'counterpoint' one another, more broadly it points to what he describes as the 'fluidity of function' between the playwright and his 'collaborators' (2017b: 3), a fluidity that productively destabilizes the conventional (in Britain) priority of text over performance (see 2017b: 2). In relinquishing playwriterly 'authority' in this way, Stephens does not see himself as abdicating responsibility but rather as empowering directors, artistic teams and performers to bring their 'energy' and 'spirit of fight' to his plays, which in themselves are not 'cogent representation[s]' of that which he imagined because 'imagination resists cogency. Rather [they are] fluid and contradictory and tentative and inchoate' (2017b: 5–6). Seen in this light, the rehearsal room becomes a space for imagination, creativity and improvisation on the part of the creative team and performers, rather than a place for them to sit down and read the playwright's text in a spirit of 'reverence' (Stephens 2017b: 6). This is an approach to theatre-making that, in Rebellato's words, 'disturbs the objecthood of theatre' by foregrounding the fact that no play-text – in Barthesian terminology, not even the most (supposedly) 'readerly' (*lisible*) or closed one – 'can exhaustively determine the productions that can be made of it' (2013: 24–5).[4]

This chapter focuses on two European productions of Stephens's *Pornography* – Sebastian Nübling's (Schauspiel Hannover, June 2007; Deutsches Schauspielhaus Hamburg, October 2007) and Laurent Gutmann's (La Colline Théâtre National, Paris, November 2010) – in an attempt to show, through both contextualization and close reading of certain scenographic and acting choices, what it means in practice to state that in theatre 'there's no purity of text which is received by a reader' (Stephens qtd in Radosavljević 2014: 267).⁵ As Duška Radosavljević among others has noted, and as this volume has explored in depth, Stephens's 'journey of discovery' (2013: 112) towards 'writerly'/collaborative forms of authorship has been fundamentally shaped by his immersion in German theatre, particularly his long-standing association with Nübling (b. 1960). *Pornography* itself was commissioned by the Deutsches Schauspielhaus Hamburg specifically to be directed by Nübling, and the strikingly open stage direction '*Images of hell*' that closes both the brief prologue (where the beginning of one of the 7/7 bombers' suicide speeches, aired by Al Jazeera television on 1 September 2005, is reproduced) and Scenes Seven to Two (where a series of nameless speakers/ characters tell six stories, all of which lead to the 7/7 bombings) is no doubt one of the reasons why Stephens, when first searching for a theatre willing to stage the play in the UK, was told that it was 'far too German' (qtd in Logan 2007). On his part, French actor and director Gutmann (b. 1967) discovered Stephens's work precisely via its popularity in Germany and chose to stage *Pornography* – the first production of a play by Stephens in the context of France's network of national theatres (*théâtre public*) – because of its formal audacity, which he saw as deriving from its German inception: 'It's a text that appeals to the interpretation of a director, that doesn't surrender its theatrical keys easily, less so than other frequently staged texts where I sense the economy of English theatre. That is no coincidence: *Pornography* was commissioned by a German director' (2010a; 'J'ai choisi *Pornographie* parce que c'est la plus audacieuse formellement. C'est un texte qui appelle l'interprétation d'un metteur en scène, il ne livre pas ses clés théâtrales facilement, moins que d'autres textes très scénarisés, dans lesquels je sens l'économie du théâtre anglais. Ce n'est pas un hasard: *Pornographie* est né d'une commande d'un metteur en scène allemand').⁶ A comparative analysis of Nübling's and Gutmann's respective points of access into Stephens's *Pornography* may hopefully be a first step prompting further work on the European 'directions' this play, as well as Stephens's work at large, has taken.⁷

Nübling's *Pornographie*: 'Surging images' and 'small detonators'

From a German perspective, the play-text, as Stephens's German translator Barbara Christ points out, is regarded 'as material' to be rethought and reworked with every new production.[8] In Britain, this is often associated with the *Regietheater* (normally translated as 'director's theatre') that emerged in the late 1960s and early 1970s, when 'a new breed of West German directors [including Peter Stein and Peter Zadek among others] started to offer radical reinterpretations of the classics' (Barnett 2010a: 153) aimed at making them topically relevant. However, as Peter Boenisch points out, the phrase 'director's theatre' 'effects nothing but to reify the notion of individual authorship, transferring it from the playwright to the director' (2008: 32). While this may have been true, to some extent, of those 1960s and 1970s German directors – 'visionary interpreter[s]' (Barnett 2010b: 185) or 'director-auteurs' (Radosavljević 2013: 194) – it obscures both 'the general fact that German theatre, for at least a century, has at its very heart been a "theatre beyond the text", essentially predicated on the "*Inszenierung*" (that untranslatable "in-scening" only approximately captured in the common French term *mise en scène*)' (Boensich 2008: 32), and the emergence, since the 1980s, of what Barnett calls 'postdramatic direction' (2010b: 186) and Radosavljević describes as 'collaborative performance-making methodologies' (2013: 194).[9] *Regie*, in this context, is 'an essentially collective, social and political practice' (Boenisch 2015: 7) where the director co-creates the *Inszenierung* with 'her doubles' (Pavis 2010: 399), among whom Patrice Pavis names the (often non-mimetic) actors, the playwright (if there is one), the dramaturg, the choreographer and the musician, to which no doubt should be added the scenographer. Nübling belongs to this new generation of collaborative directors who often choose to work in more or less stable creative teams, which in his case includes Swiss-born scenographer Muriel Gerstner, a key contributor to his *Inszenierung* for *Pornographie*.[10]

Klaus van den Berg has written eloquently of how, inspired by earlier models and developments, scenographers in Germany since the 1990s have substantially reimagined the relationship between text and space while still remaining within the parameters of Germany's predominantly proscenium stages. Basically, this is a 'visual dramaturgy' (van den Berg 2008: 7) that discards representational space. Rather, space becomes 'an integrated text', which 'instead of illustrating the play' or 'reproducing a text', offers 'its visual interpretation' in the form of '"surging images" that [. . .] fold a successive series of content into space and visually display its multiple references' (van den Berg 2008: 7). Gerstner (b. 1962) forms part of this generation of scenographers for whom 'space makes little sense as a realistic set' (van den Berg 2008: 12). Significantly, van den Berg points out that this scenographic revolution has been nourished by contemporary German-language playwrights such as Elfriede Jelinek or Heiner Müller who write 'in images' and create 'a theatre of space' (2008: 8). One way in which they do so, as Barnett notes, is by including 'stage directions that cannot be realized literally' (2010a: 151); instead, they invite the intervention of the director and the entire creative team in an open acknowledgement of the always unfinished nature of any play-text and hence of the fact that 'making sense' in theatre is always the result of 'collaborative co-creation' (Boenisch 2015: 7) rather than individual authorship. Stephens's *'Images of hell'* is no doubt one such 'writerly' stage direction.

Marion Hirte, who has on two occasions collaborated with the Nübling/Gerstner partnership as dramaturg, notes that Gerstner 'is often the first in the team to make crucial interpretations through her spatial designs' (Hirte n.d.). In Gerstner's own view, what informs both Stephens's writing of *Pornography* and the efforts of the speakers/characters in the play itself is the rending tension between the absence of 'the right words' and the fact that 'all we have left is the attempt to understand through words' (qtd in Schell 2014: 68; 'Gleichzeitig ist das Stück genau davon beseelt, dass die richtigen Worte zwar fehlen, uns allen aber dennoch nichts anderes bleibt, als zu versuchen, die sprachliche Verständigung aufrechtzuerhalten').[11] In what follows, I argue that the tenor of Gerstner's interpretation created a visual dramaturgy in the form of 'surging images' (van den Berg 2008: 7) that juxtaposed moments of connection and alienation, deconstruction and reconstruction in an unresolved dialectical tension that was pointedly handed over to spectators at the end of the performance.

Gerstner describes how her reading of the play-text informed the creative team's decision to keep all nine performers – eight actors plus the prompter, Friederike Trudzinski, who also participated in the performance – present on stage throughout and to give them a shared task that they would carry out together (see Schell 2014: 68).[12] She had found a postcard that showed a woman who was so absorbed in a jigsaw puzzle that 'she almost became part of it' (qtd in Schell 2014: 68; 'daß sie fast schon selbst Teil davon wird'), and her thoughts for the stage design finally crystallized around Brueghel's *Tower of Babel* (c. 1563). Thus, the stage was dominated by a huge, incomplete mosaic backdrop depicting Brueghel's painting smeared with several ominous-looking black smudges that made it look as if it was on fire, perhaps visually evoking the iconic image of the Twin Towers surrounded by dense clouds of smoke on 9/11.[13]

In both Hannover and Hamburg, all nine performers were already present on the proscenium stage while spectators took their seats in the auditorium. With the house lights still on, some of these performers, singly or in small groups, sat or stood at the ten or so tables on stage sorting out tiles and using them to complete the large, square panels that were missing from the mosaic backdrop. Some others, in the meantime, stood in front of the mosaic itself, their backs to the audience, patiently trying to fit the tiles into the empty slots. This was followed by two performers taking one of the completed panels and fitting it into the corresponding empty square in the mosaic. To conclude the opening sequence (no less than eleven minutes on DVD), while some of the performers scattered the remaining tiles on the floor, a group of four collaborated to build a scaffold by piling five tables on top of one another and push it upstage, where it was used at various points during the performance to reach the higher parts of the mosaic.

Stephens has often observed that he could not share the general sense of incredulity about the 7/7 terrorists being British; rather, he felt that both they and their 'act itself' were part of British (European) society in profoundly complex, unsettling ways that needed to be addressed, not ignored (qtd in Cramer 2008; see also Stephens 2009: xviii). His text makes this point both structurally – by placing the suicide bomber's monologue right in the middle of the play (Scene Four) – and thematically – by presenting the six monologues, all stories of 'transgression' (Stephens 2009: xviii), on an equal footing and refraining from passing moral comment on any of them. In Nübling's production, significantly, the actor who played the bomber (Samuel Weiss) was Caucasian and, in the cast list included in the programme, was simply identified as *Mitwirkend* (participant, collaborator), not as a Terrorist or Suicide Bomber, unlike the rest of the actors, who were listed as Mother, Schoolboy, Brother, Female Student, Professor and Old Woman. The Tower of Babel mosaic became instrumental in highlighting this dimension of the play-text. At the end of Scene Four, the suicide bomber left his bag, which he had been laboriously carrying and dragging along, lying prominently visible downstage centre and proceeded to add his own tile at the very bottom of the mosaic, a gesture that was heightened by the use of music and the dimming of lights. The bag remained on stage throughout the rest of the show and eventually functioned, I would suggest, as what Bert Neumann, chief scenographer at the Volksbühne Berlin since 1992 and a seminal figure for German scenography since 1990, calls 'small detonators' (*'kleine Sprengsätze'*), visual elements 'that might subvert the audience's perception' (van den Berg 2008: 11).

The explosive potential of the suicide bomber's bag became apparent in Scene One, where, as the voiceover recitation of the list of the fifty-two victims of 7/7 began, the rest of the performers together began to clear the stage of tables and chairs and place the remaining square panels in the appropriate empty spaces in the mosaic backdrop, building scaffolds with the tables as needed. With all the square panels in place, however, the mosaic remained incomplete, both because of the presence of the black smears and because of the absence of numerous individual tiles, still lying scattered across the stage. Eventually, the nine performers sat down in a semi-circle of chairs downstage, their backs to the audience, looking at the unfinished mosaic and occasionally discussing it in pairs, as if they were spectators. After a few minutes, one of them walked up to the one remaining scaffold and tried to push it stage right. After signalling he could not do it on his own, another four performers came to his aid and the scaffold was successfully removed, followed by everyone taking their chairs stage right and sitting down there again as a group, looking at the mosaic. This had the effect of foregrounding the suicide bomber's bag again as it sat on its own in the middle of the now practically bare stage. When, at the very end of the recitation, with the stage in near complete darkness, one of the performers walked up to it, unzipped it and turned it over to empty its contents, it was revealed to contain not a bomb but hundreds more tiles with which all the performers continued the task of trying to reconstruct the mosaic as the performance drew to a close. In sum, by unobtrusively yet incrementally drawing the audience's gaze towards the suicide bomber's bag and eventually disrupting automatic expectations about it, Nübling's production placed the focus on 'the fault lines of perception in the visual field' (van den Berg 2008: 12). The perceptual explosion spectators were eventually confronted with was a potent image intimating that reconstruction requires not only a collective, collaborative effort, but that it needs to cut across divisive us/them binaries if it is to be both effective and lasting.

Gutmann's *Pornographie*: Hypervisibility and the space of the intimate

Stéphane Braunschweig, Artistic Director of La Colline when Gutmann's *Pornographie* was staged, makes a distinction between 'theatre as text', where it is assumed that 'the text contains a coherence' inscribed by the playwright that must be recovered in performance, and 'theatre as material', where rather than search for 'totality' in the play-text/playwright, the director/creative team 'assemble', 'edit' and 'bind together' a range of heterogeneous 'verbal and extra-verbal fragments' in order to produce a performance (Pavis 2013: 294). In this connection, and as is the case with German *Inszenierung*, within French theatre culture the term '*mise en scène*' goes hand in hand with the 'theatre as material' notion, referring as it does to 'an autonomous production of meaning' rather than 'a translation or an illustration of the pre-existing text' (Pavis 2010: 396). Likewise, the *metteur en scène* (director) is 'semantically situated directly within the realm of art, reinforcing the ideal of artistic autonomy and freedom' (Boenisch 2015: 3).

Within this framework, Pierre Simard's 2000 essay 'Sous le signe du refus: L'accueil du théâtre britannique en France' ('Under the Sign of Refusal: The Reception of British Theatre in France') continues to be of relevance in relation to Gutmann's *Pornographie*. According to Simard, as the *passeur de texte* (text courier) of contemporary British plays to the French public, the *metteur en scène* is responsible for transferring the source work 'into a stage and aesthetic universe' that 'will produce in his/her chosen target audience' the relevant 'aesthetic, cultural and ideological echoes' only if it takes into account the specificities of French theatre culture (2000: 175; '[il] devra transférer ce dit dans un univers spectaculaire et esthétique respectueux de l'ensemble de ces paramètres s'il aspire à produire dans le public cible qu'il s'est choisi un ensemble d'échos esthétiques, culturels et idéologiques'). Among those specificities, Simard highlights a tension between universality and contextual rootedness (2000: 168; 'l'éternelle opposition entre l'universalité et l'enracinement'): while post-1956 British theatre, Simard points out, is 'open [. . .] to the sensitivities of society and the expression of its crises' ('ouvert depuis 1956 aux sensibilités de la société et a l'expression de ses crises'), French theatre tends to be defined 'by a search for universality' (2000: 179; 'les scènes françaises en quête [. . .] d'universalité'). Within this context, the director as *passeur de texte* needs to find a fertile set of cultural referents and aesthetic forms that will make it possible for him/her to transfer the complexity of the source work 'into an equivalent yet not superimposable complexity in the culture of arrival' (Simard 2000: 179; 'dans une complexité équivalente non superposable, dans la culture d'arrivée').

Two pieces printed as part of the programme for *Pornographie* published by La Colline, 'Entretien avec Laurent Gutmann' ('Interview with Laurent Gutmann') and 'Transgresser ou refuser la tyrannie de la transparence' ('To Transgress or to Reject the Tyranny of Transparency'), both confirm

Simard's diagnosis as regards French theatre's historic tendency to shun current social and political realities and, at the same time, provide clues as to how Gutmann positions himself vis-à-vis the universality/contextual rootedness divide. He states that 'It is the double movement of distance and closeness that fascinates me' (2010b: 28; 'C'est ce double mouvement d'éloignement et de rapprochement qui me passionne'), and his production of *Pornographie*, I argue, was informed by precisely this sort of (uneasy) balancing act.[14] Thus, on the one hand Gutmann explains in the interview that, following such pioneering French directors as Antoine Vitez and Jean Vilar, for a long time he tended to believe that 'current events were not worthy of theatre', since the (political) force of theatre resided in its self-reflexive artificiality (2010b: 27–8; 'J'ai grandi avec l'idée que l'actualité, par exemple, n'était pas un matériau digne pour le théâtre'; 'Pendant tout un pan du XXe siècle, nos maîtres ont redéfini le théâtre dans une sorte de sur-affirmation de sa facticité, du simulacre, revendiquant son artificialité comme une force. [. . .] un théâtre qui parle *d'abord* du théâtre' (emphasis original)). He has now, however, completely changed his mind: 'the more I go on, the more I am obsessed by the need for a theatre that helps me to think through the present moment' (2010b: 27; 'Plus j'avance en effet, plus je suis obsédé par la nécessité d'un théâtre qui m'aide à penser ce qui se passe aujourd'hui').

On the other hand, in 'Transgresser ou refuser la tyrannie de la transparence', Gutmann chooses to foreground a dimension of *Pornography* that tilts his production towards the self-reflective, universalist end of the spectrum, albeit without entirely renouncing the focus on current events. He begins by seemingly echoing Stephens (see, for example, 2009: xviii; Schultz 2010: 10) when he states that the play is not about terrorism but about transgression (see Gutmann 2010c: 2) – and, indeed, the line 'Veillez à ne jamais dépasser la ligne jaune' ('Be careful never to cross the yellow line'), delivered in voiceover at the very start of his *Pornographie*, flagged up this theme (the play-text's brief prologue was cut).[15] But unlike Stephens, who firmly ties transgression to context by referring to the third age of capitalism, consumerism, a massively overpopulated world and the objectification of others within the contemporary urban experience, Gutmann interprets transgression in a way that is less social and more focused on the individual subject: 'To transgress is to refuse the tyranny of transparency, to reconquer an intimate space', he states (2010c: 2; 'transgresser est refuser la tyrannie de la transparence, reconquérir un espace intime'). Gutmann's interest in transparency and the space of the intimate derives from two key referents within French culture, Italian philosopher Giorgio Agamben's *Qu'est-ce que le contemporain?* (2008) and French psychoanalyst Gérard Wajcman's *L'Œeil absolu* (2010), both of whom are abundantly quoted in La Colline's programme for *Pornographie* and both of whom view the contemporary moment through the dual conceptual prism of (in)visibility and the gaze.[16]

For Agamben, the contemporary artist 'must firmly hold his gaze on his own time' in order to perceive 'not its light, but rather its darkness' (2009: 44).[17] Indeed, those who can 'call themselves contemporary are only those who do not allow themselves to be blinded by the lights of the century, and so manage to get a glimpse of the shadows in those lights, of their intimate obscurity' (2009: 45). In order to pinpoint what that contemporary obscurity is about, Gutmann turns to Wajcman, director of the Centre d'étude d'histoire et de théorie du regard (Centre for the Study of the History and Theory of the Gaze) at the Université Paris 8-Vincennes-Saint-Denis, who describes the present moment as an 'age of hypervisibility' characterized by a 'desire for transparency which [. . .] aims to extort the intimate, to pull out the truth from the subject' (qtd in La Colline 2010: 15, 6; 'Le désir de transparence [. . .] se réalise en volonté d'extorquer l'intime, d'arracher sa vérité au sujet'). This is a violent, dangerous illusion of mastery that requires the traditional role of art, understood as to 'make visible', to be rethought: we need to not only 'open our eyes to the eye that watches us' (Wajcman qtd in La Colline 2010: 15; 'ouvrir l'oeil sur l'oeil qui nous regarde'), but also find ways of 'evading the all-seeing gaze' so as to defend 'the territories of the intimate', the necessarily hidden, ineffable core of each subject (Wajcman qtd in La Colline 2010: 6; 'se soustraire au regard omnivoyant', 'les territoires de l'intime'). In these circumstances, Wajcman announces a new programme for art, 'to render invisible' rather than 'reproduce the visible' (qtd in La Colline 2010: 15; 'pour énoncer à l'art un nouveau programme: L'art ne reproduit pas le visible, il rend invisible'). Gutmann believes this dictum to be an exact description not only of his production of *Pornographie* but also of the essence of Stephens's play (see 2010b: 33).

The theories of Agamben and Wajcman throw important light on Gutmann and stage designer Mathieu Lorry-Dupuy's (b. 1978) choices regarding the transformation of Stephens's '*Images of hell*' stage direction into a specific scenography. This is how Gutmann describes the stage design they jointly devised:

> the eight actors are in a hyperrealistic space, [horizontally] divided into two. The first part, downstage, the larger of the two, is empty. [. . .]

> The second part, in the distance [upstage], is a panoramic apartment behind a [transparent] sliding bay window split up into several sections, with all the rooms: [stage right to left] kitchen-cum-dining-room, living room, bedroom, bathroom. And the actors inhabit this space as if they had agreed to be completely transparent, to reveal themselves through all the gestures of everyday life. (2010b, 32; les huit acteurs sont dans un espace hyperréaliste, divisé en deux. La première partie, à la face, la plus grande, est vide. [. . .] La deuxième partie, au lointain, est un appartement panoramique, derrière une baie vitrée qui coulisse en plusieurs pans, avec toutes les pièces: salle de bain, chambre, cuisine, salon. Et les acteurs y vivent comme s'ils acceptaient d'être complètement transparents, de s'exhiber dans tous les gestes de la vie quotidienne)

When the performance began, the actors – who remained on stage throughout – consecutively stepped out of the upstage apartment area into the downstage playing space and there, 'in front of the audience, they [went] further and reveal[ed] things you do not see', a process of 'unveiling' that, according to Gutmann, sought to 'recreat[e] a space of mystery and intimacy' (2010b: 32; 'Et là, [. . .] devant le public, ils vont aller plus loin, raconter des choses qu'on ne voit pas', 'aller encore plus loin dans le dévoilement, c'est en fin de compte recréer un espace de mystère et d'intimité'). In this way, Stephens's *Images of hell* were from the start connected to the experience of living in a society of hypervisibility that both Agamben and Wajcman write about. Crucially, the audience was also exposed to the experience of hypervisibility, since the production's scenic arrangement meant that rather than being allowed to hide in the safety of a conventionally darkened auditorium, spectators and the actors/characters in the upstage apartment space became mirror images of each other, with both silently watching each other as much as the actors who stepped into the downstage area to perform their roles in episodes Seven to Two of the play-text. This mirror effect was highlighted at the very start of the performance, immediately after 'Veillez à ne jamais dépasser la ligne jaune' was heard, by keeping the eight actors just sitting there in the apartment, not saying or doing anything, not even looking at each other, for a whole two minutes, until the actor playing the working mum in episode Seven (Reina Kakudate) stood up from her position in the kitchen stage right, slid open the glass panel and walked into the playing area. In other words, throughout the performance spectators were invited to look at themselves as part of the same 'hell' of atomized hypervisibility as the actors/characters in the play.

The production's strategy to invite spectators to examine their experiences of hypervisibility was enhanced through the frequent use of direct address across the fourth wall – a motif established right at the start of the performance, when the working mum opened her monologue with a smile on her face and her gaze fixed on the audience – and the generalized deployment of other (Brechtian) distancing devices. To cite one example, when the working mum finds, 'to [her] surprise, that there are tears pouring down [her] face and falling onto the newspaper' (Stephens 2009: 216), the fact that Kakudate kept on smiling while at the same time her hands mimicked the movement of the tears falling down her face created a strikingly dissonant effect, a painful tension where spectators literally watched the invisible (the tears) trying to break through the surface of the visible (the smile). The tension was further foregrounded near the end of the episode through the treatment given to the lines, 'Are you laughing or crying? / What? / I said are you laughing or crying?' (Stephens 2009: 221), which come directly after the working mum reports that London has won the bid to host the 2012 Olympics and, like all lines in Stephens's play-text, are not assigned to any particular speaker. In Gutmann's production, Kakudate spoke rapidly and laughed excitedly as she announced the Olympic win, but then immediately the invisible (the crying hiding, once again, under the working mum's laughter) was made palpable by the simple yet effective expedient of slowing the moment down: another actor (Pauline Lorillard), who had so far been watching Kakudate's performance from one of the sofas in the apartment area, interrupted the monologue with 'Tu ris ou tu pleures?'. Kakudate turned to her deliberately to ask 'Quoi?', and Lorillard stood up, slid open one of the central glass panels and repeated, 'Je dit tu ris ou tu pleures?'. Finally, between the two aforementioned moments, the production's exploration of the smile/laughter (visibility) and tears/crying (invisibility) dialectic was orchestrated to directly involve the audience: when the working mum, once again enthusing about London's victory in the 2012 Olympic bid, quotes 'Look at the stars. See how they shine for you' from Coldplay's 2000 hit 'Yellow', Kakudate tentatively half-sang the lines in English, then looked about herself as if she had lost track of the rest of the lyrics, and eventually turned back for help to the actors in the apartment, who did not respond at all. This foregrounded interruption of the flow of the French text, which was followed by Kakudate laughing her way through the lines describing the queen knighting the ice-cream sellers in Hyde Park, had the effect of flagging up the clash between the visible surface glitter (the stars shining on Olympic London; the working mum's merriment) on the one hand, and the invisible emotional vacuum and affective isolation characterizing her existence. Sure enough, it provoked uneasy chuckles from the spectators as they, perhaps, recognized themselves in the performance's mirror. In sum, through scenographic design and non-mimetic acting strategies, Gutmann's *Pornographie* relentlessly impelled spectators to confront, both in the play and in themselves, the deceptive transparency and the intimate, affective obscurity that Agamben and Wajcman see as the 'image of hell' defining the present historical moment.

By way of conclusion

The preceding discussion of Nübling's and Gutmann's productions of Stephens's *Pornography* confirms that, in performance, fidelity to the text – the idea that a play-text can be interpreted and performed 'following the author's intentions, as if there existed a correct reading' – is no more than a (persistent) 'illusion' (Pavis 2013: 295). Instead, once and again theatre confronts us with the 'impurity' of the play-text, its open, unfinished, 'writerly' nature, and the 'inevitable and productive betrayal regarding the so-called truth of the text' (Pavis 2013: 296) that directors and creative teams need to perform. Drawing on contemporary translation theory, I have argued elsewhere in relation to film adaptation that creative teams 'refract' or 'inf(l)ect' their source material rather than simply, and passively, 'reflect' it (see Aragay 2005: 30). In the case of the two productions under examination here, Nübling and his team tapped into Stephens's *Pornography* to construct an *Inszenierung* that confronted spectators with acutely jarring images of connection and disconnection, while the mise en scène devised by Gutmann and his co-creators inf(l)ected the play-text with Agamben's and Wajcman's reflections on contemporaneity and (in)visibility. Both productions deployed scenographic and acting strategies designed to incite a process of self-examination on the part of spectators, and both emerged from a broadly Continental view of the play-text as necessarily transformable material. This approach stands in contrast with Anglo-American theatre cultures in which, as Pavis notes, 'directing a play' still predominantly means 'taking as a starting point the text's givens as unalterable, to the letter' (2013: 294).

And yet, as Boenisch has observed, 'recently, the term "theatre direction" rather than "directing"' (2015: 3) has become increasingly prominent in Britain precisely as a way to offset the text-centric connotations of the latter. In '"Changing the Conversation": Simon Stephens, Sean Holmes, and Secret Theatre', Jacqueline Bolton cogently argues that Stephens has played a key role in this connection, in the sense that '[his] experiences of working with directors, designers, dramaturgs and actors from European theatre cultures' (2016b: 340) have enabled him to legitimate 'a renewed questioning of theatrical structures and aesthetics which is impacting upon the work of established, early career, and emerging directors' (2016b: 337). Thus, as Bolton points out, during its almost two-year existence the Secret Theatre project, launched in 2013 by Stephens and the Lyric Hammersmith's Artistic Director Sean Holmes, was fuelled by a desire to challenge the 'structures of literalism' (Holmes qtd in Bolton 2016b: 339) underpinning British mainstream theatre culture – or, to go back to Stephens's own phrasing, to interrogate the imaginary 'purity of text' (qtd in Radosavljević 2014: 267). Whether or not mainstream theatre-making in the UK will continue down this path, what seems undoubtable is that Stephens's 'unhomely' receptiveness to collaborative forms of authorship has allowed creative teams in Europe and beyond – as well as, increasingly, at 'home' – to push his plays in boldly creative, exciting new directions.

Critical Perspectives

PRECURSIVE TEXTS IN THE WORK OF SIMON STEPHENS: *MOTORTOWN, BIRDLAND, PUNK ROCK*

James Hudson

In interviews, prose work and public lectures, Simon Stephens is characteristically candid in acknowledging his indebtedness to the multiplicity of writers, musicians, artists, photographers and film-makers who have influenced his work. As a playwright, he is remarkably cognizant of his theatrical lineage, and an awareness of this inheritance clearly informs his slew of celebrated adaptations of classic plays, such as *A Doll's House* (2012), *The Cherry Orchard* (2014), *The Threepenny Opera* (2016) and *The Seagull* (2017). Beyond these 'English Language Versions' of existing plays, however, it is well-established that Stephens's omnivorous appreciation of various art forms means that the influences that pervade his work comprise an eclectic bill of fare. A self-confessed 'thieving playwright' (2010c), Stephens maintains that 'the first part of any writing for me is about absorbing information and consciously looking for inspiration' (2010b). His plays are populated with influences drawn from novels, screenplays and visual artists, such as the photography of Richard Billingham and paintings of Gerhard Richter. However, of the cross-media consumption that informs his creative process, it is film and music that stand out above all. Indeed, Stephens is perhaps one of a first generation of UK dramatists who would be as likely to claim inspiration from film as from theatre, having been 'introduced to drama not through the stage but on screen' (Carr 2013: online), through both the television dramas and plays of Alan Bleasdale and Dennis Potter as well as the movies of Martin Scorsese, David Lynch and Gus Van Sant.[18] As Chapter 4 of this volume explores, Stephens equally derives much of his inspiration from music, with the sonic landscape of 1980s Manchester an omnipresent background and atmospheric lodestar; he has expressed that he would like his plays 'to inspire, excite, terrify and alarm audiences in the same way and with the same directness as music does to me' (ibid.).

Clearly the breadth of Stephens's engagement with the musical and filmic is too extensive to be usefully captured over the course of a single chapter, and that is not what is attempted here. Instead, this chapter trains its focus on Stephens's repeated strategy of redeploying these elements of recently historical and contemporary popular culture in conjunction with the reinterpretation of a seam of classic, continental avant-garde theatrical texts, specifically by Georg Büchner (1813–1837), Bertolt Brecht (1898–1956) and Frank Wedekind (1864–1918). It examines the way that canonical theatrical texts of these writers are digested alongside more recent cultural material, particularly that of film, in Stephens's plays *Motortown* (2006), *Birdland* (2014) and *Punk Rock* (2009). In doing so, it identifies processes surrounding the synthesis and rearticulation of diverse source materials that are the result of an idiosyncratic style of adaptation distinctive to Stephens in his approach to original work. In each case, Stephens extrapolates a central facet of the precursive text – the moral ambiguity surrounding Woyzeck's culpability for murder in *Woyzeck* (1913), Brecht's nascent apprehensions about the depredations of capitalism in *Baal* (1923), Wedekind's disquiet about the debilitating pressures of bourgeois socialization on adolescents in *Spring Awakening* (1906) – and, cross-pollinating these experimental pre-modernist and modernist texts with more recent film material, rearticulates it appropriately for its contemporary historical moment.

Stephens is by no means alone in engaging with his theatrical antecedents in such a fashion, and many of his contemporaries have also made practical use of source material. Latterly, Jez Butterworth's plays have become well-known for their dramatic and literary allusiveness, from the re-engineering of Shakespearean and pastoral folk myths in *Jerusalem* (2009) to *The Ferryman*'s (2017) evocation of canonical Irish playwrights like J. M. Synge, Sean O'Casey and Brian Friel. With *Dunsinane* (2010), *Caligula* (2003) and *The Suppliant Women* (2017) David Grieg has conducted his own conversations with theatrical history, these plays answering Shakespeare's *Macbeth,* adapting Albert Camus's own envisioning of classical drama, and reinterpreting Aeschylus respectively. Dennis Kelly's 2010 play *The Gods Weep* was his own variation on *King Lear*, and Zinnie Harris's *The Restless House* (2016) was a trilogy of plays that adapted the Oresteia. These modern instances, of course, are themselves part of a tradition; a profoundly dialogic medium, theatre is itself continually engaged in a process of perpetual reproduction. Brecht himself frequently worked from models, exercised by the desire to counter, rub against, or dispute the adopted work, claiming 'anyone can be creative, it's rewriting other people that's a challenge' (qtd in Thomson 1994: 25). In this, Brecht was partaking of a tradition that had perhaps already achieved apotheosis in the Renaissance poetic praxis of *imitatio*, the creative emulation of others and the adaptation of their work. As Shakespeare scholar Robert S. Miola informs us: 'According to this theory, a poet demonstrated originality not by inventing new stories

Critical Perspectives

but by adopting extant, particularly classical ones. The genius lay not in the invention but the transformation' (2000: 2). In the present historical moment, the twentieth-century notion of artistic plagiarism has perhaps ceded way to an appreciation of creativity as an endless process of the assimilation and recycling of extant materials, while the theory of intertextuality has emphasized the way that texts are constructed out of already existing discourse, with authors understood to be compiling texts from pre-existing texts. Since intertextuality is by definition a property that all texts possess, and the intertextual dimensions of a given text are not reducible to uncovering its sources or influences, this chapter does not intend to engage with the notion of intertextuality beyond this basic recognition. In the case of Simon Stephens, however, the use of a precursive text as a site of inspiration appears to be a reflex that is constitutive of his style. In excavating the archaeology of these precursive dramatic texts buried in Stephens's original plays, this chapter interrogates the nature and function of this continual process of assimilation and reinterpretation as it applies to his oeuvre. Specifically, it examines his strategy of recontextualizing the concerns of these palimpsest texts so that they have renewed relevance for his contemporary moment. If history, as Foucault reminds us, is continually produced in the present, what can Stephens's conversations with theatrical history tell us about the theatre-making of our contemporary moment and the concerns it seeks to represent?

Motortown/Woyzeck/Taxi Driver

Stephens has divulged that it was the way his plays evoked music for Ian Rickson, Artistic Director of the Royal Court from 1998 to 2006, that led to the impetus for what was to become *Motortown*:

> Ian told me that every play I'd written to date had evoked the same spirit in him as was evoked by ballads. He wanted me to write a play that had the same acerbic dissonant energy as those bands I'd loved since adolescence, like The Fall and the Butthole Surfers. (2009: xv)

Motortown is, of course, a title every bit as descriptive of a musical genre as *Country Music* (2004) and *Punk Rock*, with the first word of the portmanteau that made up the name of the legendary Detroit record company simply used in full. The title makes the play a cognate with the work of Martin Scorsese, who peppered the violence and machismo of films like *Mean Streets* (1973) and *Goodfellas* (1990) with the bold, up-tempo and emotionally raw sound characteristic of the Motown label. *Motortown* is Stephens's response to the fallout of the Iraq war mediated through his response to two precursive texts; the play transposes the eponymous character from Büchner's 1836 play *Woyzeck* onto the descent-into-hell narrative and moral indeterminacy of Scorsese's *Taxi Driver* (1976). Stephens has repeatedly been explicit about the influence of the antiheroes Franz Woyzeck and Travis Bickle upon the central character of *Motortown*, ex-squaddie Danny (see, for example, Stephens 2010d), though the play refrains from configuring its exploration of Danny's psychotic proclivities around either dehumanization or trauma arising from his experience as a soldier. What is notable about Stephens's trafficking with this pair of source texts is the way that, in cleaving to their themes and approaches, he crafts a work unaligned with predictable axioms about the deleterious effects of war, and instead offers a palimpsest text of equally troubling moral complexity.

Büchner's *Woyzeck* presaged naturalism in making the radical step of presenting Woyzeck's tragedy as attributable to a confluence of external factors rather than an individual flaw; it also anticipated expressionism with its episodic, disconnected construction, clipped dialogue and often dreamlike atmosphere. Throughout the play we see the soldier Woyzeck patronized and belittled by his social superiors and callously instrumentalized into a medical prop for the army Doctor's facetious experiments. Already experiencing apocalyptic hallucinations and suffering physically from the Doctor's insistence that he subsist on nothing but peas for three months, Woyzeck murders his adulterous lover, Marie. Left unfinished by Büchner, the play ends with Woyzeck wading deeper and deeper into the water of a nearby pond in an attempt to dispose of the murder weapon. Conversely, Paul Schrader, screenwriter of *Taxi Driver*, leant heavily upon Fyodor Dostoevsky's *Notes from Underground* (1864) in his interpretation of an outsider figure commenting caustically on society from its margins. A discharged marine, Travis takes a job as a taxi driver and becomes voyeuristically enmeshed in the seedy, crime-ridden and dysfunctional milieu of night-time New York. Paranoid and psychotic, he begins a punitive fitness regimen and instigates a murderous attack on 'Sport' Higgins's brothel, attempting to extricate the adolescent runaway Iris, a child sex worker that he has befriended. After killing three men, Travis is lauded as a vigilante hero; Iris returns to her parents and Bickle returns to his job. Very much like Dostoevsky's Underground

Man, Woyzeck and Travis are incubators of Nietzschean *ressentiment* and, in Stephens's hands, Danny becomes a distillation of both prior works' address of issues relating to masculine sexual inadequacy and class politics.

All three main protagonists are sexually repressed and, consequently, in a characteristic Freudian spiral, reel from thwarted Eros to furious Thanatos. Just as Woyzeck loses Marie to another, more archetypically masculine man in the form of the Drum Major, Travis fails in his pursuit of his object-cathexis, campaign volunteer Betsy. In an ambiguous scene that takes place in her bedroom, Marie apparently relents to the regimental Drum Major's overtures with the words 'Oh who cares! It's all the same' (Büchner 1997: 18); comparatively, in *Taxi Driver*, Betsy agrees to let Travis take her on a date but walks out, humiliated, when he gauchely takes her to a pornographic film. Stephens clearly picks up this motif in *Motortown*, with Danny suffering from similar sexual inadequacy. The very first words of the play, related by Danny's brother Lee, concern his ex-girlfriend Marley: 'She doesn't want to see you. She told me to tell you' (Stephens 2009: 143).[19] Marley knows to touch this particular nerve when deterring Danny's attempt to renew their acquaintance with searing frankness: 'This is ridiculous. You couldn't even get it up half the time. Could you though? When you think about it. Came in about two seconds when you did' (159). Just as for Woyzeck and Travis, Danny's psychotic breakdown is engendered by the loss of a female partner that they never truly possess. In each case attributable to their own lack of sexual potency, their self-loathing and guilt are displaced and projected onto others who become scapegoats for their emasculation: Woyzeck fixates on Marie's infidelity and sexual availability; Bickle deplores Sport's pimping of Iris; Danny uses the fourteen-year-old Jade as a prop to exorcize Marley's aspersions about his sexual inadequacy. Like *Woyzeck*, *Motortown* ends suspended between the murder being committed and discovered, with Danny, like Woyzeck, enduring an anxiety-fuelled twilight before he is brought to justice. As with Martin Scorsese's de-saturating of the colour-palette of the final shoot-out of *Taxi Driver* to diminish the brightness of the blood effect (and therefore obtain an 'R' rating for the film), *Motortown*'s Royal Court première, directed by Ramin Gray, deliberately used an excess of fake blood following Jade's murder, which the performers then fastidiously mopped up after the scene had ended. While both these aspects were practical ways of dealing with the messy realities of producing verisimilitude, each represent a striking aesthetic commentary on the mediation of violence in art in their own right, both being manoeuvres that magnify the impact by drawing attention to the artificiality of the spectacles they depict.

The thread of masculine sexual inadequacy articulated within each work is indivisible from the location of the issue within a specific class context that conditions how it is to be viewed as one component of a total situation. In *Woyzeck* the emphasis is less on the conventional sexual jealousy that motivates it as a revenge tragedy than on situating Woyzeck's actions inside a matrix of poverty, mental illness and the menial status which allows his social superiors to both judge and instrumentalize him. Woyzeck's accountability for his crime is not straightforward; literally a medical research-subject enduring a nutritional death-sentence, exchanging his urine for money so the Doctor can examine the effects of peas on his diet, he is also a metaphorical test case located within the heyday of the nature-versus-nurture debates of the early nineteenth century. Woyzeck is a 'working class tragedy' not simply because, as Kenneth McLeish maintains, it was 'the first stage drama ever to make tragedy from the plight of someone with no social standing' (1997: xviii), but also because it acknowledges the way that violence is an inevitable outgrowth of the material effects of living in a society based on classes. *Taxi Driver* too is emphatically framed in these same class terms, with Travis compartmentalized by his occupation and treated instrumentally by his passengers. When troubled by dark thoughts, Travis discusses his situation with fellow cabbie Wizard, who warns him about the tendency of capitalism to corrode individuality to create the sort of subject it needs: 'A man takes a job. And that job . . . you know, like, that becomes what he is. You know, you do a thing, and that's what you are. [. . .] You get a job, you become the job' (Schrader et al. 1999).

The homogeneity of class perspective advanced in *Woyzeck* and *Taxi Driver* is also shot through *Motortown*, a nihilistic envisioning of the impoverished and disaffected turning on each other in difficult times. Danny's class background is alluded to rather than given concrete exposition, revealed in fragmentary reproaches of his parents and oblique references to working-class pleasure spots in Essex. As in *Woyzeck*, it emerges most concertedly through force of contrast, where the middleclass are glimpsed unflatteringly. In *Motortown*, the middle class appear in the guise of a pair of insufferably conceited anti-war liberal swingers that proposition Danny for a threesome. When he hears that they attended the Stop the War Protest, Danny's response is utterly contemptuous: 'I wish I'd been there. [. . .] With my SA80. Sprayed the lot of yer' (200). If, as Aleks Sierz notes, critics of *Motortown* were displeased that Stephens's play did not locate the cause of

Danny's anger wholly in his wartime experiences, it is also perhaps simplistic to suggest, as Sierz goes on to do, that 'Danny's deprived background, and his family, are the cause of his problems' (Sierz 2011: 131). Instead, in reconceptualizing *Woyzeck*, Stephens's play transcends the anatomy of environmental causation proffered by Büchner; so, while Sierz's statement would certainly serve as an appropriate description of Woyzeck's plight, it is perhaps not an adequate perspective from which to apprehend the judicious balance Stephens maintains in the calculus between environment, agency and desire in his play, which the grafting of *Taxi Driver* as an additional precursive text has allowed Stephens to do.

It is certainly significant that Woyzeck, Travis and Danny all bear the imprint of recent army service; Woyzeck lives a daily regimental drudge of menial hardship, but Travis is a Vietnam War veteran emblematic of the national trauma occasioned in the United States by that conflict. How Stephens's *Motortown* extends and complicates this metaphor is therefore as much a valuable point of comparison as the foregrounding of a working-class perspective. Echoing *Taxi Driver*, *Motortown* reiterates the view that Western countries export their violence abroad, with both Travis and Danny returning to perpetrate it upon their own communities like a vicious Freudian return of the repressed. Like Travis, Danny is a recent returnee from an aggressive imperialist war begun without provocation and prosecuted with astounding destructive power; yet Stephens, like Scorsese before him, is not interested in interrogating the war with any particular specificity. Insofar as *Taxi Driver* and *Motortown* have something to say about their respective foreign wars, the point is not that either protagonist has become corrupted by the violence they have witnessed or enacted abroad, but that their appetite for destructiveness was latent within them and indeed nourished by their upbringing. When Danny cracks under pressure, it is, to use Stephens's words, the 'barely contained casual violence and racism' (2010d: 36) inherent in English society that issues forth. As Stephens has maintained, since the military is a part of, not separate from our culture: 'if those boys [soldiers] are violent, chaotic or morally insecure, it's because they are a product of a violent, chaotic and morally insecure culture' (qtd in Abrahams 2006: online). On their return from service, Travis and Danny re-encounter their own culture with a heightened appreciation of their diminished status, see a panorama of perpetual exploitation and generalized criminality, and internalize it as a dog-eat-dog state of nature, pledging themselves to a Hobbesian war of all against all. Travis is confounded by permissiveness and the decline of conservatism he sees in the multiracial identities and sexual licentiousness he observes from his taxi; Danny's furious racist diatribe in Scene Six is a condensation of reactionary nativist and anti-multiculturalist tropes that echoes the familiar far-right victimology that locates the cause of supposed 'community decline' in allegedly incompatible racial and cultural admixing:

> They're Hasidic Jews in swimming pools. They're lesbian cripples with bus passes. They're niggers, with their faces all full of their mama's jerk chicken, shooting each other in the back down Brixton high street until the lot of them have disappeared. They're little dickless Paki boys training to be doctors or to run corner shops and smuggling explosives in rucksacks onto the top decks of buses. [. . .] I fought a war for this lot. (188)

The key to both protagonists' animus is the sense is of having lost something, be it moral fibre for Travis or the privileges of white skin for Danny. Both indulge in reactionary laments for discipline and authority while being simultaneously tempted by that which they decry. Demonstrating classic fetishist behaviour, they both know and do not know what they are doing, acknowledge and deny their urges and are attracted and repulsed by the vulnerable Iris/Jade figures onto whom they project their own desires. As Stephens has stated:

> I knew that this play, so inspired by Martin Scorsese's *Taxi Driver*, needed a character akin to that played by Jodie Foster [Iris] in the movie. A scarred angel whom the protagonist mistakenly feels he can save. A delusion that leads to brutal murder. In the time of Vietnam this was played out against her pimps and traffickers. In the more morally chaotic time of *Iraq 2 – The Sequel* it was played out on her. (2010d: 36)

This statement is key to understanding Stephens's adaptive process in his reinterpretation of palimpsest texts, as it is here where *Motortown* departs from its precursors in offering its own interrogation of motive and causation in its exploration of contemporary violence. Both *Woyzeck* and *Taxi Driver* postulate confusion concerning morality and causality, and Stephens's interest in *Motortown* is aligned along the same axis of investigating culpability and moral complexity in a configuration where the main – and putatively most attractive – character is a murderer with a series of fixations and attachments. Each work explores rather than explains these obsessions, figuring the protagonists principally as victims of their own circumstances and pathologies. *Woyzeck* displaces conventional notions of causation representative of its time: the aggressor is also the victim. *Taxi Driver* pushes this complication of ethical binaries in a different direction, where the murderous acts of the reactionary vigilante do, in their own small way, 'clean up the streets', and Travis's repressed and homicidal urges are partially validated by rescuing Iris. *Motortown* pushes this moral uncertainty to yet another extreme, with Danny's torture and murder of Jade encapsulating perfectly the deluded and contradictory logic of the doctrine of liberal interventionism manifested by the US/UK powers in the Iraq war: like the wholesale cataclysm visited on the people of Iraq, a population that hawkish pre-war rhetoric claimed the invasion was specifically intended to save, Danny's initial interest in rescuing Jade gives way to unhinged, egomaniacal masculine posturing and murderous violence. It is emphatically not that the Iraq war was a potentially emancipatory military enterprise that tragically went wrong, but that it was only ever self-serving, predatory and imperialistic, and, like Danny's tarrying with Jade, any interest in helping was only ever untaken in bad faith.

Birdland/Baal

Stephens acknowledges the use of Brecht's *Baal* as a precursive text for *Birdland* in his opening note to the published text (2014c: 3).[20] It is a pleasing symmetry to note that Brecht was accused of plagiarizing none other than Büchner in his composition of *Baal*,[21] and it is easy to see the armature of *Woyzeck* undergirding Brecht's play about an amoral and dissolute lower-class anti-hero at odds with those around them. At the same time, this makes *Woyzeck* something of an ur-text to *Birdland* as well as *Motortown*, albeit at one further remove and after Büchner's original had passed through Brecht's guts, as it were. Brecht's Baal is a singer and poet, which Stephens updates into Paul, the singer-songwriter of a globally popular music duo whose amazing success, hedonistic excesses and Icarus-esque decline the play chronicles. In doing this Stephens references Alan Clarke's 1982 BBC adaptation of the play, where the musician David Bowie played Baal, thereby grafting a further real-life parallel to the work.

The opening scenes of *Birdland* are a schematic reproduction of the opening scenes of *Baal*. *Baal* begins with the eponymous central character taking up with Johanna, the fiancée of the impressionable and naïve Johannes, after Baal repudiates his current lover Emelie as the four of them visit an inn together. The ingénue Johanna confesses her humiliation and confusion in a post-coital scene with an exaggeratedly indifferent Baal. She subsequently drowns herself in the river, information which is relayed to Baal in the following scene by a pair of sisters who visit the singer in his room for yet another of his sexual assignations. In *Birdland* the progression is largely identical over the course of the first five scenes. Johnny, Paul's bandmate, informs Paul of his depth of feeling for his girlfriend Marnie, who is scheduled to join them on their world tour. Once again, two couples endure an embarrassing scene over a meal, here occasioned by Paul's hundred-thousand pound inducement for his companion, Annalisa, to kiss Marnie. As with *Baal*, the scene immediately following this shifts to the aftermath of Paul and Marnie's infidelity, as Paul casually teases her about whether or not he will decide to inform Johnny of their tryst. Marnie kills herself by jumping from the roof of the hotel, and, similarly to Baal, Paul learns of the suicide from a pair of sex-workers claiming to be sisters. Thereafter, *Birdland* departs from its source-text, both plays developing into episodic fragments that demonstrate the monumental egoism of their protagonists, with Baal abandoning his pregnant lover and Paul increasingly becoming a monster of vanity. There is concordance of sorts in the resolution of both plays: Baal murders his boon companion Ekart in an argument over their sexual claim to a waitress, though a strong subtextual undercurrent suggests that it is a violent eruption of their latent homosexual desire for each other (as Ekart says, 'why shouldn't I have women? Am I your lover?') (Brecht 1970: 56). In *Birdland* it is the band's manager, David, who is the enabling friend to Paul, satiating his whims before pulling the plug on his excesses by revealing that the Byzantine amounts of money Paul has been spending was not actually his, but a loan advanced by the record company and secured against future expected profits. In this he is like Ekart, who abets Baal's profligate life but also is the one that ends the sequence of debauch.

Ronald Gray says that *Baal* 'has no concern at all with poverty or with criticism of capitalism' (1976: 20). While it is true that Brecht composed the play before he adopted Marxist thought as an organizing principle within his work, he did later reflect that it showed how artists not seeking to profit from their work were inimical to capitalism. As he stated: 'Baal's art of living shares the fate of all arts under capitalism: it is warred upon. Baal is asocial, but in an asocial society' (qtd in Ewan 1970: 98). It is this notion of the artist under capitalism that provides the basis for the connective tissue between *Baal* and *Birdland*, with both Baal and Paul avatars of creation and destruction, simultaneously creative and productive artists who are nevertheless vampirically extractive of the essences of people around them. The important difference is that Brecht's Baal is resolutely indigent and unconcerned with capitalizing on his artistic talent, but his contemporary analogue Paul knows only profit with his crude equation of monetary value as the sole calculus of essential worth. The real horror of Stephens's transposition is in the way that his updated incarnation of Baal pridefully monetizes his own artistic value, and in doing so becomes an emblem of contemporary capitalism. This is what makes *Birdland* a *Baal* for our time. In Paul, Stephens augments and accelerates destructive tendencies only nascent in Baal to formalize a critique adequate to encompass the liabilities, malfunctions and depredations of the debt-fuelled conspicuous consumption and predatory financial chicanery that characterizes neoliberal capitalism. Paul can only navigate personal relationships through the medium of transactions – his reunion with his father involves him paying off an extortionate loan trifling to him but crippling to his father, and Paul nevertheless expects his father to pay him back. When visiting Marnie's bereaved parents Paul pointedly and deliberately offers to buy them luxury items as if their grief is redeemable through auction.

While both Baal and Paul have absolute freedom from moral scruples in the way they use others as mere props for their own satisfaction, their other defining feature is their relentless appetite. *Birdland* begins with Paul's ostentatious admiration of a peach: 'This is a really spectacular peach. It's absolutely fucking unbelievably fresh' (8). This attitude towards food expands to encompass more conspicuous and outlandish consumption, from artisan shoes to private helicopters. Baal moves through the play, in the words of Frederic Ewan 'wasting not only himself but other people as well, consuming, consuming, and never satisfied' (Ewan 1970: 95). Stephens accentuates this aspect of Paul, an attribute which, as Andrew Haydon notes, was ramped up in Carrie Cracknell's Royal Court production: 'He is always eating. More and more. Other characters comment on it. The amount he eats, the way he eats repulses them. [. . .] He's got fat' (2014b: online). Stephens updates Baal in Paul by linking his insatiable appetite and instinctive consumerism to an unabashed admiration for capitalism, proclaiming that the price of something is the only determinant of its value, and that the market system is the force responsible for raising living standards worldwide: 'This is the best time we've ever lived in. [. . .] Globally. Look at the statistics' (10). On the face of it, this makes Paul's reckless and extravagant debt-fuelled spending an obvious metaphor for the systemic risk, lack of moral hazard and institutional rot that led to the Credit Crunch, global financial crisis and subsequent Great Recession brought about by the banking system and the financial services industry in 2008. This was a parallel which escaped few critics, with Stewart Pringle of *Exeunt* describing Paul as 'rotting into the subprime' (Pringle 2014). While Paul is a walking aberration and repudiation of essential human goodness and solidarity, his views are entirely inkeeping with the mainstream of capitalist thought as it is applied in metric-led technocratic neoliberal governance and conceptualized by advocates of globalization and economic liberalization. Baal uses others instrumentally out of atavistic appetite; Paul uses others according to the dominant economic and political notions of our time.

Punk Rock/Spring Awakening/Elephant

A host of influences feed into Stephens's 2009 play *Punk Rock*, but prime among them, as with *Birdland* and *Motortown*, is an avant-garde German play written over a hundred years ago. In this instance, the play that most informs Stephens's text is Frank Wedekind's *Spring Awakening*, a *fin de siècle* work that deals uncompromisingly with the tragedy engendered when nascent adolescent sexuality comes up against the repressive strictures of a hidebound and uncomprehending bourgeois morality. As with *Motortown*, film also provided a repository of influence for Stephens's play, with Gus Van Sant's *Elephant* (2003) an important contributing factor.

Elephant is Van Sant's response to the 1999 Columbine High School massacre, and *Punk Rock* follows it in dealing with the subject of a school shooting. Like *Spring Awakening*, it stages the familiar teenage experience of the woeful mismatch between apparently abstruse formal education and the confused and inexpert apprehension of sexual maturity and adult responsibility. An attempt to render an objective, distanciated perspective on a complex and emotive issue, Van Sant's *Elephant* is resolutely remote, affectless and non-sensationalistic, aligning with no specific characters and instead mainly composed of Steadicam shots that track over the shoulder of the students, charting their discontinuous interconnectedness over the course of the school day. This dispassionate approach is maintained throughout, even as the duo of shooters conduct their violent rampage over the last half hour of the film. By contrast, *Spring Awakening* is a remarkably torrid and emotionally febrile account of awkward sexual misadventure, child abuse and punitive reactionary authoritarianism that leads to rape, suicide and a botched abortion. The mixing of these two approaches from the inherited material makes Stephens's *Punk Rock* a distinctive and effective blend. The play adopts the non-judgemental posture of *Elephant* in offering open yet provocative questions but, equally, gives an uncompromising account of the quandaries confronted by the youths it depicts that recalls the frank investment in adolescent interiority favoured by *Spring Awakening*.

Punk Rock is an adaptation in the mould of *Motortown* rather than *Birdland*, in that it distils the essence of its precursive texts rather than replicating elements of scene and structure. As with *Spring Awakening*, there is a distinct social pecking order in the group of students, but unlike the strategy of transposing and updating identifiable characters from precursive texts evident in *Motortown* and *Birdland*, the students of *Punk Rock* are vibrant and original twenty-first-century creations, even if Stephens sustains clear resonances between the issues that afflict his grammar-school students and their predecessors. As with *Spring Awakening*, the educational context of the play is crucial. Studying for mock exams that will both validate the school fees paid by their parents and provide an indication of their destination in terms of a career or an elite university, the students of *Punk Rock* are consumed with anxiety and terrified of failure. In *Spring Awakening*, Moritz is permanently anxious about his schooling and, while he passes his mid-term exams, becomes so traumatized by his subsequent failure to improve and eventual expulsion from school that he commits suicide. As with Moritz, who reads *Faust* and Homer, and does Greek, Latin and quadratic equations, the students of *Punk Rock* are generally portrayed as articulate, knowledgeable and interested in the world around them: even discounting the remarkable intellectual facility of Chadwick, who variously parses Paul Dirac, anti-matter and the size of the universe, topics like architecture and the history of Stockport are casually thrown around in common-room conversation. Similarly to *Spring Awakening*, there is the sense that the real and important knowledge transactions occurring are in the students' interrogation of each other's aspirations and anxieties rather than in their formal teaching: both plays feature the youngsters asking frequent questions about themselves and their situation, looking for and yielding insights which set curriculums are inadequate to teach and exams are inadequate to test. The youth of both *Spring Awakening* and *Punk Rock* long for escape from provincial life, which in the former play is relayed by Ilse's scandalous reports of her wild bohemian excursions, and in the latter in reiterated wishes 'Just to get out' (2011: 330) of Stockport.[22] In William's mind this is represented by his 'life's ambition' (312) to study at Cambridge University, but for Cissy it could be 'Edinburgh. Glasgow. Dublin. Paris. Anywhere apart from here' (351).

Stephens's students, like Wedekind's over a hundred years before, are afraid of their bodies: how they appear, how they work, what they might be capable of. They share an incredulity at adult life and behaviour frequently characterized by imaginative projections concerning how they would treat their children if they were adults: while Moritz hypothesises that having brothers and sisters share beds might prevent his future progeny from being as tense and frightened as he is, in *Punk Rock* the three female students' estimation of their own parenting runs all the way from 'putting them in a cupboard' (349) to 'Tennis lessons. Football lessons. Ballet lessons. Anything they want' (350). Here Stephens preserves the sense, inherited from *Spring Awakening*, that while the present is, to use a pair of words iterated through the text, 'unsettling' and 'unnerving', all sense of prospect is caught up in strangulated adolescent fears.

While they dramatize very different things, the final scene of *Punk Rock* echoes the climate of thought broached in the final action of *Spring Awakening*. At the end of *Punk Rock*, William, the shooter, is incarcerated in a medium security hospital with a seemingly endless questionnaire designed by psychiatrists to evaluate his mental state. Rather than his mock exams, which represented a possible pathway to a positive future, William must now complete this test which will evaluate neither his knowledge nor his capacity to think but which, over the course of 1,800 questions, will apparently tell others who he is. After the play's nervous kinetics, not to mention its horrifying finale, there is a self-contained and studious atmosphere. However, William is interrupted by the unexpected appearance of Nicholas, one of the students that he murdered, who enters, sits across from him, says nothing and then abruptly exits, 'as *though he'd forgotten something and has to rush to get it*' (406–7). A comparable sense of contemplation and uncertainty characterizes the final enigmatic scene of *Spring Awakening*. Like William, Melchior has extracted himself from his educational environment as he flees reform school and an uncertain future awaits. Entering a graveyard at night, he comes across the resting places of Moritz and Wendla, the latter having died as a result of her attempt to abort Melchior's baby. As with William, Melchior encounters his dead friend when Moritz appears and attempts to convince Melchior to join him among the dead: 'infinitely above all despair and rejoicing' (Wedekind 2009: 66). In both plays the apparition is a powerful coup de théâtre that takes the audience suddenly out of the pre-existing naturalistic co-ordinates and presents an abject stage spectacle of thwarted youth and potential by producing an almost Shakespearean ghost. Melchior nearly succumbs, but decides instead to follow a mysterious Masked Man who enters the graveyard and sardonically deflects Moritz's pitiable entreaties to his friend to give up on life. The Masked Man offers no guarantees other than to introduce Melchior 'to every single interesting thing in the world' (Wedekind 2009: 69). Melchior submits to an unknown future, metaphorically on the cusp of a rapidly modernizing and mechanizing twentieth century, a punctual point in history that prompted Edward Bond, translator of the 1974 text of the play, to ask: 'Did the Masked Man lead Melchior to die in the First World War, going straight from spring to winter?' (Bond 2009: xxix).

William is shaken by Nicholas's appearance, and ends the play expressing the aspiration for a regular life: 'Just be normal. Go to hospital one day and get my head sorted out. Buy a small house. Not spend too much money' (410). The pathos in these lines is all the more evident because of the way that William has foreclosed on any positive future by perpetrating what Stephens has called a 'murderous suicide' (qtd in Love 2016b: 1). No clear motive or explanation for the shooting is offered, nor is one evident from the sequence of events in the play. William's disappointment in being romantically rebuffed by Lilly and his strange reaction to the death of Mr Lloyd would not appear to constitute significant enough reasons for the extremity of his actions. He is a witness to Bennett's bullying rather than the object of it, and the revelation of his dead brother is only referred to fleetingly. He affects to prefer being alone at the outset but can interact with others well enough; only his tendency towards fabulism marks him out as being in any way different from the crowd. This corresponds well with the presentation of the killers in *Elephant*, who are shown playing violent videogames and watching Nazi documentaries together, but also playing Beethoven's *Moonlight Sonata*, eating breakfast and kissing in the shower. The film declined to offer anything other than an indistinct composite picture rather than anything that prescribed a direct aetiology of the incident. In keeping William's motivation fundamentally enigmatic Stephens is consistent with the approach pursued by Van Sant's film, which in itself was a response to the general societal incomprehension at what motivated the Columbine killers Dylan Klebold and Eric Harris themselves. Speaking to *Time Out*, Van Sant remarked that he had put a phrase that the Columbine killers wrote down in the mouths of the killers in his film:

They wrote a list of things they wanted to do, and at the end of it was to have fun. 'One: Get Joshua Jackson. Two: Storm the library. Three: Have fun.' That's a quote. (qtd in Said 2004: 18)

William refuses to offer up any significant rationale for his deed beyond the bland pabulum, 'I did it because I could. I did it because it felt fucking great' (408). Exposing a lacuna in both motive and meaning in favour of an emphatic insistence on the primacy of the sensory and affective potency of the deed itself, it adds up to, as Stephens says, a 'narcissistic nihilism' (qtd in Love 2016b: 1) that succinctly characterizes the lethal, inarticulate, uncomprehending destructiveness of not only William, but, as we have seen, of Danny and Paul as well.

Conclusion: Towards an adaptive originality

William's statement 'it felt fucking great' is not only a possible reference to *Elephant*, but almost certainly also a verbatim lifting of a notorious phrase from Sarah Kane's play *4.48 Psychosis* (2000). While this chapter has focused on Stephens's engagement with canonical modernist and pre-modernist avant-garde dramatic texts, there remains much to say about the influence of the generation of playwrights that precede him. Moreover, even with the attention paid to canonical palimpsest texts rather than these less overt influences, this chapter cannot hope to encompass the true extent of Stephens's manipulations of prior texts. Stephens has written an English-language version of Odön von Horváth's 1932 political whirlwind *Kasimir and Karoline* under the title *The Funfair* (2015), as the opening play for the Manchester theatre venue HOME, consciously undated to address the political salience of the rise of UKIP and Nigel Farage. *Carmen Disruption* (2012) twists Bizet's opera *Carmen* (1875) into a fragmented text about social breakdown under late-capitalism, with Stephens's image of a dying Europe, as Dan Rebellato observed 'never more bracingly caught than in the enormous gored bull dying at the centre of the Almeida stage' (Rebellato 2015). Stephens has also reimagined Alfred Jarry's grotesque, scatological 1896 pastiche of *Macbeth*, *Ubu Roi*, in the form of the *Trial of Ubu* (2010), and provided a version of Euripides's *Medea* set in late 1970s Manchester with *Blindsided* (2014).[23] Some of these instances might qualify as more thoroughgoing adaptations than original plays fashioned from precursive templates, others are certainly less moored to their predecessors;

all nonetheless function as repurposed and rearticulated prior texts that appraise the fears, anxieties and malfunctions of the contemporary world that Stephens habitually lays bare.

While it is clear that his promiscuous appropriation of influence can be plotted on a continuum from merely finding inspiration in a song or an image, to the assimilation and adaptation of an entire prior work, his imaginative process as a playwright is always, in essence, adaptive.

THE DIRECTORS

Andrew Haydon

One of the most striking features about Simon Stephens as a playwright is the unusual extent to which he gives his directors autonomy. In a domestic theatre culture that often prides itself on the power vested in The Writer, Stephens is interesting for the way in which he seems fascinated by directors, and by the endless possibilities for his plays that they might create. It is clear that he counts his many directors as artists, collaborators and equals, rather than servants tasked with executing a playwright's minutely detailed orders. It is fascinating to note the extent to which these directors of world première productions have often shaped the play itself; how their notes and cuts may often become part of the fabric of the 'extant text by Simon Stephens' – an ironic contrast to the process in Germany, where a particular staging may eviscerate the script, but the published version handed by Stephens to his German agent remains intact.

Marianne Elliott *directed the world premières of* Port, Harper Regan *and* The Curious Incident of the Dog in the Night-Time, *as well as reviving* Port *for the National Theatre in 2013. She has been an associate director at the Royal Exchange Theatre, Manchester and the National Theatre, London. She is now the Artistic Director of Elliott Harper Productions, whose inaugural production was the UK première of Stephens's* Heisenberg. *This interview took place on 16 November 2015.*

How did your working relationship with Simon begin?
I liked his writing from the very early days when he was a really young writer. I saw *Bluebird*; I think I read *Bluebird*, and I think it was because of that that Sarah [Frankcom] and I really wanted him to be a resident writer at the Royal Exchange. It was then working with him around the Royal Exchange that I got very close to him and we started working together a lot. And then, only recently, when we were being interviewed about *Curious Incident*, we realised that we had not only lived very close to each other in Stockport as children but that we actually used to get the same bus to school, and used to wait at the same bus stop every morning. And he remembered me! [. . .] There are lots and lots of similarities between us because we were brought up within a half-mile radius of each other in a very specific town, so I think I really connect to Simon's work – not all of it, but a lot of it – on a really fundamental level. It's hard to articulate exactly what it is.

The plays of Simon's that you've directed [Port, Harper Regan, The Curious Incident of the Dog in the Night-Time] *are all very different. Did you approach directing each of them differently?*
I don't think so. I approached them all in the same way I always approach a script, in terms of the amount of research and the amount of prep and the amount of thinking and the design work. [. . .] I do a lot of work on the characters' back stories, and on their through-lines and objectives and the super-objectives of each character. I work out why the characters are speaking when they're speaking and exactly what it is that they're saying. So it's all very character-driven. I do a lot of work with the actors, we improvise a lot, scenes before and after the actual written scenes. I think that Simon works quite musically; his rhythms are so important, I would never ignore any of his punctuation. For example, he might put four full stops in a sentence of only five words and things like that are quite important in terms of how the character is feeling. And there's usually a lot of subtext as well, which is what I love about his work. There are lots of things that aren't said, that can't be said, and a huge amount of feeling beyond what is actually written down.

He's very free with directors and allows them carte blanche, really. He allows them to do all sorts of sacrilegious things to his writing that a lot of other writers wouldn't allow. He's worked with some German directors who are very free with his texts indeed. I haven't been in the past, I've been pedantically respectful. That isn't to say he hasn't rewritten them with my requests but, as far as the actors are concerned, we try to follow what he's trying to say.

You can do some really fascinating things with the actors on his texts. For example, you can work on objectives, as per normal, but you can also work on subconscious objectives; objectives that the characters aren't aware of. And that's really brilliant. It's really exciting doing work like that. There's a lot of subconscious in Simon's writing, I think he mines quite a lot of depth that he doesn't even know about. I remember when we started work on *Port*, there were something like fifty different ways of naming death in the script, and he had never seen that. But he was dealing, at the time, with his father's death and, although he was writing about a very different subject, this still came out in the writing.

Port is, really, about the end of eras. It's snapshots of different moments from Rachael's life. And each snapshot means that it's the end of a certain era and the beginning of a new one. That means there's all sorts of murky juicy waters that you find yourself in, when you really get to the bottom of what he's writing about. It's very rich.

You first directed Port *at the Royal Manchester Exchange in 2002. What was it like to revive the play at the National Theatre eleven years later?*
The biggest thing was that second time around we were producing the show in a vast proscenium arch space – the Lyttleton – which is used mainly for classic plays which are usually more verbose than modern plays. It's used for plays that are already well known; are more sure-fire hitters. The stage is very high from the auditorium so it presents the play with a kind of reverence. So it's quite difficult to get small intimate textual moments across in the Lyttleton. The Royal Exchange, on the other hand, is built to be intimate – not one seat is more than 30ft away from the stage. We decided to embrace the largeness of the stage at the National Theatre and put these characters and the minutiae of their lives in this vast concrete landscape, so you're always seeing the microcosmic within the macrocosmic. You're always putting them in the context of the world around them. That made it much more of a political play than it had maybe been at the Royal Exchange.

I didn't think I'd ever want to redo a show of anything I'd already done. [. . .] But I really thoroughly enjoyed doing *Port* again. I think probably because it has a lot of me in it that I'm not aware of. The whole experience was just as rich the second time, even though we were doing it a different way. I don't think we did anything the same, apart from use the Stone Roses song at the end ['This Is the One', 1989]. And we didn't set out to do the opposite, but I thought there was still something very live about that play. I'd wanted to make it about death, the first time. With the second production I wanted to make it more about growing up in Manchester.

Was there a feeling of having to explain *Manchester when you were doing it in London?*
That is a good question. I don't think there was ever a feeling that we had to explain Manchester, but to portray it very authentically. [. . .] It's a big theatre, so it has a more wide-ranging audience than, say, the Cottesloe [now Dorfman, at the National Theatre] where we did *Harper Regan*. We were grateful for that, because a lot of people, wherever they were from, they really connected to that story. And yet [. . .] a few London reviewers drew comparisons with [the long-running ITV soap opera set in a fictional town in the north of England] *Coronation Street,* just because of the northern accents. Really extraordinary. It's so completely the opposite to *Coronation Street*. Still, it's got northern accents, so people put the two together.

You directed Harper Regan *in 2008, with Lesley Sharp in the eponymous role. Yet I understand that in early drafts the title character was originally male – Seth Regan. What do you make of Stephens's female characters?*

It was handed to me as a play about a woman. I think Simon's really, really good at writing female characters. He's got a lot of very strong women in his life and he always has had. And he just sort of *gets* them, I think. And he writes them in a very detailed, sensitive way, and they have a huge amount of strength in them. I think he enjoys writing about women. And there aren't that many interesting writers out there putting interesting female characters at the forefront of their stories. Particularly stories where they're not victimised, where you get to understand the character, warts-and-all, and get to empathise with them all the way through, even though they've got some massive hurdles that they have to cross. And sometimes they don't cross them particularly heroically. So it's extraordinary to come across a writer who is (a) interested and (b) sensitively executing material for women. I'm surprised that he ever wrote Harper Regan as a man; it must have been a very early version. As far as I'm concerned, she is absolutely, totally female, that character.

Sarah Frankcom *joined the Royal Exchange Theatre, Manchester, as Literary Manager in 2000. She became an Artistic Director of the theatre in 2008, becoming the sole Artistic Director in 2014. In 2019 she was appointed director of London Academy of Music and Dramatic Art. She directed the world premières of* On the Shore of the Wide World, Punk Rock *and* Blindsided. *This interview took place on 22 November 2015.*

The first play of Simon's that you directed was On the Shore of the Wide World, *at the Royal Exchange, Manchester.*

Simon and I talked about that play quite recently because someone quite well-known asked him 'Why can't you go back to writing nice family dramas?' And I don't think that's a play that's a 'nice family drama'. I think there's a lot more going on. But it's ostensibly something recognisable, that people can relate to. It doesn't scare the horses, formally. I'm really fond of that play. It interests me when I go back to it because I always admire it more than I think I'm going to. [. . .] That play is in part a meditation on how an alcoholic affects a family. Really, it's a play about recovery. [. . .]

In that first production, we cut a scene from the play in which Christopher comes back as a ghost. In terms of the architecture of the play it's a scene that doesn't bear any relationship to any other, either tonally, or in terms of narrative. It's completely out of the blue. I couldn't make the scene work, and the actor couldn't make the scene work, so on the first or second preview I cut it. And it never returned. Of course, now it's the scene that interests me most about the whole play. Sebastian Nübling came to see the production [. . .] and I just remember him saying to me afterwards how *horrified* he was that that scene wasn't there! And I remember thinking [of Simon], 'Oh, this is really interesting, you're having parallel relationships. There are two things happening here. There's how you are working within a very traditional, very UK theatre-writing system, and there's also how you are starting to develop some of your sensibilities somewhere else'.

Ramin Gray *was Artistic Director of Actors Touring Company from 2011 to 2018, and was previously an associate director of the Royal Court Theatre, London, where he directed the world première of* Motortown. *This interview took place on 27 February 2016.*

How did you come to direct Motortown *at the Royal Court?*
It was the 50th anniversary of the English Stage Company. I'd been at the Court since 2000, which is when Simon joined as writer-in-residence. I think we always had a mutual respect and admiration but also a slightly guarded thing. I don't know that he particularly liked my work and I'm not sure I was especially enamoured with some of his work. I was international associate, so I was always looking at plays by Jon Fosse, Roland Schimmelpfennig and Marius von Mayenburg, and I found some of his writing to be a little bit sentimental, actually, for my taste. His background as a teacher means that there's something in some of his early plays that feels like the best part of a teacher: 'I want these characters to do better; these people are in trouble, how can I help them?' But I remember vividly Simon coming to see *Ladybird*, a play by Vassily Sigarev, which had the actor Danny Mays in it.[24] And I remember when the lights came up he turned and said to me, 'I'm going to write something for Danny Mays'.

He was commissioned by Ian [Rickson] to write something for the Royal Court Downstairs. And he came in one day and said, 'Is Ian in?' And I said 'No'. And he said 'Look, I've written my commission. Here it is'. And I said, 'Oh. Great. I'll give it to Ian'. And he gave it to me and, of course, I read it. And I was completely blown away by it. I thought. This. Is. Amazing. Of course, Ian came in the next day, and I said 'It's come in. It's fucking amazing. Have a read'. Ian read it, came back, said 'This is great. We should do it'. And I said 'We should'. And Ian said, 'Will you phone up, err . . . Peter Gill and see if he's free? No. Roger Michell. Will you phone up Roger

Michell and see if he's free?' So I phoned up Roger Michell and he read it and he said, 'yeah, it's great. It's a shame there isn't a scene where all eight of them do something. I really like it, but no thanks'. So I offer it to so-and-so, and to so-and-so; and this with about eight directors I had to send it to. And I was just combusting with thwarted-ness. And eventually Ian went, 'You quite like this, don't you?' And I said 'I fucking love it', and he said 'why don't you do it?' and I said 'Ok'.

He then said 'We've got no money'. And I said, 'that's fine. I don't need anything for this'. I knew exactly how I wanted to do it. I knew what I had to do was make something that looked like a William Forsythe show.[25] That's the truth of it. So the aesthetic – grey dance floor and some chairs – is pure Forsythe. And I remembered what Roger Michell had said, and I thought he's right actually: you do need to do something with all eight actors, you can't have them all sitting in their dressing rooms coming on and doing one scene and going off. And if I'm not going to have a set, I'm going to need to do something. So I set about looking for a choreographer. Hofesh Shechter had just arrived in the UK and he'd done some stuff at The Place,[26] and we talked, and I liked him, and I said, 'do you want to work with me?'. And he said 'Is it a play?'. So I sent it to him, we started talking, and it was the beginning of a really happy collaboration. Throwing Hofesh in was sort of like a curve ball.

What appealed so much to you about the play?
Simon, brilliantly, wrote that play with the characters having the [intended] actors' names. And that really turned me on. There is an infinitesimal amount of material between the actor and the audience. And once you realise that, you realise you don't need a set. It has what I call 'Forest of Arden' lines, so a character will say 'Oh, so this is Foulness Island', and you know exactly where you are. You don't need to have an island set.

So, we got Danny Mays and we got a really good company of actors around him. I knew two things. I knew that Jade [Ony Uhiara] would be shot and I knew that it would be fantastic if there could be a lot of blood. So all I did was ask for a pump under the floor that would pump huge amounts of blood. And I needed some school chairs, like the ones used in *The Events*.[27] It's all the same aesthetic as *The Events*, really. And then I needed something to get from scene to scene. The action couldn't be continuous. The image I used with Hofesh [was], 'If we're building a wall, the bricks are Simon's scenes, and you're going to make the mortar to hold the wall up'.

There were two other things. I needed some English music. It's an English play. It's not a British play, it's an English play. It's about England. It's about a working-class Englishman [. . .] So I needed some English music, and I found – oddly, on Radio 3 – a two-piece band from Leeds called That Fucking Tank. And I had that, and a bit of Purcell. I had 'Dido's Lament', an incredibly beautiful piece of music, as everybody wiped up the enormous amount of blood. Which I nicked from Alain Platel.[28] But at its core, the reason it was brilliant wasn't any of those things, but because Danny Mays gave a knockout brilliant performance. It was just one of those things that worked.

How would you describe the aesthetic of the play, or your production of it?
There's a really weird line in the play. They're on Foulness Island, and he's torturing the girl, and he's screaming orders at her and he says 'Put your hand on the floor. Put your hand on the floor'. And I said, 'Simon, they're on an island, surely you'd say "put your hand on the ground"'. And he said 'Oh, yeah. Shall I change it?' And I said, 'Nah, it's ok. Leave it. Leave it. It's wonderful, because you're writing for the theatre. You're not writing naturalism'.

Another thing – I was a bit nervous, because I'd been directing all these weird foreign plays so I was worried that he might not take me seriously as a director of – on the face of it – a naturalistic British play. So I said to him 'we should do a Royal Court thing, we should do research. We can go to all the locations of the play. We can go to Foulness Island, we can go to military barracks and all that sort of shit'. And Simon's reaction was really interesting. He kind of flinched and he said 'Really?' And I was like 'Yeah, why not? It'll be really interesting!'. And I can't remember how he put it but I got the sense that he was saying 'too much light shed on this thing might make it crumple'. And that was a really key moment in our relationship. Because he was steering me away from doing the naturalistic sort of thing, which I never wanted to do anyway. So we found ourselves in sync.

So it opened and it was running at the Court at the time when *Look Back in Anger* would have been playing fifty years before and it was about an angry young man and it sat in that space in a really pure way. And I think we were all really, really proud of it. I was proud of it. Danny was proud of it. Simon was really proud of it. Hofesh was really proud of it. And it divided people. Some people loathed Hofesh's work. 'What are those silly dancing chairs. What are they? Take them away. Don't fuck about'.

Sean Holmes *was Artistic Director of the Lyric Hammersmith, London, from 2009 to 2018. He directed the British premières of* Pornography, A Thousand

Stars Explode in the Sky, Morning *and the first major UK revival of* Herons. *This interview took place on 24 March 2016.*

How did you arrive at your aesthetic for Pornography?
I think I'm probably in more of a position to articulate it now than I was then because I think that it was probably the beginning of a journey towards a more deconstructed, metaphorical language of theatre. For me, the real breakthrough for that play and that design was that every scene took place in the theatre. So the bar was exactly the same as the Traverse stage, the tube train was exactly the same as the Traverse stage. That liberated us from the literalism of 'let's pretend that this eight-foot square is now the tube carriage'. You know, 'let's *not* pretend that wobbling on top of two chairs put together is "being in a tube carriage"; let's sit opposite each other on this empty stage but let's be in a tube carriage'. And that seemed to work really well. [. . .] I also think it's one of the first times that I said – and only because I knew the writer who had done it – 'oh, sod this, we need to create something ourselves'. I wouldn't have used the word at the time but I suppose I was my own dramaturg. That second section of rehearsal in Birmingham, we basically – probably not with the rigour that I would apply now but with a kind of instinct – we chopped, changed and moved things around in a way that I felt worked.

Morning *was the next play of Simon's that you directed.*
In terms of the production, *Morning* was really a response to *Three Kingdoms*. [. . .] You know what's really interesting? I think my most important relationship with Simon is not with his plays, in funny way. I think there are other people, like Sarah [Frankcom], or Marianne [Elliot], who are more consistently directors of Simon's plays, if you see what I mean. Whereas I think what is interesting is the joint artistic journey that we've been on together since *Pornography*, and particularly through the Lyric, which I think reached its height with *Three Kingdoms*. And with *Morning*, both of us were trying something in response to what we saw Sebastian [Nübling] doing with the Junges Theater in Basel. So, if you were going to say 'who's done the landmark productions of Simon's plays?', it would probably be Marianne who's in that really tight director/writer relationship with him. But with us it's been more a case of, like, together we've been able to push ourselves and the language of what we're putting onstage.

So, originally, *Morning* came out of a workshop with three young people from our young company at the Lyric and three young people from the

Junges Theater, Basel. But – unlike with *Three Kingdoms*, where at the heart of the play was the gesture of international collaboration – it felt like a play that was about the concerns of young people in these different countries, and [that internationalism] didn't quite make sense; it would have felt odd to just have kids from Switzerland and England in it, without crowbarring that idea in. So in the end there were two separate productions, here and in Switzerland. That was also a play where we swapped the genders, so in the original draft the murderers were boys.

In 2016, the Lyric Hammersmith staged the first major British revival of Herons. *How closely did you work with Simon on this revival?*
Simon had very little to do with that production; so, there, his absence was as important as his involvement. And his maturity to be able to allow us that freedom, in the same way that he would allow theatres overseas that freedom. *Herons* is set in a very specific milieu – white working-class, East End – and it seems to me that [Simon is exploring] a world in which the weak bully the weaker, and the logic of the society that can push people into that behaviour [. . .] One of the first lines of the play is 'everyone's always lying' and it's a world in which everyone is always imposing their truth. So it's obvious that Scott's brother horribly murdered this girl, yet the first scene is Scott insisting that this is not the case, through violence, fear and intimidation. I think we live in a world where this happens all the time, where truths are imposed upon us.

Joel [Horwood][29] and I really deliberately attacked that play dramaturgically. We cut at least a third, if not half of the play. It's interesting, when you're working in a more metaphorical and abstract space, and you're working with images, you suddenly understand why the Germans cut so much, because psychological backstory is just unnecessary [. . .] That production of *Herons* was born out of *Pornography*, through *Morning*, through *Three Kingdoms*, through Secret Theatre.[30] What I really liked about *Herons,* was I felt really in charge of the decisions. The whole process behind it was really rigorous: the design, the lighting, the confidence and the ownership of the young performers, of all the performers, it felt like that's what we wanted to do in that moment with that play. And that came from Simon's willingness, freedom and trust to just let us do it.

Katie Mitchell *is a freelance theatre director who works across the UK and Europe, previously associate director at both the Royal Court and the National Theatre. She directed the world première of* Wastwater, *the UK première of* The

Trial of Ubu *and Stephens's version of* The Cherry Orchard. *This interview took place on 5 February 2016.*

You've directed both original works by Stephens and his adaptations, or 'versions', of canonical texts. Is working on 'a version' like working on 'a Simon Stephens play'?
No. I don't think it is, because whenever you do a version, you've always got an intermediary. For *The Cherry Orchard*, for example, we were working very much from Helen Rappaport's literal translation from the Russian, and from her amazing footnotes. That means that you've got this almost scientific document. So you're trying to follow that document and honour it. [Original] writing is not like that, it has more freedom in it.

You directed Wastwater *at the Royal Court Theatre Downstairs in April 2011. What was the genesis of this production?*
Dominic [Cooke, then Artistic Director of the Royal Court] wanted very much to encourage Simon formally, [so] the genesis was from Dominic initially pushing and setting new formal rules for Simon to write within. Dominic sent the script over to me when I was working in Copenhagen and, well, it's just a masterpiece, isn't it? I was very, very happy. Because it's formally exquisite, and radical, and the content is really important. The way the story plays itself out in that strange sequence of relationships is exquisite. [. . .] If you were to look at it from a feminist point of view, the balance of the three women is amazing as well – twenties, thirties, fifties [. . .] so it's well thought-through in terms of gender too. [. . .]

A real hidden and brilliant colleague on that play, though, was [the designer] Lizzie Clachan.[31] Because what she did, together with Paul Handley,[32] the production manager, was just incredible. To deliver – on that money, at that speed – those three different environments . . . It was an amazing piece of set design and production management. Because the play only really works formally if you move really quickly from one naturalistic environment to the next. Long scene changes would formally destroy the movement of the piece.

Did the play change much in rehearsals?
We did want it to have a coda, which actually we put in but then we took out. There was this fourth scene. It was there in one of the previews. The curtain went down, and then it went up again and we just saw the empty warehouse, and a loud airplane just flying over. It was to last not seconds

but *minutes*. It would have been great. Really amazing! I can't remember our reasoning. [. . .] It's night, isn't it, when they're in the warehouse? So it was just that moment when dawn comes up and the birds start to sing, and this amazing sunlight flooded into the warehouse and an airplane flies over. But we lost our nerve. We said, 'we'll do that in Germany, we can't do that here'.

Carrie Cracknell *directed* Birdland, *loosely based on Brecht's play,* Baal, *at the Royal Court Theatre Downstairs in 2014. Prior to this, she directed Stephens's version of* Henrik Ibsen's A Doll's House *at the Young Vic in 2012. This interview took place on 14 March 2016.*

Did you approach Birdland *as an adaptation of Brecht's original play?*
No, I didn't spend a lot of time considering that original text within the process; the relationship [between the two plays] felt quite loose and transient [in comparison to] the experience of working on *A Doll's House*. What I tried to do was unlock the play that I thought Simon was trying to write and find a language for that. Which I think is the job of a director working with a living writer – to reflect back to him what he has written and ask him to clarify what he was trying to say.

In Simon Stephens: A Working Diary, *there's a fascinating entry from 14th January 2014, where he reflects on the re-writes he is making during rehearsals for* Birdland: *'I tried to reign back on the misogyny in that first draft', he writes. 'It's alarming to me that when I was writing so unconsciously I should produce a character whose apparent hatred of women was so inchoate and uncontrolled' (2016: 19). Could you talk about this issue of misogyny in* Birdland?
Interestingly, we did a reading of *Birdland* in the rehearsal room during the process of *Blurred Lines*.[33] So, of course, I was looking at the play through a very particular set of goggles – I mean, that's my set of goggles generally – but I was in a very particular place because of what I was making and where my mind was. I guess Simon was very conscious of that, and in that reading he saw that there were structural elements of the play which were really gendered, and that it was quite violent in terms of its gender politics. He felt that that was very much the action of the central male character – and I think that was true, that's who he was writing and it was the world he was writing about – but I also think there were political questions about the wider connotations of that violence that weren't being addressed. So, yeah, we had that conversation and I think some notes that I had given were thrown into relief by that reading and he became much

clearer about what he'd written. [He saw] a play that came very much from an unconscious set of drivers or an unconscious set of things that were being worked through.

I'd always assumed that the structural elements of violence were a direct inheritance from Brecht's play. How did the play change, after that reading?
There was a recalibration after that and it became more about why the protagonist, Paul, was falling apart, and what the world he was living within was doing to him, and the ways in which he was lashing out at both the men and women in his life. I think that was a useful and interesting recalibration and it made the play more complex. Some of the most interesting scenes in the play concerned the break-up between the two [male] friends, and the relationship between the father and son.

Do you consider that part of your job as a feminist director is to reduce the amount of violence against women on stage?
I have a responsibility as a maker, yes, to ask questions about what we're representing on stage, whether that's about women being sexualised, whether that's about women not being the protagonist, whether it's about using sexual violence against women as a plot development point, and to ask whether that happens in a way that is casually culturally reinforcing, as opposed to [deliberately culturally] challenging. I think [the former] happens an enormous amount, particularly in television drama but also in film and theatre. There's a fundamental question about the normalisation of sexual violence. It's something that happens on an unbelievable scale and there are lots of really complex forces at work around that – about why men do that to women, why we constantly make culture about men doing that to women – and there are some big and thorny questions to ask about that. I worry that simply restating that in a non-questioning way isn't helping that narrative move forward.

It came also from a conversation with Nick Payne during *Blurred Lines* in which he felt there's an enormous amount of male responsibility regarding this. As he put it, rape is a male problem: why are we not talking to men about it? Why is it considered to be a female problem? Because the violence and fucked-up-ness lives in men. Women have to survive that and move forward through it and, in a way, be permanently marked by it – but at its core it's about male weakness. And I found that really provocative, and really interesting, and so for me that is an ongoing, burning conversation that we should be having within culture.

NOTES

Introduction

1. Stephens, Word document titled 'questionnaire_munich', n.d.
2. The exam boards are AQA and Eduqas/WJEC. The other play is Dennis Kelly's *DNA* (2008).
3. Stephens's astonishing productivity as a writer has necessitated a selective approach to his corpus. Co-authored works – such as *Marine Parade* (2010, with singer-songwriter Mark Eitzel) or *A Thousand Stars Explode in the Sky* (2010, with David Eldridge and Robert Holman) or *Fatherland* (2018, with Scott Graham and Karl Hyde) – together with Stephens's new versions of classic texts (by, for example, Chekov, Ibsen and Horváth), are omitted from this study.
4. I thank Stephens's English agency, Casarotto, Ramsay and Associates, and particularly Emma Magnus, for this information.
5. See, for example, Boenisch (2015), and Scheer (2019).
6. 'Britain's best kept secret is that it has a culture of new writing directors who respect the fact that on this model the writer is the *artist* and the director is the *interpreter*' (Whybrow 2007).
7. See Bolton (2011: 90–145).
8. An illustrative example of this is Nübling introducing Stephens to one of his favourite theatre companies, the Sheffield-based experimental ensemble, Forced Entertainment. Stephens had never previously heard of Forced Entertainment.
9. See also Bolton (2012a).
10. In 1996 *The Policy for Drama of the English Arts Funding System* stated that 'the work of living playwrights is essential to the continuing vitality and cultural relevance of drama' (8). Following the Peter Boyden Report in 1999, Arts Council England negotiated with the Treasury a £25 million increase in theatre subsidy.
11. In his survey of British theatre, *State of the Nation: British Theatre Since 1945*, Michael Billington, for instance, closes his book with the ringing declaration that '[t]he health of British theatre over the past sixty years has depended heavily on its dramatists and their ability to reflect the state of the nation [. . .] the future of theatre rests with its playwrights' (2007a: 404, 411).

Notes

12. Stephens, Word document, 'Thoughts on Fear', 2008.
13. Ibid.
14. Ibid.
15. I am reminded of Roland Barthes's elegant formulation: 'There is no official decree or supernatural intervention which graciously dispenses the theatre from the demands of theoretical reflection' (1972: 73).
16. Stephens, 'Thoughts on Fear'.

Chapter 1

1. Stephens, handwritten diary entry, 4 January 2000. (Monday 3 January 2000 was a Bank Holiday).
2. Stephens, handwritten diary entry, 20 February 2000.
3. For an excellent critical discussion of this, see Holden (2017).
4. Stephens, handwritten diary entry, 23 June 2000.
5. Stephens, handwritten diary entry, 12 July 2000.
6. Stephens, handwritten diary entry, 16 May 2000.
7. Stephens, handwritten diary entry, 27 May 2000.
8. Ibid.
9. Stephens, 23 June 2000.
10. While by no means wanting to suggest that the writers and directors that led the workshops at the Royal Court were practitioners of the 'stultifying pedagog[y]' Jacques Rancière discusses in his oft-cited essay, it is interesting to reflect on how pedagogical practices of new play development might inflect dramaturgical models. The teaching Rancière criticises is that which cleaves to 'the logic of straight, uniform transmission: there is something – a form of knowledge, a capacity, an energy in a body or a mind – on one side, and it must pass to the other side. What the pupil must *learn* is what the schoolmaster must *teach* her' (2009: 14). Rancière's analysis offers a compelling explanation for the construction and continued presence of 'elders', 'gurus', 'fathers' or, indeed, Darth Vaders within cultures of new play development.
11. Stephens, handwritten diary entry, 2 June 2000.
12. Stephens, handwritten diary entry, n.d., c.September 2000.
13. Ibid.
14. Ibid.
15. Ibid.
16. Ibid.
17. Ibid.

Notes

18. Ibid.
19. Stephens, handwritten diary entry, 15 September 2000.
20. Ibid.
21. *One Minute* (2003), a commission for Actors' Touring Company, is discussed in Chapter 2.
22. This and all subsequent references to the play are taken from *Plays: 1* (2005).
23. In the 1945 General Election Phil Piratin (1907–1995), a member of the Communist Party of Great Britain, was elected MP for Mile End in Stepney, London. Stephens moved to Stepney in 1994.
24. This and all subsequent references to the play are taken from *Plays: 1* (2005).
25. Stephens, letter to Mel Kenyon, 9 August 2001.
26. Stephens, handwritten diary entry, 11 July 2000.
27. Stephens, handwritten diary entries, 8 and 9 May 2000.
28. Russell's complaints of his mum 'buying the most expensive toilet paper' and one time even 'tipp[ing] a bus conductor' (87) wink slyly to Liubov Andryeevna Ranyevskaia's squandering of money on lunches and beggars in *The Cherry Orchard*. The (failed) magic trick by the character of the 'Fat Man' echoes the rather more successful trompe-l'oeil performed by Charlotta in the same play.
29. This and all subsequent references to the play are taken from *Plays: 1* (2005).
30. Stephens, letter to Mel Kenyon.
31. Ibid.
32. Ibid.
33. Stephens, handwritten diary entry, 16 March 2000.
34. Stephens, 4 January 2000.
35. Stephens, handwritten notes, n.d.
36. Stephens, 20 February 2000.
37. Stephens, letter to Mel Kenyon.
38. Stephens, handwritten notes, n.d.
39. Stephens, handwritten diary entry, 2 July 2001.
40. This and all subsequent references to the play are taken from *Plays: 1* (2005).
41. Stephens, Word document titled 'programme notes', 16 October 2002.
42. Ibid.
43. Stephens, handwritten diary entry, n.d., c.July 2000.
44. Stephens, 'programme notes', 16 October 2002.
45. Stephens's first-born son.
46. Stephens, handwritten diary entry, 12 December 2000.

Notes

47. This and all subsequent references to the play are taken from *Plays: 2* (2009).
48. Stephens, handwritten diary entry, 9 October 2002.
49. Stephens, Word document titled 'Notes for Royal Exchange Programme', n.d.
50. Ibid.
51. Unless specified otherwise, this and all subsequent references to the play are taken from *Plays 3* (2011).
52. Stephens, Word document titled 'it is something of a tradition in British rehearsal rooms for a rehearsal to start with a read', n.d.
53. Simon Stephens, Word document titled 'THEMES', n.d.

Chapter 2

1. Stephens, Word document titled 'Hanover lecture Jan 2008'.
2. Ibid.
3. Ibid.
4. Ibid.
5. Ibid.
6. Stephens, Word document titled 'Athens Motortown November 2007'.
7. All further references to this text are taken from *Plays: 2* (2009).
8. An early draft of *Motortown* (dated 20 July 2005) contains a stage direction suggesting that the characters' names should be those of the actors.
9. See also Bolton (2014a).
10. All further references to this text are taken from *Plays: 2* (2009).
11. Amanda (Milly) Dowler was thirteen years old when she was abducted on her way home from school in Walton-on-Thames, Surrey, England, on 21 March 2002.
12. All further references to this text are taken from *Plays: 2* (2009).
13. Stephens was in fact father to two boys, Oscar and Stanley, at the time of writing *One Minute*.
14. Stephens, handwritten diary entry, 19 September 2002.
15. Sarah Payne was abducted near the home of her grandfather in Kingston Gorse, West Sussex, England, on 1 July 2000.
16. All further references to this text are taken from *Plays: 3* (2011).
17. All further references to this text are taken from *Plays: 2* (2009).
18. Stephens, Word document titled 'Sea Wall Dublin Festival Intro 110215'.
19. All further references to this text are taken from *Plays: 3* (2011).
20. Stephens, Word document titled 'Hamburg rehearsal notes for Punk Rock 010310'.

21. Stephens, Word document titled 'Initial notes to self pre first draft October 07'.
22. Stephens, 'Hamburg rehearsal notes'.
23. Stephens, handwritten diary entry, 10 July 2000.
24. Ibid.
25. Stephens, Word document titled 'treatment 2', n.d.
26. Stephens, Word document titled 'Fugue – initial notes', n.d.

Chapter 3

1. Teater No99 ceased operations in 2019 (https://no99.ee/). For a discussion of the company's work, see Epner (2013).
2. Stephens, Word document titled 'Lullaby Burn draft 010908'.
3. All further references are taken from this published text.
4. Stephens, Word document titled 'Interview Simon Stephens with Ariane de Waal 1_3 Dec 2014'.
5. Stephens, Word document titled 'Wastwater Blog for RC 130311'.
6. Ibid.
7. Ibid.
8. Stephens, 'Wastwater Blog'.
9. Mitchell directed the first major revival of Crimp's 1997 *Attempts on Her Life* (2007, National Theatre), *The Country* (2000, Royal Court) and *The City* (2008, Royal Court).
10. For an extended discussion of 'expressive realism' and its counterpoint, 'critical method', see Bolton (2011: 146–98).
11. Stephens, Word documents titled 'Part One', 'Katie Mitchell questions for Part 2' and 'Katie Mitchell questions on Part Three'. n.d.
12. Stephens, 'Part One'.
13. Ibid.
14. Ibid.
15. Stephens, Word document, 'My thoughts on working with Katie Mitchell', n.d.
16. Stephens, Word document titled 'Hamburg Rehearsal Notes for Punk Rock 010310'.
17. Stephens, 'Katie Mitchell questions on Part Three'.
18. Ibid.
19. Milošević was president of Serbia (1989–97) and president of the Federal Republic of Yugoslavia (1997–2000). His five-year trial for genocide and crimes against humanity, during which Milošević conducted his own

Notes

defence as he refused to accept the legitimacy of the court (which had not been convened according to UN agreement), ended without a verdict upon Milošević's death in his prison cell in 2006. During his term of office, Taylor was accused of war crimes and crimes against humanity as a result of his involvement in the Sierra Leone Civil War (1991–2002). He was found guilty in April 2012 of all eleven charges levied by the Special Court, including terror, murder and rape.

20. Stephens, Word document 'Every play I ever wrote was about travel', n.d.
21. All further references to the text are taken from *Plays: 4* (2015).
22. Both productions opened with Stephens's rewriting of *Ubu Roi* as a curtain-raiser, a heavily condensed and stripped-back text inspired by Kenneth McLeish's 1997 translation.
23. There is a resemblance here with Marianne Elliott's imagining of 'Christopher Boone' in her production of *The Curious Incident of the Dog in the Night-Time*.
24. Stephens, Word document titled 'Trial of Ubu initial notes 130209'.
25. Stephens, Word document titled 'B Christ Questions UBU 191109'.
26. Saunders cites Max Stafford-Clark, John Bull and Vera Gottlieb among these commentators (2008: 3-6).
27. Grochala (2017) develops this analysis in some detail, mapping Zygmunt Bauman's analysis of 'liquid modernity' (2012) – the contemporary dislocation between power and politics caused by increasing globalization – onto the dramaturgical structures of contemporary political theatre.
28. See Stephens (2016: 265).
29. Tennant trained at the Drama Centre, London, under the late Reuven Adiv. Adiv had been taught by, and then taught alongside, Lee Strasberg, the Polish-American actor and director credited with developing 'the Method' approach to acting, derived in part from the teachings of Stanislavski. Tennant has to date appeared in over fifty stage productions, at theatres including the National Theatre, the Royal Shakespeare Company, Liverpool Everyman, Soho Theatre, the Young Vic and Royal Court, and worked with several of the UK's most sought-after directors, including Erica Whyman, Sean Holmes, Michael Boyd, Anna Mackmin, Roxana Silbert, David Farr, Robert Icke, Nancy Meckler and Maria Aberg.
30. Julia Lochte of the Thalia Theater, Hamburg, was also dramaturg on the production.
31. Tennant confirms that during the early stages of rehearsal he 'kept phoning Simon who kept saying "just go with [Nübling], go with him, go with what he wants"' (2016a).
32. See Poll (2016: online), Costa (2012: online) and Love (2012: online). Costa and Love's pieces focus specifically on Nübling's production of *Three Kingdoms*; Poll addresses Stephens's oeuvre more broadly, returning to

criticisms first advanced in her review of *Birdland* for the *British Theatre Guide* (2014: online).
33. Stephens, Word document, '9 Questions to Simon Stephens', May 2013.
34. Ibid.
35. My thanks to Kara McKechnie for translating this article for me.
36. For example: Edward Bond and William Gaskill, John Osborne and Anthony Page, Arnold Wesker and John Dexter, Michael Frayn and Michael Blakemore, Tom Stoppard and Peter Wood, David Hare and Richard Eyre, Alan Bennett and Nicholas Hytner, Caryl Churchill and Max Stafford-Clark and, more recently, David Eldridge and Rufus Norris.
37. See Bolton (2011: 174–98).

Chapter 4

1. Stephens, Word document, 'INTERVIEW WITH SIMON STEPHENS', 26 April 2006. The interviewer is identified as 'JD'.
2. Ibid.
3. Ibid.
4. In 2016, the album was ranked No. 2 among the top 'Albums of the Year' for 1979 by *NME* (see https://www.nme.com/bestalbumsandtracksoftheyear/1979-2-1045405).
5. Stephens, Word document titled 'Metal Box Draft 290811'.
6. Ibid.
7. All further references to this text are taken from *Plays 4* (2015).
8. Stephens, Word document, 'Is that me*', n.d.
9. For a detailed discussion of the use of silence in debbie tucker green's plays see Massana (2020).
10. For a questioning of this position, see Adiseshiah and Bolton (2020).
11. The original company of actors comprised Nadia Albina, Hammed Animashaun, Leo Bill, Cara Horgan, Charlotte Josephine, Adelle Leonce, Katherine Pearce, Billy Seymour, Sergo Vares and Steven Webb. Together with Holmes and Stephens, the creative associates included Ellen McDougall, Anrizé Kene, Hyemi Shin, Lizzie Powell and Nick Manning. For a longer discussion of Secret Theatre, and links to reviews of the productions created by the ensemble, see Bolton (2016b).
12. Bond's trilogy of plays, *Have I None*, *The Under Room* and *Chair* played in the studio space at the Lyric Hammersmith from 19 April 19 to 26 May 2012.
13. These were written by Mark Ravenhill, Hayley Squires, Joel Horwood and Caroline Bird.

Notes

14. In the Lyttleton Theatre, *The Doctor's Dilemma* (1906) by George Bernard Shaw was playing in repertory with *The Last of the Haussmans* (2012), a new play by Andrew Beresford, starring Julie Walters and Helen McCrory. In the Olivier, *Timon of Athens* was playing, directed by the National's Nicholas Hytner and starring Simon Russell Beale in the eponymous role.

15. A third UK tour was planned, and the production was due to return for a limited London run, in 2020/21.

16. See also Stephens talking about his involvement in rehearsals for *Three Kingdoms*: 'In rehearsal my work was also, weirdly to respond to my own text [. . .] I had to dislocate my rehearsing-self from my writing-self [. . .] I helped them edit and cut the play [. . .] Sometimes I would be writing to their command. I loved this. It felt like being a writer on Tin Pan Alley or a Hollywood studio'. (Bolton 2012b: vi–vii)

17. 'To what end the hard work of dramatic form? Why build a theatre, disguise men and women, torture their memories, invite the whole town to assemble at one place if I intend to produce nothing more with my work and its representation, than some of those emotions that would be produced as well by any good story that everyone could read by his chimney-corner at home?' (Lessing 1769 [1962]: 426)

18. When the play transferred to the Apollo in the West End, Katy Rudd became Resident Director. She describes one aspect of rehearsing new actors into the cast: 'As we only get snippets of each scene, I improvise with the actors around the text so that they have a clear idea of the 'whole picture'. For example, I get the actors to improvise the Christmas where Christopher gets given the train track, because it seems to be a rare happy memory in the Boone household [. . .] Because actors think in pictures and, you know, if they have a memory, it's easy to see it when they're talking about it' (2015). This approach corresponds closely to the process of improvising that Nicholas Tennant describes when talking about rehearsal rooms in England (see Chapter 3).

19. See Bolton (2016a) for a GCSE study guide to the play.

20. See Bell (2016), for an insightful discussion of this.

21. Stephens, Word document titled 'Why Write?', 8 March 2001.

Chapter 5

1. Micaëla's opening monologue, for example, contains lyrics from Sonic Youth's 'Expressway to Your Skull' (1986) (Stephens 2014a: 6–7). Later in the play, The Singer speaks lines which riff on Daft Punk's 'Touch' (2013) (14). Some of Escamillo's lines are lifted from Kraftwerk's 'Hall of Mirrors' (1977) (26).

2. The term 'panorama' play is mine. I distinguish the 'panorama' play from the 'state of the nation' plays closely associated with the works of David Hare,

Notes

David Edgar and Howard Brenton. Instead, for me, the 'panorama' play is closer to the work made by playwrights in the 1930s and 1940s. Elmer Rice's *Street Scene* (1929) comes to mind.

3. The Royal Court Theatre is often seen as emblematically representative of this. Ian Rickson, who was Artistic Director of the Royal Court from 1998 to 2006, has spoken of 'the importance of surrendering your ego to the world of the play' when you are directing (2007: 21).
4. Stephens's published letter to Matthew Jocelyn, director of the Canadian premiere of *Harper Regan* (Canadian Stage, Toronto, 2015), an apparently less 'writerly' play-text than *Nuclear War*, praised the way in which the director 'pushed [the play] to places [he] had never imagined possible' (2015e) through a balletic/operatic treatment, sculptural design, and non-mimetic acting.
5. My thanks to the Deutsches Schauspielhaus Hamburg and La Colline for supplying DVD recordings of both productions and to my research assistant Marta Tirado for her efficient support in the early stages of researching this essay.
6. All subsequent translations from French are mine, unless otherwise stated.
7. Non-Anglophone European productions of *Pornography* include *Pornography* (Teatr Dramatyczny, Warsaw, Poland, 2008, dir. Grażyna Kania), *Pornografi* (Aalborg Teater, Denmark, 2009, dir. Rune David Grue), *Pornografi* (Odense Teater, Denmark, 2010, dir. Peter Dupont Weiss), *Pornographie* (Théâtre de Poche, Brussels, Belgium, 2014, dir. Olivier Coyette) and *Pornografia* (La Farinera del Clot, Barcelona, Spain, 2018, dir. Iban Beltran).
8. Email from Christ to the author of this chapter, 15 August 2017.
9. *Inszenierung* 'is situated somewhere between a production, the idea or concept that drives it, and its realisation in each performance' (Boenisch 2015: 20).
10. Gerstner has worked in close association with Nübling and with musician Lars Wittershagen since 2000.
11. Translations from German are mine, with the help of Anja Burkhardt.
12. The prompter in Nübling's *Pornographie* displayed the markedly anti-illusionistic role traditionally played by prompters in German theatre, where they operate generally as stage managers and often appear on stage both during the performance and at intermissions (see Hadley Denton 2007: 249). Trudzinski, for example, announced the titles of Scenes Seven to Two, which Nübling's production derived from the play-text's 'Seven Ages of Man' template.
13. I thank my student Lina Katzmarcik for drawing my attention to this.
14. That the production was walking a very fine line is confirmed by some of the responses it gave rise to. For Stephens's French translator Séverine Magois, 'something didn't work' in Gutmann's production; 'I think that what was lacking was a sense of urgency, or the sense that the attacks happened. They became some kind of secondary event in the background' (email to the author of this chapter, 24 July 2017). In contrast, for the critic of the left-wing daily

newspaper *L'Humanité*, 'For once, this is not a detached kind of theatre' but 'A political theatre that makes sense' (S. 2010: 19; 'Pour le coup, ce n'est pas là un theatre distancié'; 'Un theatre politique qui fait sens').

15. The wording of the official announcement used by the RATP (Paris and Île-de-France transport network) and mostly by the SNCF (French rail network) is, in fact, 'Veuillez vous éloigner de la bordure du quai' ('Please keep away from the edge of the platform'). The reference to the 'yellow line' in Gutmann's production nevertheless made sense to French audiences, as in Francophone contexts the phrase 'dépasser la ligne jaune' (or, more often, 'franchir la ligne jaune') is used to refer to acts of (perceived) transgression, while elsewhere 'crossing the red line' is the preferred expression.

16. It is worth noting here that besides his practical training as an actor, Gutmann has a master's degree in political science and philosophy.

17. As far as I have been able to ascertain, Wajcman's work has not been translated into English. Agamben's 'What Is the Contemporary?' has been published in English with his 'What Is an Apparatus?' and 'The Friend' (Agamben 2009). The third section of the French translation of Agamben's essay, published in 2008, is reproduced in its entirety in La Colline's *Pornographie* programme (see La Colline 2010: 25–6); rather than translate it into English myself, I use the published English version for my quotations.

18. For a more complete list of Stephens's film and television influences, see Kellaway (2009: online) and A.B. (2014: online).

19. All further references to the text are taken from *Plays 2* (2009).

20. All further references are taken from this published text.

21. See Brecht (1970: xi–xii).

22. All further references to the text are taken from *Plays 3* (2011).

23. See Bolton (2014b) for an account of the relationship between these texts.

24. *Ladybird* was directed by Ramin Gray at the Royal Court Theatre Upstairs in March 2004.

25. William Forsythe is an American dancer and choreographer. He is based in Germany and works largely in mainland Europe.

26. Hofesh Shechter is an Israeli dancer, choreographer and composer based in London.

27. Gray directed David Greig's *The Events* for Actors Touring Company in 2013.

28. Alain Platel is a Belgian choreographer. He founded the dance company les ballets c de la B in 1984.

29. Joel Horwood is a British playwright. He joined the Lyric Hammersmith as an artistic associate in 2015.

30. See Chapter 4 of this volume for a discussion of this project.

Notes

31. Lizzie Clachan is a British theatre designer who works across the UK and Europe. In 1998 she was a co-founder of the theatre company Shunt.
32. Paul Handley was Head of Production at the Royal Court Theatre from 1999 to 2012.
33. Cracknell directed Nick Payne's *Blurred Lines* at The Shed, National Theatre, London, in January 2014.

BIBLIOGRAPHY

Archive: Simon Stephens

Stephens's personal archive comprises a (paper and digital) collection of diaries, letters, working notes and play drafts dating from 1999. It is not categorized; as such, individual items have been identified in the footnotes which accompany each chapter by the type of document, its title and date (where provided).

A.B. (2014), 'Why He Writes', *The Economist*, 4 April. https://www.economist.com/prospero/2014/04/04/why-he-writes (accessed 14 September 2020).
Aberg, Maria (2012), 'Maria Aberg Production 2012', n.d. https://www.rsc.org.uk/king-john/past-productions/maria-aberg-production-2012 (accessed 28 August 2020).
Abrahams, Nadia (2006), 'Simon Stephens: Interview', *Time Out*, 19 April. http://www.timeout.com/london/theatre/features/244/Simon_Stephens-Interview.html (accessed 30 August 2010).
Adiseshiah, Siân and Jacqueline Bolton (2020), 'debbie tucker green and (the Dialectics of) Dispossession: Reframing the Ethical Encounter', in Siân Adiseshiah and Jacqueline Bolton (eds), *debbie tucker green: Critical Perspectives*, 67–88, Cham: Palgrave.
Agamben, Giorgio (2009), *What Is an Apparatus? and Other Essays*. Trans. David Kishik and Stefan Pedatella. Stanford: Stanford University Press.
Albeiz, Sean (2003), 'Know History! John Lydon, Cultural Capital and the Prog/Punk Dialectic', *Popular Music*, 22 (3): 357–74.
Anderson, Gordon (2010), Unpublished interview with Jacqueline Bolton, London, 5 May.
Animashawun, Ola (2011), '*Wastwater*: Simon Stephens and Katie Mitchell' [podcast], Royal Court Theatre. Link no longer available (accessed 15 June 2018).
Aragay, Mireia (2005), 'Reflection to Refraction: Adaptation Studies Then and Now', in Mireia Aragay (ed.), *Books in Motion: Adaptation, Intertextuality, Authorship*, 11–34. Amsterdam and New York: Rodopi.
Arts Council of England (1996), *The Policy for Drama of the English Arts Funding System*. London: Arts Council of England.
Barnett, David (2010a), '"I've been told . . . that the play is far too German": The Interplay of Institution and Dramaturgy in Shaping British Reactions to German Theatre', in Rebecca Braun and Lyn Marven (eds), *Cultural Impact in the German Context: Studies in Transmission, Reception and Influence*, 150–66. New York: Camden House.
Barnett, David (2010b), 'Christoph Marthaler: The Musicality, Theatricality and Politics of Postdramatic Direction', in Maria M. Delgado and Dan Rebellato

Bibliography

(eds), *Contemporary European Theatre Directors*, 185–203. London and New York: Routledge.

Barnett, David (2016), '"This Is Why I'm Really Excited by British Theatre in the Next Five Years": David Barnett in Conversation with Simon Stephens', *Contemporary Theatre Review*, 26 (3): 311–18.

Barthes, Roland (1972), 'The Tasks of Brechtian Criticism', in Richard Howard (trans.), *Critical Essays*, 71–6. Evanston: Northwestern University Press.

Barthes, Roland (1974), *S/Z*. Trans. Richard Miller. Oxford: Blackwell.

Barthes, Roland (1977), *Image, Music, Text*. Trans. Stephen Heath. London: Fontana Press.

Basset, Kate (2012), '*Morning* review', *The Times*, 9 September.

Baudrillard, Jean (2002a), 'The Spirit of Terrorism', in *The Spirit of Terrorism*, 1–34. London: Verso.

Baudrillard, Jean (2002b), 'Hypotheses on Terrorism', in *The Spirit of Terrorism*, 49–84. London: Verso.

Baumann, Zygmunt (2003), *Liquid Love*. Cambridge: Polity Press.

Baumann, Zygmunt (2012), *Liquid Modernity*. Cambridge: Polity Press.

BBC News (n.d.), 'Victims of the Bombings'. http://news.bbc.co.uk/1/shared/spl/hi/uk/05/london_blasts/victims/default.stm (accessed 7 September 2020).

Bell, Charlotte (2016), 'Seeing Like a Classroom: Theatre and Performance in Education', *Studies in Theatre and Performance*, 36 (2): 145–58.

Belsey, Catherine (1980), *Critical Practice*. London: Routledge.

Benedict, David (2008), '*Harper Regan* review', *Variety*, 28 April.

Billington, Michael (2001), '*Herons* review', *Guardian*, 23 May.

Billington, Michael (2004), '*Country Music* review', *Guardian*, 29 June.

Billington, Michael (2007a), *State of the Nation: British Theatre Since 1945*. London: Faber and Faber.

Billington, Michael (2007b), 'Women of Troy', *Guardian*, 29 November. https://www.theguardian.com/stage/2007/nov/29/theatre.euripides (accessed 1 September 2019).

Billington, Michael (2008), 'Harper Regan', *Guardian*, 24 April.

Billington, Michael (2009a), 'Don't Let Auteurs Take Over in Theatre', *Guardian*, 14 April. https://www.theguardian.com/stage/theatreblog/2009/apr/14/auteur-theatre (accessed 1 September 2019).

Billington, Michael (2009b), '*Punk Rock* review', *Guardian*, 10 September.

Billington, Michael (2012), 'Three Kingdoms – Review', *Guardian*, 9 May. https://www.theguardian.com/stage/2012/may/09/three-kingdoms-review (accessed 22 January 2021).

Billington, Michael (2014), '*Birdland* review – Ceaselessly Inventive Critique of Rock Stardom', *Guardian*, 10 April.

Boenisch, Peter (2008), 'Exposing the Classics: Michael Thalheimer's *Regie* Beyond the Text', *Contemporary Theatre Review*, 18 (1): 30–43.

Boenisch, Peter (2015), *Directing Scenes and Senses: The Thinking of Regie*. Manchester: Manchester University Press.

Bolton, Jacqueline (2011), *Demarcating Dramaturgy: Mapping Theory onto Practice*, unpublished doctoral thesis, University of Leeds.

Bibliography

Bolton, Jacqueline (2012a), 'Capitalizing (on) New Writing: New Play Development in the 1990s', *Studies in Theatre and Performance*, 32 (2): 209–25.

Bolton, Jacqueline (2012b), 'Preface', in *Three Kingdoms*, v–xiii. London: Methuen.

Bolton, Jacqueline (2013), 'Simon Stephens', in Dan Rebellato (ed.). *Modern British Playwriting 2000-2009: Voices, Documents, New Interpretations*. London: Bloomsbury Methuen.

Bolton, Jacqueline (2014a), 'Introduction and Commentary', in *Simon Stephens: Pornography*, vii–lxxiv. London: Methuen.

Bolton, Jacqueline (2014b), 'Introduction', in *Blindsided*, iii–xii. London: Bloomsbury Methuen.

Bolton, Jacqueline (2015), 'Introduction', in *Harper Regan*, 3–24. London: Bloomsbury Methuen.

Bolton, Jacqueline (2016a), *Simon Stephens's The Curious Incident of the Dog in the Night-Time: Essential Guides for Exam Study*. London: Methuen Bloomsbury.

Bolton, Jacqueline (2016b), '"Changing the Conversation": Simon Stephens, Sean Holmes and Secret Theatre', *Contemporary Theatre Review*, 26 (3): 337–44.

Bond, Edward (2012), 'The Bochum Talk – The Third Crisis: The State of Future Drama', 22 September. https://static1.squarespace.com/static/5bf729daf83 70a9b693e71d4/t/5bfc69e9f950b7c1e48c27df/1543268841982/bochumtalk.pdf (accessed 24 August 2019).

Bradley, Jack (2006), Unpublished interview with Jacqueline Bolton, London, 7 August.

Bragg, Melvyn (1994), 'Dennis Potter interview with Melvyn Bragg', *Without Walls Special*, Channel 4, 5 April.

Brecht, Bertolt (1970), *Collected Plays Vol 1: 1918–1923*. Eds John Willett and Ralph Manheim. London: Methuen.

Brown, Georgina (2009), '*Punk Rock* review', *Mail on Sunday*, 13 September.

Büchner, Georg (1997), *Woyzeck*. Trans. Gregory Motton. London: Nick Hern Books.

Butterworth, Jez (2009), *Jerusalem*. London: Nick Hern Books.

Butterworth, Jez (2017), *The Ferryman*. London: Nick Hern Books.

Campbell, Chris (2011), '*Wastwater*: In Conversation with Simon Stephens' [podcast], Royal Court Theatre (accessed 15 June 2018).

Carr, Ellen (2013), 'Writing with Simon Stephens', *A Younger Theatre*, 30 January. http://www.ayoungertheatre.com/writing-with-simon-stephens/ (accessed 18 November 2017).

Christ, Barbara (2017), Email correspondence with Mireia Aragay, 15 August.

Costa, Maddy (2012), 'Three Kingdoms: The Shape of British Theatre to Come?', *Guardian*, 16 May. https://www.theguardian.com/stage/theatreblog/2012/may/16/three-kingdoms-shape-british-theatre-or-flop (accessed 2 October 2017).

Costa, Maddy (2016), 'Northern Spirit', *Contemporary Theatre Review*, 26 (3): 387–90.

Coveney, Michael (2008), '*Harper Regan* review', *WhatsOnStage*, 24 April. http://www.whatsonstage.com/west-end-theatre/reviews/04-2008/harper-regan_19622.html (accessed 7 August 2014).

Crawley, Peter (2016), 'Song From Far Away – review: Feats of Stage Poetry Lighten the Dark and Unknowable', *The Irish Times*, 14 July.
Cramer, Steve (2008), '*Pornography* – Simon Stephens Interview', *The List* 607, 17 July. http://www.list.co.uk/article/10159-pornography-simon-stephens-interview (accessed 2 December 2010).
Crimp, Martin (1999), *Attempts on Her Life*. London: Faber and Faber.
Cusack, Niamh (2015), Unpublished interview with Jacqueline Bolton, London, 27 July.
Derbyshire, Harry (2008), 'The Culture of New Writing', *Contemporary Theatre Review*, 18 (1): 131–4.
Edgar, David and Amanda Whittington (eds) (2013), *Agreements and Contracts: A Working Playwright Guide*, The Writer's Union. https://writersguild.org.uk/wp-content/uploads/2019/08/WGGB-Working-Playwright-Agreements-and-Contracts-August-2019.pdf (accessed 29 November 2020).
Elliott, Marianne (2015), Unpublished interview with Jacqueline Bolton, London, 19 August.
Epner, Luule (2013), 'Postdramatic Textual Strategies: The Case of Theatre NO99', in Guna Zeltiņa with Sanita Reinsone (eds), *Text in Contemporary Theatre: The Baltics Within the World Experience*, 166–74. Newcastle upon Tyne: Cambridge Scholars.
Ewan, Fredric (1970), *Bertolt Brecht: His Life, His Art and His Times*. Bath: Calder and Boyars.
Fischer-Lichte, Erika (2008), 'Patterns of Continuity in German Theatre: Interculturalism, Performance and Cultural Mission', in Simon Williams and Maik Hamburger (eds), *A History of German Theatre*, 360–77, Cambridge: Cambridge University Press.
Frankcom, Sarah (2010), Unpublished interview with Jacqueline Bolton, online, 28 June.
Frankcom, Sarah (2014), Unpublished interview with Jacqueline Bolton, online, 14 February.
Gardner, Lyn (2003), 'One Minute review', *Guardian*, 9 June.
Gardner, Lyn (2014), '*Blindsided* – review', *Guardian*, 31 January.
Gardner, Lyn (2015), '*Song From Far Away* – review', *Guardian*, 6 September.
Gompertz, Will (n.d.), 'New Playwrights Courting Success', http://news.bbc.co.uk/1/hi/programmes/newsnight/8815455.stm (accessed 11 September 2020).
Gray, Ramin (2010), Unpublished interview with Jacqueline Bolton, London, 24 May.
Gray, Ronald (1976), *Brecht the Dramatist*. London: CUP.
Greig, David (2003), *Caligula*. London: Faber and Faber.
Greig, David (2010), *Dunsinane*. London: Faber and Faber.
Greig, David (2017), *The Suppliant Women*. London: Faber and Faber.
Grochala, Sarah (2017), *The Contemporary Political Play: Rethinking Dramaturgical Structure*. London: Bloomsbury Methuen.
Gutmann, Laurent (2010a), 'Lever de rideau (5): Laurent Gutmann monte *Pornographie*'. Interview with Aurélien Ferenczi. *Télérama*, 9 December.

Bibliography

http://www.telerama.fr.scenes/lever-de-rideau-5-laurent-gutmann-monte-pornographie,63484.php (accessed 5 July 2017).

Gutmann, Laurent (2010b), 'Entretien avec Laurent Gutmann', in *Pornographie de Simon Stephens, mise en scène Laurent Gutmann: Cahier-programme*, 27–33. Paris: La Colline Théâtre National. http://www.colline.fr/sites/default/files/archive/0.956777001289815658.pdf (accessed 5 July 2017).

Gutmann, Laurent (2010c), 'Transgresser ou refuser la tyrannie de la transparence', in *Pornographie de Simon Stephens, mise en scène Laurent Gutmann: Cahier-programme*, 2. Paris: La Colline Théâtre National. http://www.colline.fr/sites/default/files/archive/0.956777001289815658.pdf (accessed 5 July 2017).

Haddon, Mark (n.d.). http://markhaddon.com/writing/fiction (accessed 28 August 2020).

Haddon, Mark (2013), 'Mark Haddon on The Curious Incident of the Dog in the Night-Time', *Guardian*, 13 April. http://www.theguardian.com/books/2013/apr/13/mark-haddon-curious-incident-book-club (accessed 4 August 2020).

Hadley Denton, Eric (2007), 'The Technological Eye: Theater Lighting and *Guckkasten* in Michaelis and Goethe', in Evelyn K. Moore and Patricia A. Simpson (eds), *The Enlightened Eye: Goethe and Visual Culture*, 239–64. Amsterdam and New York: Rodopi.

Hare, David (2005), *Obedience, Struggle and Revolt*. London: Faber and Faber.

Harris, Zinnie (2016), *This Restless House*. London: Faber and Faber.

Hart, Christopher (2009), 'Punk Rock review', *Sunday Times*, 13 September.

Haydon, Andrew (2012), 'Three Kingdoms: Lyric Hammersmith', 10 May. http://postcardsgods.blogspot.com/2012/05/three-kingdoms-lyric-hammersmith.html (accessed 25 August 2020).

Haydon, Andrew (2013), 'Theatre in the 2000s', in Dan Rebellato (ed.), *Modern British Playwriting 2000–2009: Voices, Documents, New Interpretations*, 40–98, London: Methuen.

Haydon, Andrew (2014a), 'Carmen Disruption review – "Delights in Being Counterintuitive"', *Guardian*, 18 March.

Haydon, Andrew (2014b), '*Birdland* – Royal Court', 15 April. http://postcardsgods.blogspot.co.uk/2014/04/birdland-royal-court.html (accessed 12 April 2018).

Hebdige, Dick (1979), *Subculture: The Meaning of Style*, London: Routledge.

Hemming, Sarah (2012), '*Morning* review', *Financial Times*, 11 September.

Hirte, Marion (n.d.), 'Porträt Muriel Gerstner', Goethe Institut. http://www.goethe.de/kue/the/bbr/bbr/ag/ger/por/deindex.htm (accessed 6 July 2017).

Hitchings, Henry (2009), 'Punk Rock review', *Evening Standard*, 9 September.

Hitchings, Henry (2012a), 'Three Kingdoms review', *Evening Standard*, 9 May. https://www.standard.co.uk/culture/theatre/three-kingdoms-lyric-hammersmith-review-7727877.html (accessed 22 January 2021). .

Hitchings, Henry (2012b), '*Morning* review', *Evening Standard*, 10 September.

Holden, Nicholas (2017), 'Building the Engine Room: A Study of the Royal Court Young Peoples' Theatre and Its Development into the Young Writers' Programme', unpublished doctoral thesis, University of Lincoln.

Holmes, Sean (2010), Unpublished interview with Jacqueline Bolton, 22 June, London.
Holmes, Sean (2013a), 'Maybe the Existing Structures of Theatre in This Country, Whilst Not Corrupt, Are Corrupting', *WhatsOnStage*, 18 June. https://www.whatsonstage.com/london-theatre/news/sean-holmes-maybe-the-existing-structures-of-theat_31033.html (accessed 26 August 2014).
Holmes, Sean (2013b), Unpublished interview with Jacqueline Bolton, London, 21 November.
Hutton, Dan (2013), 'Maria Aberg', *Exeunt*, 22 April. http://exeuntmagazine.com/features/maria-aberg/ (accessed 28 August 2020).
Ilter, Seda (2015), 'Rethinking Play Texts in the Age of Mediatization: Pornography', *Modern Drama*, 58 (2): 283–62.
Innes, Christopher (2011), 'Simon Stephens', in Martin Middeke, Peter Paul Schnierer and Aleks Sierz (eds), *The Methuen Guide to Contemporary British Playwrights*, 445–65. London: Methuen.
Jester, Caroline and Caridad Svich (eds) (2017), *Fifty Playwrights on Their Craft*. London: Bloomsbury Methuen.
de Jongh, Nicholas (2004), 'Country Music review', *Evening Standard*, 29 June.
Kane, Sarah (2000), *4.48 Psychosis*. London: Methuen.
Kellaway, Kate (2009), 'How Simon Stephens's Plays Are Galvanising British Theatre', *Guardian*, 30 August. http://www.guardian.co.uk/stage/2009/aug/30/simon-stephens-theatre-punk-rock (accessed 14 September 2020).
Kelly, Dennis (2008), *DNA*. London: Oberon Books.
Kelly, Dennis (2010), *The Gods Weep*. London: Oberon Books.
Kingston, Jeremy (2003), '*One Minute* review', *The Times*, 10 June.
Lacey, Stephen (1995), *British Realist Theatre: The New Wave in Its Context*. London: Routledge.
La Colline (2010), *Pornographie de Simon Stephens, mise en scène Laurent Gutmann: Cahier-programme*. Paris: La Colline Théâtre National. http://www.colline.fr/sites/default/files/archive/0.956777001289815658.pdf (accessed 5 July 2017).
Lan, David (2012), 'A Leap in the Dark', 17 May. https://matttrueman.co.uk/2012/05/guest-post-a-leap-in-the-dark-by-david-lan.html (accessed 29 August 2020).
Lane, David (2010), 'A Dramaturg's Perspective: Looking to the Future of Script Development', *Studies in Theatre and Performance*, 30 (1): 127–42.
Ledger, Adam J. (2016), '"It's Not about Fucking It Up": *The Trial of Ubu*, the Text and the Director', *Contemporary Theatre Review*, 26 (3): 345–56.
Lehmann, Hans-Thies (2005), 'Theater Denken, Risiken Wagen, Formeln Nicht Glauben', *Theater der Zeit* (3): 12–13.
Lessing, Gotthold Ephraim (1769 [1962]), *The Hamburg Dramaturgy*. Trans. Helen Zimmern. New York: Dover Publications.
Logan, Brian (2007), 'One Day in July', *Guardian*, 19 June. https://www.theguardian.com/stage/2007/jun/19/theatre (accessed 1 September 2019).
Love, Catherine (2012), 'Three Kingdoms: New Ways of Seeing, Experiencing, Expressing', *Love Theatre*, 12 May. http://lovetheatre21.wordpress.com/2012/05

Bibliography

/12/three-kingdoms-new-ways-of-seeing-experiencing-expressing/ (accessed 2 October 2017).

Love, Catherine (2013), 'As You Like It, Royal Shakespeare Theatre', *Exeunt*, 12 June. https://catherinelove.co.uk/2013/06/12/as-you-like-it-royal-shakespeare-theatre/ (accessed 28 August 2020).

Love, Catherine (2016a), 'New Perspectives on Home: Simon Stephens and Authorship in British Theatre', *Contemporary Theatre Review*, 26 (3): 319–27.

Love, Catherine (2016b), 'Introduction and Commentary' to *Simon Stephens: Punk Rock*, London: Methuen.

Lukowski, Andrzej (2012), '*Morning* review', *Time Out (London)*, 13 September.

Magois, Séverine (2017), Email correspondence with Mireia Aragay, 24 July.

Marmion, Patrick (2004), '*One Minute* review', *Time Out*, 11 February.

Marmion, Patrick (2012), 'The Curious Incident of the Dog *in the Night-Time* review', *Daily Mail*, 10 August.

Massana, Elisabeth (2020), 'Cartographies of Silence in debbie tucker green's *truth and reconciliation*', in Siân Adiseshiah and Jacqueline Bolton (eds), *debbie tucker green: Critical Perspectives*, 257–76, Cham: Palgrave

Maxwell, Dominic (2013), '*The Curious Incident of the Dog in the Night-Time* review', *The Times*, 14 March.

McCauley, Alistair (2001), '*Herons* review', *Financial Times*, 24 May.

McCauley, Alistair (2004), 'Country Music review', *Financial Times*, 30 June.

McLeish, Kenneth (1997), 'Introduction' to *Woyzeck* by Georg Büchner. London: Nick Hern Books.

Metabolic Studio (n.d.). https://metabolicstudio.org/about (accessed 13 September 2020).

Mitchell, Katie (2009), *The Director's Craft*. Abingdon: Routledge.

Miola, Robert S. (2000), *Shakespeare's Reading*. Oxford: Oxford University Press.

Morrison, Blake (1997), *As If*. Cambridge: Granta.

d'Monté, Rebecca and Graham Saunders (eds) (2008), *Cool Britannia? British Political Drama in the 1990s*. Basingstoke: Palgrave Macmillan.

Mottram, Harry (2015), 'The Curious Incident of the Relaxed Performances: How One Play Changed Theatre', *Children's Theatre Magazine*, n.d. https://www.harrymottram.co.uk/2017/12/13/childrens-theatre-magazine-feature-the-curious-incident-of-the-relaxed-performances-how-one-play-changed-theatre-2/ (accessed 28 August 2020).

Mountford, Fiona (2008), '*Harper Regan* review', *Evening Standard*, 25 April.

Neill, Heather (2008), '*Harper Regan* review', *The Stage*, 24 April.

Nield, Sophie (2016), 'Reading *Three Kingdoms* as a Woman: Criticism, Misogyny and Representation', *Contemporary Theatre Review: Backpages*, 26 (3): 396–9.

NME (2016), 'Albums and Tracks of the Year: 1979', 10 October. https://www.nme.com/bestalbumsandtracksoftheyear/1979-2-1045405 (accessed 25 August 2020).

Nübling, Sebastian (2015), 'Foreword', in Simon Stephens, *Plays 4*, xi–x, London: Methuen.

Parker, Christian (2016), 'Ruthless Compassion: A Case for Simon Stephens', *Contemporary Theatre Review*, 26 (3): 393–6.

Bibliography

Pavis, Patrice (2010), 'The Director's New Tasks', in Maria M. Delgado and Dan Rebellato (eds), *Contemporary European Theatre Directors*, 395–411, London and New York: Routledge.

Pavis, Patrice (2013), *Contemporary Mise en Scène: Staging Theatre Today*. Trans. Joel Anderson. London and New York: Routledge.

Peter Boyden Associates (1999), *Roles and Functions of the English Regional Producing Theatres – Final Report*.

Poll, Melissa (2014), 'What About the Birds?', *British Theatre Guide*, 16 April. https://www.britishtheatreguide.info/features/what-about-the-birds-96 (accessed 29 November 2020).

Poll, Melissa (2016), 'When Little Is Said and Feminism Is Done', *Contemporary Theatre Review/Interventions*, 26 (3). https://www.contemporarytheatrereview.org/2016/when-little-is-said-and-feminism-is-done/ (accessed 2 October 2017).

Pringle, Stewart (2014), 'Birdland', *Exeunt Magazine*, 11 April. http://exeuntmagazine.com/reviews/birdland/ (accessed 7 April 2018).

Public Image Ltd (1979), *Metal Box*. Virgin Records.

Radosavljević, Duška (2013), *Theatre-Making: Interplay between Text and Performance in the 21st Century*. Basingstoke and New York: Palgrave Macmillan.

Radosavljević, Duška (2014), 'Theatre as an Intellectual Concertina: Simon Stephens in Conversation with Duška Radosavljević', in Margherita Laera (ed.), *Theatre and Adaptation: Return, Rewrite, Repeat*, 255–67. London: Bloomsbury Methuen.

Ramsey, Seb (2016), 'New Year's Eve 2016 – Party Party Party', *Manchester Evening News*, 1 January. https://www.manchestereveningnews.co.uk/news/greater-manchester-news/manchester-new-years-eve-pictures-10673770#rlabs=10%20p%241 (accessed 2 July 2020).

Rancière, Jacques (2009), *The Emancipated Spectator*. Trans. Gregory Elliott. London: Verso.

Rebellato, Dan (2005), 'New Theatre Writing: Simon Stephens', *Contemporary Theatre Review*, 15 (1): 174–8.

Rebellato, Dan (2007), 'From the State of the Nation to Globalization: Shifting Political Agendas in Contemporary British Playwriting', in Nadine Holdsworth and Mary Luckhurst (eds), *A Concise Companion to Contemporary British and Irish Drama*, 245–62. Oxford: Blackwell.

Rebellato, Dan (2009), 'When We Talk of Horses: Or, What Do We See When We See a Play?' in Stephen Bottoms (ed.), *Performance Research*. Special Issue: *Performing Literatures*, 14 (1): 17–28.

Rebellato, Dan (2010), 'Katie Mitchell: Learning from Europe', in Maria M. Delgado and Dan Rebellato (eds), *Contemporary European Directors*, 317–38. London: Routledge.

Rebellato, Dan (2012), 'Three Kingdoms', *Spilled Ink*. http://www.danrebellato.co.uk/spilledink/2013/3/12/three-kingdoms (accessed 24 August 2020).

Rebellato, Dan (2013), 'Exit the Author', in Vicky Angelaki (ed.), *Contemporary British Theatre: Breaking New Ground*, 9–31. Basingstoke and New York: Palgrave Macmillan.

Bibliography

Rebellato, Dan (2015), 'Theatre Review of the Year: 2015', 17 December. http://www.danrebellato.co.uk/spilledink/2015/12/17/theatre-review-of-the-year-2015 (accessed 2 February 2018).

Reinelt, Janelle (2007), 'Selective Affinities: British Playwrights at Work', *Modern Drama*, 50 (3): 305–45.

Rickson, Ian (2007), 'Ian Rickson'. Interview with Mireia Aragay and Pilar Zozaya in Mireia Aragay et al. (eds), *British Theatre of the 1990s: Interviews with Directors, Playwrights, Critics and Academics*, 15–26. Basingstoke and New York: Palgrave Macmillan.

Robinson, Gerry (2000), *The Creativity Imperative: Investing in the Arts in the 21st Century*. London: Arts Council of England

Rudd, Katy (2015), Unpublished interview with Jacqueline Bolton, London, 24 July.

S., M.–J. (2010), 'Voir le monde depuis le dessous des cartes', *L'Humanité*, 20 November: 19.

Safi, Michael (2016), '"Like a Beautiful Painting": Image of New Year's Mayhem in Manchester Goes Viral', *Guardian*, 3 January. https://www.theguardian.com/uk-news/2016/jan/03/like-a-beautiful-painting-image-of-new-years-mayhem-in-manchester-goes-viral (accessed 2 July 2020).

Said, S. F. (2004), 'Shock Corridors', *Sight and Sound*, 14 (2): 16–18.

Sakelliradou, Elizabeth (1999), 'New Faces for British Political Theatre', *Studies in Theatre and Performance*, 20 (1): 43–51.

Scheer, Anna Teresa (2019), *Christoph Schlingensief: Staging Chaos, Performing Politics and Theatrical Phantasmagoria*. London: Methuen Bloomsbury.

Schell, Desiree (2014), 'Dramatischer Text und Theater. Simon Stephens' *Pornographie* in der Regie von Sebastian Nübling (2007) – Eine Analyse'. Diplomarbeit Mag. Phil., Universität Wien.

Schrader, Paul. (1999), *Taxi Driver*. Culver City, CA: Columbia TriStar Home Video.

Schultz, Anne-Kathrin (2010a, 2008), 'Entretien avec Simon Stephens', in *Pornographie de Simon Stephens, mise en scène Laurent Gutmann: Cahier-programme*, 7–11. Paris: La Colline Théâtre National. http://www.colline.fr/sites/default/files/archive/0.956777001289815658.pdf (accessed 5 July 2017).

Sereny, Gita (1972), *Cries Unheard: The Untold Story of Mary Bell*. London: Eyre Methuen.

Seymour, Richard (2018), 'No One Knows', *Patreon*, 15 February. https://www.patreon.com/posts/no-one-knows-17021568 (accessed 7 May 2018).

Shore, Robert (2012), '*Morning* review', *Metro (London)*, 11 September.

Shuttleworth, Ian (2004), '*One Minute* review', *Financial Times*, 11 February.

Shuttleworth, Ian (2009), '*Punk Rock* review', *Financial Times*, 11 September.

Shuttleworth, Ian (2014), 'Blindsided, Royal Exchange Theatre, Manchester – review', *Financial Times*, 31 January.

Sidi, Nick (2015), Unpublished interview with Jacqueline Bolton, London, 24 July.

Sierz, Aleks (2001), '*Herons* review', *What's On*, 30 May.

Sierz, Aleks (2004), 'Breaking In', *The Stage*. www.thestage.co.uk/features/feature.php/3373/breaking-in-simon-stephens (accessed 3 August 2010).

Bibliography

Sierz, Aleks (2008), 'Playwright Simon Stephens on *Harper Regan*', *TheatreVOICE*, 20 October. http://www.theatrevoice.com/audio/playwright-simon-stephens-on-harper-regan/ (accessed 9 September 2020).

Sierz, Aleks (2011), *Rewriting the Nation: British Theatre Today*. London: Methuen Drama.

Sierz, Aleks (2012), 'Award-Winning Playwright Simon Stephens Rewrites Jarry's King Ubu', *TheatreVOICE*, 7 February. http://www.theatrevoice.com/audio/award-winning-play wright-simon-stephens-rewrites-kingubu/ (accessed 25 July 2015).

Simard, Jean-Pierre (2000), 'Sous le signe du refus: L'accueil du théâtre britannique en France', in Nicole Boireau (ed.), *Le Théâtre britannique contemporain en France (1945-1998)*. Special issue, *Coup de Théâtre* 16: 167–82. http://radac.fr/index.php/revue/#toggle-id-20 (accessed 5 July 2017).

Sloterdijk, Peter (1983 [1987]), *The Critique of Cynical Reason*. Trans. Michael Eldred. Minneapolis: University of Minnesota Press.

Spencer, Charles (2001), '*Herons* review', *Daily Telegraph*, 24 May.

Spencer, Charles (2004a), '*One Minute* review', *Daily Telegraph*, 10 February.

Spencer, Charles (2004b), '*Country Music* review', *Daily Telegraph*, 30 June 2004.

Spencer, Charles (2007), 'Women of Troy: Euripides All Roughed Up', *The Telegraph*, 30 November.

Spencer, Charles (2014), '*Birdland*, Royal Court Theatre, review', *The Telegraph*, 10 April.

States, Bert O. (1985), *Great Reckonings in Little Rooms: On the Phenomenology of Theatre*. Los Angeles: University of California Press.

Stephens, Simon (2005a), *Plays: 1*. London: Methuen.
  Bluebird (1998).
  Herons (2001).
  Port (2002).
  Christmas (2003).

Stephens, Simon (2005b), *On the Shore of the Wide World*. London: Methuen.

Stephens, Simon (2009), *Plays: 2*. London: Methuen.
  One Minute (2003).
  Country Music (2004).
  Motortown (2006).
  Pornography (2007).
  Sea Wall (2008).

Stephens, Simon (2010a). Unpublished interview with Jacqueline Bolton, London, 24 May.

Stephens, Simon (2010b), 'Interview: Simon Stephens, Playwright'. *The Scotsman*, 21 September. http://www.scotsman.com/news/interview-simon-stephens-p laywright-1-811347 (accessed 12 October 2017).

Stephens, Simon (2010c), 'Sarah Kane's Debut Play *Blasted* Returns'. *Guardian*, 24 October. http://www.theguardian.com/stage/2010/oct/24/sarah-kane-blas ted (accessed 10 August 2017).

Stephens, Simon (2010d), 'Keynote Address: Writing Black People', *Contemporary Drama in English*, (17): 19–36.

Bibliography

Stephens, Simon (2011a), *Plays: 3*. London: Methuen.
   On The Shore of the Wide World (2005).
   Marine Parade (2010).
   Harper Regan (2008).
   Punk Rock (2009).
Stephens, Simon (2011b), 'Sky Diving Blindfolded: Or Five Things I Learned From Sebastian Nübling', Theatertreffenblog, 9 May. https://theatertreffen-blog.de/tt11/2011/05/09/skydiving-blindfolded/ (accessed 25 August 2020).
Stephens, Simon (2011c), *Wastwater*. London: Methuen.
Stephens, Simon (2012), Unpublished interview with Jacqueline Bolton, London, 18 January.
Stephens, Simon (2013a), Unpublished interview with Jacqueline Bolton, London, 24 October.
Stephens, Simon (2013b), *The Curious Incident of the Dog in the Night-Time*. London: Bloomsbury Methuen.
Stephens, Simon (2013c), 'The Third Man', *Film International*, (65): 9–11.
Stephens, Simon (2014a), *Blindsided*. London: Bloomsbury Methuen.
Stephens, Simon (2014b), *Carmen Disruption*. London: Bloomsbury Methuen.
Stephens, Simon (2014c), *Birdland*. London: Bloomsbury Methuen.
Stephens, Simon (2014d), 'Simon Stephens: The Tracks of My Plays', *Guardian*, 21 April. https://www.theguardian.com/stage/2014/apr/21/simon-stephens-tracks-plays-playlist-birdland (accessed 10 September 2020).
Stephens, Simon (2015a), *Plays: 4*. London: Bloomsbury Methuen.
   Three Kingdoms (2011).
   The Trial of Ubu (2010).
   Morning (2012).
   Carmen Disruption (2014).
Stephens, Simon (2015b), 'Simon Stephens: My Favourite Living Writer? Robert Holman, Dramatist of Secrets and Shyness', *Guardian*, 10 March. https://www.theguardian.com/stage/2015/mar/10/simon-stephens-robert-holman-favourite-living-writer-a-breakfast-of-eels (accessed 13 September 2020).
Stephens, Simon (2015c), 'The Nature of Dramatic Action', 17 March. https://www.writeaplay.co.uk/live-online-workshop-simon-stephens/ (accessed 3 September 2020).
Stephens, Simon (2015d), 'Manchester is Richer than Ever in Theatrical Potential', *Guardian*, 19 May. https://www.theguardian.com/stage/2015/may/19/simon-stephens-manchester-home-funfair (accessed 25 October 2016).
Stephens, Simon (2015e), 'A Letter from Simon Stephens to Matthew Jocelyn', *Canadian Stage*, n.d. https://www.canadianstage.com/Online/default.asp?doWork::WScontent::loadArticle=Load&BOparam::WScontent::loadArticle::article_id=B2DDFF43-7FDD-44CC-AABE-21F9929184FD (accessed 27 June 2017).
Stephens, Simon (2015f), Unpublished interview with Jacqueline Bolton, London, 28 July.
Stephens, Simon (2015g), *Song from Far Away*. London: Bloomsbury Methuen.
Stephens, Simon (2015h), *Heisenberg: The Uncertainty Principle*. London: Bloomsbury Methuen.

Stephens, Simon (2016), *Simon Stephens: A Working Diary*. London: Bloomsbury Methuen.
Stephens, Simon (2017a), *Rage*. London: Bloomsbury Methuen.
Stephens, Simon (2017b), *Nuclear War*. London: Bloomsbury Methuen.
Stephens, Simon (2018), *Fatherland*. London: Bloomsbury Methuen.
Stephens, Simon (2019a), *Maria*. London: Bloomsbury Methuen.
Stephens, Simon (2019b), *Light Falls*. London: Bloomsbury Methuen.
Sutton, Adrian (2015), Unpublished interview with Jacqueline Bolton, London, 24 July.
Taylor, Paul (2004), '*Christmas* review', *Independent*, 14 January.
Taylor, Paul (2008), '*Harper Regan*, National Theatre: Cottesloe, London', *Independent*, 25 April.
Taylor, Paul (2014), '*Birdland*, theatre review: Sherlock's Moriarty Andrew Scott Is Excellent', *Independent*, 10 April.
Taylor, Paul (2015), 'Song From Far Away – Young Vic review: A Searching Study of Emotional Insufficiency', *Independent*, 7 September.
Tennant, Nicholas (2016a), Unpublished interview with Jacqueline Bolton, London, 16 April.
Tennant, Nicholas (2016b), Personal email correspondence with Jacqueline Bolton, 19 May.
Theater Talk (2014), 'The Curious Incident with [sic] the Dog in the Night-Time', 12 November. https://www.youtube.com/watch?v=svdl_ee22-w (accessed 28 August 2020).
The Lowry (2020), '*Curious Incident of the Dog in the Night-Time* to Launch Third UK Tour at The Lowry', 4 March. https://thelowry.com/2020/03/04/curious-incident-of-the-dog-in-the-night-time-to-launch-third-uk-tour-at-the-lowry/ (accessed 28 August 2020).
Thompson, Jessie (2014), 'Fear and Loathing in Late Capitalism: An Interview with Simon Stephens', *The Quietus*, 27 April. https://thequietus.com/articles/15091-simon-stephens-birdland-theatre-interview (accessed 18 June 2020).
Thompson, Laura (2012), '*The Curious Incident of the Dog in the Night-Time* review', *Daily Telegraph*, 4 August.
Thompson, Peter (2013), 'Introduction: The Privatisation of Hope and the Crisis of Negation', in Peter Thompson and Slavoj Zizek (eds), *The Privatization of Hope: Ernst Bloch and the Future of Utopia*, 1–20. London: Duke University Press.
Thomson, Peter and Glendyr Sacks (eds) (1994), *The Cambridge Companion to Brecht*. Cambridge: Cambridge University Press.
Tomlin, Liz (2007), 'Beyond interpretation', unpublished paper presented at Performing Literatures, Workshop Theatre, Leeds: University of Leeds, UK, 30 June–1 July.
Treadaway, Luke (2015), Unpublished telephone interview with Jacqueline Bolton, 14 July.
Tripney, Natasha (2012), 'Hardcore Critical Girl-on-Girl Action', *Exeunt*, 21 May. http://exeuntmagazine.com/features/critical-girl-on-girl-action/ (accessed 25 August 2020).

Bibliography

Trueman, Matt (2013), 'Review: *As You Like It*', Royal Shakespeare Theatre, 15 May. http://matttrueman.co.uk/2013/05/review-as-you-like-it-royal-shakespeare-theatre.html (accessed 26 August 2014).

Trueman, Matt (2016), '*Herons* (Lyric Hammersmith)', *WhatsOnStage*, 22 January. https://www.whatsonstage.com/london-theatre/reviews/herons-lyric-hammersmith_39570.html (accessed 28 August 2020).

Turner, Cathy and Synne Behrndt (2008), *Dramaturgy and Performance*. Basingstoke: Palgrave Macmillan.

Ue, Tom (2014), 'Adapting *The Curious Incident of the Dog in the Night-Time*: A Conversation with Simon Stephens', *Journal of Adaptation in Film and Performance*, 7 (1): 113–20.

Van den Berg, Klaus (2008), 'Contemporary German Scenography: Surging Images and Spaces for Action', *Contemporary Theatre Review*, 18 (1): 6–19.

Walker, Nicola (2015), Unpublished interview with Jacqueline Bolton, London, 27 July.

Waters, Steve (2007), Unpublished interview with Jacqueline Bolton, London, 22 November.

Wedekind, Frank (2009), *Spring Awakening*. Trans. and Intro. Edward Bond and Elisabeth Bond-Pablé. London: Methuen.

WhatsOnStage (2012), 'Review Round-Up: *Three Kingdoms* Divides the Critics', 9 May. https://www.whatsonstage.com/west-end-theatre/news/review-round-up-three-kingdoms-divides-the-critics_4378.html (accessed 1 July 2019).

Whybrow, Graham (2007), Unpublished interview with Jacqueline Bolton, London, 19 November.

Williams, Holly (2017), 'Review: Nuclear War at the Royal Court', *Exeunt*, 24 April. http://exeuntmagazine.com/reviews/review-nuclear-war-royal-court/ (accessed 29 July 2020).

Wolf, Matt (2006), 'Rainbow Kiss/Motortown review', *International Herald Tribune*, 24 May.

Worthen, W. B. (2005), *Print and the Poetics of Modern Drama*. Cambridge: Cambridge University Press.

Worthen, W. B. (2010), *Between Poetry and Performance*. Oxford: Wiley-Blackwell.

Young, Stuart (2017), 'The Ethics of the Representation of the Real People and Their Stories in Verbatim Theatre', *Studies in Theatre and Performance*, 9 (1): 21–42.

Žižek, Slavoj (1989), *The Sublime Object of Ideology*. New York: Verso.

CONTRIBUTORS

Mireia Aragay is Professor of English Literature, Drama and Theatre at the University of Barcelona. She is Principal Investigator of the Contemporary British Theatre Barcelona research group (www.ub.edu/cbtbarcelona/) and has published widely in the field, including the co-edited volumes *British Theatre of the 1990s: Interviews with Directors, Playwrights, Critics and Academics* (2007), *Ethical Speculations in Contemporary British Theatre* (2014), *Of Precariousness: Vulnerabilities, Responsibilities, Communities in 21st-Century British Drama and Theatre* (2017) and *Affects in 21st-Century British Theatre: Exploring Feeling on Page and Stage* (2021), as well as the special issue 'Theatre and Spectatorship' (*Journal of Contemporary Drama in English*, 2016).

Andrew Haydon was a freelance theatre critic based in Manchester. He wrote for (among others) *The Guardian, The Financial Times, Nachtkritik .de, Frakcija, KulturPunkt.hr, Színház, The Stage* and *Time Out*. His account of British theatre in the 2000s is published in *Decades – Modern British Playwriting: 2000-2009* (2013). 'A Brief History of English Theatre Criticism Online' was published in *Theatre Criticism: Changing Landscapes* (2016) and his chapter on European productions of Sarah Kane and Mark Ravenhill is included in *Contemporary European Playwrights* (2020).

James Hudson is Senior Lecturer in Theatre at the University of Lincoln. He has published work on Edward Bond, Sarah Kane, Howard Barker, David Greig and Chris Thorpe. He is currently co-editing a themed journal issue on right-wing politics and performance (*Studies in Theatre and Performance*, 2021) and is the author of the forthcoming monograph *Contemporary British Theatre and Reactionary Ideology* (2022).

Caridad Svich is a playwright. Her first independent feature film (as co-screenwriter) *Fugitive Dreams*, based on her play, received its world premiere at the 2020 Fantasia Film Festival in Montreal. She has received the 2018 Ellen Stewart Award for Career Achievement in Theatre from ATHE, the 2012 OBIE for Lifetime Achievement, the 2011 American Theatre Critics Association Primus Prize for *The House of the Spirits,* based on Isabel Allende's novel. She is Associate Editor at *Contemporary Theatre Review*, and *Hedwig and the Angry Inch* (2019) is her most recent book.

INDEX

7/7 52–3, 57, 60, 62, 90, 177, 180, 181
9/11 52, 53, 179

Aberg, Maria 134–5, 224 n.29
acting 5, 10, 18, 36, 103, 109, 110–12, 119, 143, 177, 187, 224 n.29, 227 n.4
  ensembles 2, 3, 91, 132–5, 139–41, 145–7, 149–50, 153, 219 n.8, 225 n.11
actors 4, 5, 6, 8, 18, 19, 27, 33, 36, 37, 43, 47, 55–6, 63, 64, 76, 77, 81, 96, 100, 101, 112–14, 118, 132, 135, 147, 149, 151, 154, 178, 188, 207, 211
  as characters 5, 18, 27, 36, 43, 55–6, 63, 101, 112–14, 132
Actors Touring Company 65, 169, 210, 221 n.21, 228 n.23
Aeschylus 24, 190
Agamben, Giorgio 184, 185, 187, 228 n.17
alienation 53, 59, 126, 128, 132, 173, 179
Almeida Theatre, London 162, 204
al-Qaeda 45, 52, 59
Anderson, Gordon 16, 20, 46, 47, 65, 67, 68, 84, 87
antagonism 118–20, 123, 154
anxiety 8, 59, 67, 168, 173, 201, 205
Arts Council
  England 7, 219 n.10
  of Great Britain 6
As You Like It 57, 134
atomization 59, 62, 128, 186
audience 5, 9, 17, 36, 42, 43, 44, 47–8, 55–7, 65, 66, 67, 76, 80, 101, 117–20, 124, 132, 138, 151, 154, 158, 159, 166, 173, 180, 182, 201, 211. *See also* spectators
auteur 4, 89–90, 97, 135, 178
authorial 152
  authority 102, 104, 114, 116, 176
  function 5
  intention 9, 137, 166, 187
  voice 9, 107, 152

authorship 9, 18, 50, 61, 62, 92, 97, 99, 105, 152, 178, 179
  collaborative 64, 175, 177, 188

Baal 11, 162, 190, 197–200, 216
Barnett, David 178, 179
Barthes, Roland 98, 176, 220 n.15
Baudrillard, Jean 59–61
Belsey, Catherine 97–8
Berg, Klaus van den 178–81
Berliner Theatertreffen 49, 64
Billington, Michael 30, 41, 74, 89, 163, 219 n.11
Birdland 10, 11, 124, 157, 158, 161–3, 165, 190, 197–200, 201, 216, 224 n.32
Blindsided 88, 157, 158–60, 162, 204, 209
Bloch, Ernst 20
Bluebird 9, 20–3, 39, 40, 46, 67, 206
Boenisch, Peter 137–8, 150, 178, 188, 219 n.5, 227 n.9
Bond, Edward 31, 84, 94, 133, 134, 159, 160, 203, 225 n.36, 225 n.12
Brecht, Bertolt 11, 159, 162, 190, 197, 198
Brennan, Paul 111
Brenton, Howard 107, 226 n.2
British theatre 4, 6, 7, 8, 50, 84, 88, 91, 107, 110, 113, 121, 134, 135, 148, 153, 175, 182, 219 n.11
Broadway 137, 157, 167, 174
Brokaw, Mark 165–6
Büchner, Georg 11, 190, 192–3, 195, 197
Bush Theatre, London 23, 24, 75
Butterworth, Jez 6, 190

capitalism 58, 59, 93, 107, 161, 163, 183, 190, 194, 198–200, 204
Carmen Disruption 4, 17, 21, 88, 124, 157, 160–2, 169, 174, 204
Carver, Raymond 35, 50
causality 42, 79, 82–3, 84, 99, 195, 196–7

Index

character 5, 8, 15–17, 22, 27, 36, 40, 43, 45, 47, 56, 61–2, 64, 76, 101, 108, 131, 132, 146, 151, 159–60
  biography 84–5, 96, 98–100, 150, 207, 209
  establishment of 110–13, 142
  objective 16–17, 28, 62
  psychological complexity of 78, 80–1, 84–5
Chekov, Anton 25, 88, 89, 107, 219 n.3
Cherry Orchard, The 25, 89, 107, 189, 215, 221 n.28
Christ, Barbara 57, 106, 177
Christie, Bunny 137, 140, 143, 152
Christmas 19, 23–7, 38, 39, 43, 46, 87
Clachan, Lizzie 162, 215, 229 n.31
class 19, 25, 29, 35, 41, 80, 82, 95, 107, 128, 171, 193, 194–5, 197, 212, 214
Cocker, Jarvis 124, 173
Cohen, Phil 125
collaboration 2, 3, 4, 7, 9, 10, 50, 64, 87, 88, 90, 92, 102, 107, 121, 140, 147, 150, 176–9, 188
Columbine High School shooting 52, 78–9, 200, 203
Constable, Paule 90, 137, 152
consumerism 58, 94, 119, 183, 199
contradiction 45, 57, 85, 93–4, 120, 121, 123, 125–6, 128, 154–5, 168
Cooke, Dominic 15, 28, 215
Country Music 19, 37–42, 47, 67, 124, 191
Country Teasers, The 124, 164
Coveney, Michael 75
Cracknell, Carrie 11, 101, 162, 163, 164, 199, 216–17
Crimp, Martin 62, 95, 169, 176, 223 n.9
Curious Incident of the Dog in the Night-Time, The 1, 9, 10, 91, 121, 125, 135–53, 157, 164, 167, 174, 206, 207, 224 n.23
Cusack, Niamh 146, 149, 152
cynical reason 93–5

Damian, Diana 115, 116
death 29, 36, 37, 45, 113, 156, 169, 207, 208
delight 20
desire 16–17, 20, 21, 22, 34, 44, 58, 60, 70, 73, 120, 166, 168, 169, 170, 173, 195

despair 8, 21, 129, 130, 154, 155, 164, 202
Deutsches Schauspielhaus Hamburg 4, 160, 176, 177, 227 n.5
dialogue 62, 81, 84–5, 99, 167
directing 4, 15, 19, 28, 89, 90, 92, 95–102, 103–7, 110–20, 131–2, 137–8, 146–52, 177–9, 181–2, 187–8, 206–17, 227 n.3
directors 2–9, 63, 87, 91, 120–1, 153, 154, 176, 178, 182, 187, 206–17, 219 n.6, 220 n.10
disability 133, 134
A Doll's House 89, 189, 216
Dostoevsky, Fyodor 192
dramatic
  action 16, 17, 28, 42
  craft 7, 18, 80, 81
  fiction 25, 27, 56
  literature 81, 156

ecological disaster 50, 51, 84, 93–5
Edgar, David 6, 107, 226 n.2
Eitzel, Mark 87, 124, 164, 165, 219 n.3
Eldridge, David 87, 219 n.3
Elliott, Marianne 3, 11, 13, 14, 18, 35, 36, 70, 91, 135, 136, 138, 140, 141, 143, 144, 145, 146, 147–52, 165, 206–9
empathy 20, 22, 59, 61, 67, 69, 70, 132, 209
ensemble 2, 3, 91, 132–5, 139–40, 141, 145, 146–8, 150, 153, 219 n.8
Epner, Eero 112
Euripides 24, 68, 88, 204
European theatre 3, 11, 49, 50, 52, 67, 87, 89, 91, 110, 111, 137, 151, 175–88
European Union 50

Fall, The 123, 124, 164, 191
Fatherland 175, 219 n.3
film, influence on Stephens's plays 109, 189, 190, 192, 200, 203, 228 n.18
Fischer-Lichte, Erika 4, 5
Forsythe, William 211, 228 n.25
Frankcom, Sarah 2, 11, 13, 14, 18, 19, 36, 42, 44, 47, 49, 121, 153, 154, 158, 172, 173, 206, 209–10, 213
Frantic Assembly 91, 137, 139–41, 146, 152, 175
French theatre 182–4, 228 n.15
Funfair, The 175, 204

Index

Gardner, Lyn   89, 159
gender   8, 19, 35, 56, 63, 116, 133, 134, 214, 215, 216
German-language theatre   4, 50, 87, 119, 135, 177, 178, 227 n.12
Gerstner, Muriel   63, 178, 179, 227 n.10
ghosts   25, 33, 37, 43, 44, 204, 209
globality   8, 9, 45, 50, 51, 57, 58, 109, 119, 125, 135, 153, 157, 174, 197, 199, 200
globalization   59–60, 61, 91, 108, 116, 117, 200, 224 n.27
Goodman, Joel   168
Graham, Scott   91, 137, 140, 141, 147, 175, 219 n.3
Gray, Ramin   11, 47, 55, 57, 76, 169, 193, 210–12
Greig, David   174, 228 n.27
Grochala, Sarah   108, 224 n.27
Gutmann, Laurent   10, 176, 177, 181–7, 228 n.16

Haddon, Mark   1, 91, 135, 136, 139, 152, 157
Hampstead Theatre, London   88, 103
Hare, David   96, 107, 121, 225 n.36
Harper Regan   2, 4, 11, 21, 52, 68–75, 84, 206, 207, 208, 209, 227 n.4
Haydon, Andrew   117, 162, 199
Hebdige, Dick   123, 125–6, 130
Heisenberg: The Uncertainty Principle   14, 88, 157, 158, 165–7, 169, 206
Hemming, Sarah   132
Herons   4, 19, 27–33, 36, 41, 46, 91, 155, 213, 214
Hirte, Marion   179
Hoggett, Steven   91, 137, 140, 141, 147
Holman, Robert   84, 87, 123, 154, 219 n.3
Holmes, Sean   2, 3, 11, 64–5, 90–1, 121, 125, 131–4, 136, 188, 212–14, 224 n.29, 225 n.11
HOME, Manchester   175, 204
hope   20, 21, 22, 29, 30, 32, 35, 45, 46, 53, 75, 128, 154, 155, 160, 171
Horváth, Ödön von   175, 204, 219 n.3
Horwood, Joel   214, 225 n.13
Hove, Ivo van   3, 151, 165
hypervisibility, age of   10, 181, 184–6
Hytner, Nicholas   64, 68, 69, 225 n.36, 226 n.14

Ibsen, Henrik   88, 89, 216, 219 n.3
ideology   176
   ruling   125
   social   93–4
imagination   27, 46, 51, 59, 63, 64, 101, 107, 120, 138, 150, 163, 176
improvisation   112–13, 135, 141, 149, 150, 176
individualism   82, 107
Inszenierung   178, 182, 187, 227 n.9
internet   45, 51, 53, 59, 60, 72, 73, 74, 82
intertextuality   191
intimacy   22, 39, 41, 74, 129, 185
Iraq, 2003 invasion of   51, 52, 53, 192, 197
isolation   21, 34, 58, 59, 62, 82, 171, 174, 187

Jarry, Alfred   102, 103, 104, 106, 204
Jeffreys, Stephen   15
Jelinek, Elfriede   168, 179
Junges Theater, Basel   124, 129, 213, 214
juxtaposition   10, 85, 123, 155

Kakudate, Reina   185–6
Kane, Sarah   6, 62, 169, 176, 204
Kelly, Dennis   190, 219 n.2
Kenyon, Mel   24, 28, 30
Knight, Imogen   162, 169, 170, 171

La Colline Théâtre National Paris   10, 176, 181, 182
Lan, David   15, 88
Ledger, Adam J.   103, 104, 105
Lehmann, Hans-Thies   119
Lessing, Gotthold Ephraim   150, 226 n.17
Light Falls   14, 124, 157, 158, 171–3, 175
Literary Management   6–7
live
   event of theatre   17, 120
   performance   5, 7, 20, 32, 87
   situation   27
liveness   5, 9, 47, 48
Lloyd, Matthew   18, 19
Longhurst, Michael   162
Lorillard, Pauline   186
Love, Catherine   116, 134
Lydon, John   126, 127, 129
Lyric Hammersmith, London   2, 4, 65, 90, 91, 108, 115, 124, 125, 129, 131, 132, 133, 188, 212, 213, 214, 225 n.12, 228 n.29

247

Index

McCauley, Alistair   30, 41
McLeish, Kenneth   106, 194, 224 n.22
McPherson, Conor   24
Manhattan Theatre Club, New York   165, 167
Maria   21, 157, 158, 171–2
Marine Parade   87, 219 n.3
masculinity   116, 155, 163, 197
  and heterosexuality   116
  and sexual inadequacy   193, 194
Mays, Daniel   2, 55, 56, 57, 210, 211, 212
Metal Box   124, 126, 127, 129, 130, 131
metaphor   5, 25, 30, 36, 55, 58, 61, 63, 68, 76, 77–8, 89, 132, 154, 213, 214
Miller, Arthur   24, 151
mise en scene   4, 103, 132, 167, 178, 182, 187
misogyny   24, 115–16, 216
Mitchell, Katie   3, 11, 88–90, 95–7, 98–100, 101, 102, 103, 104–5, 107, 214–16, 223 n.9
morality   8, 19, 29, 45, 48, 49, 52, 53, 54, 58, 69, 73, 82, 84, 95, 102, 115, 116, 117, 128, 130, 156, 159, 164, 172, 180, 190, 192, 195, 196, 197, 199, 200
Morning   1, 11, 91, 124, 125–32, 213–14
Morrison, Blake   29
Motortown   1, 2, 4, 10, 11, 21, 46, 51, 52–7, 75, 80, 84, 94, 101, 124, 136, 190, 191–7, 200, 201, 210–12
Munich Kammerspiele   4, 90
music, influence on Stephens's plays   39, 123–4, 128, 131, 161, 164, 189, 207

narrative   16–17, 19, 21, 33, 42, 63, 65, 66, 90, 92, 115, 116, 126, 170
  dramatic   15, 45, 47, 70, 73, 100, 115
  fictional/fictive   20, 58, 114
  implied   25, 33
  realist   20, 26, 78
  structure   19, 67
nation   8
  and nation-state   108, 109
National Theatre   2, 42, 45, 64, 68, 69, 91, 125, 136, 137, 140, 141, 146, 153, 157, 206, 208, 214, 224 n.29, 226 n.14, 229 n.33
naturalism   20, 44, 50, 83, 84, 88, 90, 167, 192, 203, 212, 215

neoliberalism   61, 161, 199–200
new play development   6, 7, 13, 15, 220 n.10
new writing   5–6, 7, 13, 24, 90, 129, 133, 219 n.6. *See also* new play development
Nield, Sophie   115, 117
noir   21, 109, 115–16
Nübling, Sebastian   3–4, 10, 17, 49, 57, 63, 64, 85, 87, 90, 101, 102, 104, 105, 107–20, 123, 126, 129, 131, 134, 137, 149, 154–5, 160, 161–2, 167, 168, 171, 176–81, 187, 210, 213, 219 n.8, 224 nn.31–2, 227 nn.10, 12
Nuclear War   17, 21, 88, 129, 157, 158, 169–71, 176, 227 n.4

O'Neill, Eugene   24, 68
One Minute   52, 64, 65–8, 80, 84, 87, 221 n.21, 222 n.13
On the Shore of the Wide World   11, 19, 42–6, 47, 49, 68, 209
optimism   20, 27, 30, 31

Parker, Christian   44, 48
Parker, Mary-Louise   166
Pavilion Theatre, Brighton   23
Pavis, Patrice   137, 178, 187
Payne, Nick   217, 229 n.33
Pinter, Harold   99, 130
play-texts   5, 6, 9, 14, 18, 46, 62, 87, 96–8, 102, 112, 113, 114, 118, 135, 137–8, 176, 177, 179, 182, 187
  function of   47, 91, 112, 114
  reading of   92, 95, 96–8, 135, 187
  staging of   62–5, 87, 92, 113, 118, 135, 137–8, 179, 187
'playwright-artist/director-interpreter'   9, 91, 120
playwrights   1, 5–9, 13, 15–17, 63–4, 78, 84, 87, 98, 113–14, 120, 133, 153, 175, 176, 178, 181–2, 205, 219 nn.10–11
playwriting   15–17, 28–9, 67, 80, 85, 87, 88, 89, 100, 139, 155, 174
political theatre   83, 108, 224 n.27, 227 n.14
Poll, Melissa   115, 224 n.32
Pornographie   10, 63–4, 90, 137, 153, 177–81, 227 n.12

248

Index

Pornography 1, 4, 10, 11, 46, 51, 53, 54, 57–65, 68, 82, 84, 85, 87, 88, 90, 92, 94, 131, 140, 176–88, 212–13, 214, 227 n.7
pornography 45, 50, 69, 70, 72–3, 74, 109, 163, 193
Port 1, 4, 11, 14, 19, 21, 33–7, 41, 45, 46, 47, 171, 206, 207–8
postdramatic, the 62, 110, 178
Potter, Dennis 30, 189
poverty 80, 194, 198
Public Image Ltd 124
Punk Rock 1, 4, 10, 52, 78–83, 84, 85, 90, 99, 124, 128, 190, 191, 200–4, 209
punk subcultures 123, 129

race 56, 133, 196
  and racism 53, 73, 195, 196
Radosavljević, Duška 177, 178
Rage 157, 158, 167–8
Ravenhill, Mark 6, 225 n.13
realism 20, 33, 44, 78, 81, 107, 119, 150, 167, 168, 172, 173
  expressive 98, 118, 223 n.10
  mimetic 20, 27, 88, 118
  psychological 22, 56, 150
  'Royal Court' 30, 32, 44
  social 5, 19, 32, 46, 119, 129
Rebellato, Dan 20, 27, 31, 46, 55, 66, 76, 89, 107, 108, 109–10, 119, 175, 176, 204
Regietheater 4–5, 91, 137, 149, 167, 178
representation 5, 55, 67, 76, 114, 115, 117, 133, 176, 178
  dramaturgy of 77, 118, 120
  mimetic 55, 101
Rickson, Ian 13, 15, 124, 191, 210, 227 n.3
Roberts, Ferdy 90, 112
rock 'n' roll 159, 162, 164
Royal Court Theatre 2, 6, 13–16, 19, 23, 28, 30, 31, 37, 40, 41, 44, 46, 55, 67, 83, 88, 96, 124, 155, 162, 169, 170, 174, 210, 212, 214, 215, 216, 220 n.10, 224 n.29, 227 n.3
  Young Writers' Festival 9, 20
Royal Exchange Theatre 2, 4, 13, 14, 15, 18, 19, 33, 36, 37, 42, 44, 46, 49, 158, 172, 173, 206, 208, 209
Royal Shakespeare Company 88, 134, 224 n.29

Rudd, Katy 136, 140, 144, 145, 226 n.18

Saunders, Graham 108, 224 n.26
scenography 176–7, 178–9, 180, 184, 187
Schauspiel Essen 4, 103
Schauspiel Hannover 4, 10, 57
Schimmelpfennig, Roland 67, 110
Scorsese, Martin 189, 191
Scott, Andrew 2, 76, 162, 163
Sea Wall 2, 75–8, 163, 165, 167
Secret Theatre 2, 3, 91, 125, 132–5, 136, 188, 214, 225 n.11
Semper, Ene-Liis 108
Seymour, Richard 79, 82, 83
Shaham, Rinat 2, 160
Shakespeare, William 6, 19, 24, 190
Sharp, Lesley 2, 74–5, 209
Shin, Hyemi 131, 225 n.11
Shuttleworth, Ian 67, 159, 160
Sidi, Nick 14, 141, 142, 146, 147
Sierz, Aleks 5, 29, 194–5
Simard, Pierre 182–3
Sloterdijk, Peter 93
Smits, Eelco 165
Song from Far Away 3, 124, 157, 158, 164–5
spectators 5, 17, 20, 22, 33, 37, 40, 45, 48, 61, 67, 71, 76, 78, 85, 91, 99, 119, 159, 163, 166, 179, 185. *See also* audience
Spencer, Charles 30, 41, 67, 89, 163
Spring Awakening 11, 190, 200–4
Stafford-Clark, Max 15, 110, 224 n.26, 225 n.26
Stanislavski, Konstantin 112, 150, 224 n.29
'state of the nation' play 107–10, 119, 219 n.11, 226 n.2
Stockport 14, 33–4, 36, 42, 158, 160, 201, 206
subtext 17, 80, 99, 158, 207
Sutton, Adrian 138, 145, 148, 149

Taxi Driver 191–7
Taylor, Paul 74, 163
Teater No99 3, 4, 90, 112, 223 n.1
Tennant, Nicolas 110–19, 134, 149, 224 nn.29, 31
Thalheimer, Michael 4, 138

Index

Thalia Theater, Hamburg   167, 171
Theatre Writers Union   6
Third Man, The   109
Thompson, Peter   20
A Thousand Stars Explode in the Sky   87, 219 n.3
Three Kingdoms   4, 17, 65, 90–1, 92, 94, 107–20, 123, 124, 126, 131, 132, 133, 134, 137, 149, 153, 213, 214, 224 n.32, 226 n.16
Tomlin, Liz   7
Toneelgroep Amsterdam   4, 103, 151, 165
Traverse Theatre, Edinburgh   65, 131
Treadaway, Luke   137, 140, 147
Trial of Ubu, The   4, 88, 90, 92, 102–7, 204
tucker green, debbie   130, 225 n.9

Van Sant, Gus   189, 200, 203

'visual dramaturgy'   10, 178, 179

Wajcman, Gérard   10, 184, 185, 187
Walker, Nicola   141, 142, 148, 149–52
'War on Terror'   45, 52, 57, 60
Wastwater   11, 88, 90, 92–107, 214, 215
Wedekind, Frank   11, 190, 200
West End, London   137, 157, 165
Whybrow, Graham   5, 15, 16, 83, 219 n.6
Worthen, W. B.   7, 92, 107, 110, 119
Woyzeck   11, 133, 190, 191–7

Yates, Daniel B.   116
Young Vic, London   88, 107, 165, 216

Zadek, Peter   4, 178
Žižek, Slavoj   93–4

www.ingramcontent.com/pod-product-compliance
Lightning Source LLC
Chambersburg PA
CBHW062134300426
44115CB00012BA/1914